Photographer's Guide to the Sony DSC-RX100

Photographer's Guide to the Sony DSC-RX100

Getting the Most from Sony's Pocketable Digital Camera

Alexander S. White

White Knight Press
Henrico, Virginia

Published by
White Knight Press
9704 Old Club Trace
Henrico, Virginia 23238
www.whiteknightpress.com

ISBN: 978-1-937986-08-7 (paperback)
       978-1-937986-09-4 (e-book)

Printed in the United States of America

This book is dedicated to my wife, Clenise.

Contents

Author's Note and Acknowledgments

In mid-2009, I began working on my first guide book to a digital camera, the Leica D-Lux 4. I was attracted to that camera because it provided a strong set of advanced features, including manual controls and many settings for creative photography. In addition, all of these capabilities were provided in a very compact framework, and the camera yielded high-quality images. I went on from that project to publish books about other advanced compact models from Leica, Panasonic, Canon, Nikon, and Fujifilm.

As I work on one book, I keep an eye on the marketplace for small digital cameras to see what new features and improvements will be offered by these and other manufacturers. In the past, it has often been difficult to choose what model to work on next. When I saw the announcement for the Sony Cybershot DSC-RX100, though, it did not take long for me to decide that this camera is a winner, and one that deserves a book. So, even though I had not previously included a Sony model in this series of "Photographer's Guide" books, I decided with no hesitation to turn my attention to this great little camera.

As with previous books, I turned to the extremely knowledgeable and helpful contributors to the forums at dpreview.com for assistance in checking over a draft of this book to help improve the discussion of photographic topics and the camera's features. I received tremendous assistance from several contributors to the "Sony Cyber-shot Talk" forum. I am particularly grateful to John Barr, Kushal Dutt, Rick Evertsz, Chris Fox, Ira Gluck, Cosmo Genovese, Lawrence Kwan, Sam Kwan, John Laninga, Dirk Leas, David McAughtry, Mark Power, Jason Prince, Al Sorkin, and Nathan Wolfson. Any remaining errors or omissions are, of course, solely my responsibility.

All photographs in this book that illustrate the capabilities or features of the Sony Cyber-shot DSC-RX100 camera are ones that I took with the RX100. The photographs that show the camera's controls were taken with a Sony DSLR-A850, using a Sony 50mm macro lens and a Sony f/2.8 SAM 28-75mm zoom lens.

Finally, as with all of my earlier books, the greatest support in every possible way, from joining me on trips to take photographs for this book to editing and proofreading the final text, has come from my wife, Clenise.

Introduction

This book is a guide for users of the Sony Cyber-shot DSC-RX100 digital camera, one of the most capable compact digital cameras on the market today. If you are reading this book, chances are you already believe that the RX100 is one of the best choices currently available in the realm of small digital cameras. But I'll still mention some of the features that make it an outstanding choice in my opinion.

For me, the single factor that distinguishes the RX100 from the large numbers of competing models is its amazingly small size. This camera, unlike the great majority of current models with such advanced features, is not just portable but "pocketable." It will fit readily into a jacket or trousers pocket or purse and can be held unobtrusively in one hand when you don't want to call attention to your camera. But, despite this great degree of portability, the camera doesn't give up much in the way of capability.

Perhaps the greatest feature of the RX100 apart from its small size is the unexpectedly large size of its image sensor, the crucial component where light is gathered to form your images and videos. This very small camera comes equipped with a 1"-type sensor, which is twice as large as the sensor in the Fujifilm X10, and more than twice as large as those in many other small cameras in this class. The RX100 boasts 20.2 megapixels of effective resolution, and has a 3-inch (7.6-cm) LCD display with more than 1,000,000 pixels of resolution.

The RX100 also is well-equipped with advanced shooting features. You can set the camera to its Intelligent Auto or Superior Auto shooting mode and get great results most of the time with no further settings. However, the camera also offers full manual control of focus and exposure, continuous shooting, exposure bracketing, RAW format, excellent low-light performance, and numerous special features, including a variety of Scene mode choices and Picture Effect settings for manipulating images. The RX100, like many of its contemporaries, includes a built-in HDR (High Dynamic Range) shooting option. The RX100 also provides HD (high-definition) video shooting with the ability to control aperture and shutter speed while shooting movies.

The RX100 is not the perfect camera, of course; no camera can serve as the ideal tool for all situations. In this case, the major drawbacks often cited are that the camera lacks an optical viewfinder and an accessory shoe that could be used to attach items such as an external viewfinder or flash. There also is no built-in way to attach filters or other accessories to the lens, though there are work-around solutions to both of these deficiencies, discussed in Appendix A. There are not many physical controls, and those that exist are rather small and can be hard to press accurately. Also, I have found myself mistakenly pressing the red Movie button numerous times, because it is located in a place where it is natural to grip the camera. All in all, though, the RX100's virtues far outweigh its negatives.

This introduction to the camera's features is not complete, but it serves to illustrate that the Sony RX100 has an impressive set of capabilities that should be attractive to serious photographers—those who want a camera that gives them numerous options for creative control of their images and that can be carried around at all times, so they will have a substantial photographic apparatus with them when a good picture-taking opportunity arises.

My goal with this book is to provide a thorough and useful guide to the camera's features, explaining how they work and when you might want to use them. The book is aimed largely at beginning and intermediate photographers who are not satisfied with the technical documentation that comes with the camera and who need a more user-friendly explanation of the camera's many controls and menus. For those who are seeking more advanced information, I provide some discussion of topics that go beyond the basics, and I include in the appendices information that should help you uncover additional resources.

Finally, one note on the scope of this guide: I live in the United States, and I bought my camera in the U.S. market. I am not very familiar with the variations for cameras sold in Europe or elsewhere, such as different batteries or chargers. The photographic functions are generally not different, though, so this guide should be useful to photographers in all locations. It should be noted that the frame rates for high-definition (HD) video are different in different areas; the version of the RX100 sold in the U.S. uses the 60 frames per second setting for progressive video, whereas cameras sold in Europe use 50 frames per second. The video functions and operations are not different, just the frame rates. I have stated measurements of distance and weight in both the Imperial and metric systems, for the benefit of readers in various countries around the world.

Chapter 1: Preliminary Setup

Setting Up the Camera

I will assume your Sony Cyber-shot DSC-RX100 has just arrived at your home or office, perhaps purchased from an internet site or a retail store. The box should contain the camera itself, battery, combination battery charger/AC adapter, wrist strap, two adapters for attaching a shoulder strap (though no shoulder strap is supplied), micro USB cable, and the brief instruction pamphlet. There may also be a warranty card and some advertising flyers. There is no CD with software or a user's guide; the software programs supplied by Sony are accessible through the camera itself or over the internet.

To install PlayMemories Home, the Sony software for viewing and working with images and videos, you need to connect the RX100 to a Windows computer by the USB cable, with no memory card in the camera. (If you have a Macintosh or other non-Windows computer, you have to use other software, such as Adobe's Photoshop, Lightroom, or Photoshop Elements, or Apple's iPhoto or Aperture.) Then, you need to navigate on the computer to the icon for the camera's storage media and find the file called PMHOME.exe. You double-click on that file to install the software. You also can install Sony's Image Data Converter software, which converts the camera's RAW images so you can edit them on the computer. That software is available for download from http://www.sony.co.jp/imsoft/

Win for Windows PCs and http://www.sony.co.jp/imsoft/Mac for Macintosh computers.

You might want to attach the wrist strap as soon as possible, because it can help you keep a tight grip on the camera. The strap can be attached to the small mounting lug on either the left side or the right side of the camera. I will admit that I have never attached the strap myself, though, because this camera is so small that I find I can hold it firmly in my hand without much risk of dropping it, even without a strap. See Appendix A for discussion of a custom grip that can also be of great use.

Charging and Inserting the Battery

The Sony battery for the DSC-RX100 is the NP-BX1. With this camera, the standard procedure is to charge the battery while it's inside the camera. To do this, you use the supplied USB cable, which plugs into the Sony AC adapter or into a USB port on your computer. There are pluses and minuses to this type of onboard battery-charging. On the positive side, you don't need an external charger and the camera can charge automatically when it's connected to your computer. You also can find many portable charging devices with USB ports; many newer automobiles have USB slots where you can plug in your RX100 to keep up its charge.

The main drawbacks are that you cannot use the camera very easily while the battery is charging, and you cannot charge another battery outside of the camera. One solution to this situation is to purchase at least one extra battery and a device that will charge that battery outside of the camera. I'll discuss batteries, chargers, and other accessories in Appendix A.

For now, let's get the battery charged by inserting it into the camera and connecting the charger. You first need to open the battery compartment door on the bottom of the camera and put in the battery. You can only insert it fully into the camera one way; the way I prefer to do this is to look for the four gold-colored metal contact squares on the end of the battery, and insert the battery so those four squares are positioned close to the front of the camera as the battery goes into the compartment, as shown in Figures 1-1 and 1-2. You may have to nudge aside the small blue latch that holds the battery in place.

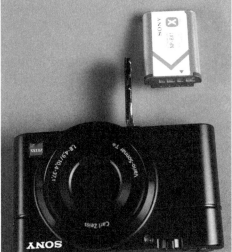

Figure 1-1:   Battery lined up for insertion into RX100

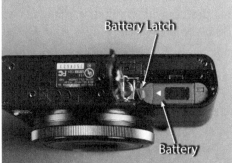

Figure 1-2:   Battery inserted and secured by latch

With the battery inserted and secured by the blue latch, close the battery compartment door and slide the ridged latch on the compartment door to the closed position. Then plug the larger, rectangular end of the USB cable into the corresponding slot on the AC adapter/charger, which is model number AC-UD11 in the United States. Plug the smaller end of the cable into the micro USB port on the upper part of the camera's right side as you hold it in shooting position, as shown in Figure 1-3.

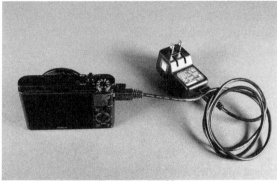

Figure 1-3: AC Adapter Plugged into RX100

Plug the AC adapter into a standard electrical outlet. An orange lamp in the center of the On/Off switch on top of the camera will light up steadily while the battery is charging; when it goes out, the battery is fully charged. The full charging cycle should take about 155 minutes. (If the charging lamp flashes, that indicates a problem with the charger or a problem with the temperature of the camera's environment.)

Inserting the Memory Card

The RX100 does not ship with any memory card. If you turn the camera on with no card inserted, you will see the error message NO CARD in the upper left corner of the screen. If you ignore this message and press the shutter button to take a picture, you may be fooled into thinking that the camera is storing it in internal memory, but that is not the case. Actually, the camera will temporarily store the image and play it back if you press the Playback button, but the image will not be permanently stored. Some other camera models have a small amount of built-in memory so you can take and store a few pictures even without a card, but the RX100 does not have any such safety net.

To avoid the frustration of having a great camera that can't save any images, you need to purchase and insert a memory card. The RX100 uses two basic types of memory storage. First, it can use all varieties of SD cards, which are quite small—about the size of a large postage stamp. These cards come in several varieties, as shown in Figure 1-4.

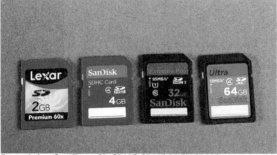

Figure 1-4:   Card Types: SD, SDHC, SDHC 32GB, SDXC

The standard card, called simply SD, comes in capacities from 8 MB to 2 GB. A higher-capacity card, SDHC, comes in sizes from 4 GB to 32 GB. The newest, and highest-capacity card, SDXC (for extended capacity) comes in sizes of 48 GB, 64 GB, and up; this version of the card can have a capacity up to 2 terabytes (TB), theoretically, and SDXC cards generally have faster transfer speeds than the smaller-capacity cards. There also is a special variety of SD card called an Eye-Fi card, which I will discuss a bit later in this chapter.

The RX100 also can use micro-SD cards, which are smaller cards, often used in cell phones and other small devices. These cards operate in the same way as SD cards, but you have to use an adapter that is the size of an SD card in order to use this tiny card in the RX100 camera, as shown in Figure 1-5.

In addition to using the various types of SD cards, the RX100, being a Sony camera, also can use Sony's proprietary storage devices, known as Memory Stick cards. These cards are similar in size and capacity to SD or SDHC cards, but with a slightly different shape, as shown in Figure 1-6. They come in various types, according to their capacities. The ones that can be used in the RX100 are the Memory Stick PRO Duo, Memory Stick PRO-HG Duo, Memory Stick Duo, and Memory Stick Micro (M2). The Memory Stick Micro, like the micro-SD card, requires an adapter for use in the camera.

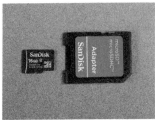

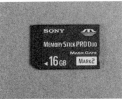

Figure 1-5: Micro-SD Card and Adapter   Figure 1-6: Memory Stick PRO Duo

What type and size of card should you use? In my experience, the type does not matter. Any of the various types of SD or Memory Stick cards should work just fine. The factors that do matter are capacity and speed. The capacity to choose depends on your needs and intentions. If you're planning to record a good deal of high-definition (HD) video or large numbers of RAW photos, you should get a large-capacity card, but don't get carried away—the largest cards have such huge capacities that you may be wasting money purchasing them.

There are several variables to take into account in computing how many images or videos you can store on a particular size of card, such as which aspect ratio you're using (16:9, 3:2, 4:3, or 1:1), picture size, and quality. To cut through the complications, here are a few examples of what can be stored on an 8 GB SD card or Memory Stick card. If you're using the standard 3:2 aspect ratio and Large size images, you can store about 355 RAW images (the highest quality), 290 high-quality JPEG images (Large size and Fine quality), or about 1200 of the lower-quality Standard images.

If you're interested in video, here are some guidelines. You can fit about 40 minutes of the highest-quality high-definition (HD) video on an 8 GB card. That same card will hold almost five hours of video at the lowest quality, 640 x 480 pixels, also known as VGA quality. Note, though, that the camera is limited to recording just about 29 minutes of video in any one sequence. An 8 GB card can hold intermediate amounts of video at quality levels between the highest-quality HD and VGA.

One other consideration is the speed of the card. A high rate of speed is important to get good results for recording images and video with this camera. You should try to find a card that writes data at a rate of 6 MB/second or faster to record HD video. If you go by the Class designation, a Class 4 card should be sufficient for shooting stills, and a Class 6 card should suffice for recording video. Newer cards, such as the SanDisk Extreme Pro, and Lexar Professional, shown in Figure 1-7, come with the UHS designation, for ultra high speed; these cards have roughly the same speed as a Class 10 card. If you choose one of these, you should have no problems with any level of video recording. A fast card also will help when you set the camera for continuous shooting of still images.

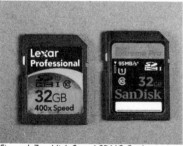

Figure 1-7:   High-Speed SDHC Cards

Finally, you need to realize if you have an older computer with a built-in card reader, or just an older external card reader, there is some chance it will not read the newer SDHC cards. In that case, you would have to either get a new reader that will accept SDHC cards, or download images from the camera to your computer using the USB cable. Using the newest variety of card, SDXC, also can be problematic with older computers. In mid-2010 I tried a 64GB SDXC card, and my MacBook Pro could not read it at all at first, even when I left it in the camera and connected the camera to the computer by USB cable.

More recently, the situation has improved. If your computer has a recent version of the operating system, it will be able to read SDXC cards if you use a compatible card reader. Specifically, the cards can be read by Windows 7; Windows Vista with Service Pack 1 or 2; and Windows XP with a software patch for reading the exFAT file system. That patch is available at http://www.microsoft.com/downloads. For Macintosh computers, you need Mac OS X version 10.6.6 or later; otherwise, you need a patch such as one I found at www.sonnettech.com, the web site for a company that makes SDXC card readers.

As I write this, 64 GB SDXC cards cost about $55.00 and up, and prices are dropping. So, if you don't mind the risk of losing a great many images or videos if you lose the card, you might want to choose an SDXC card with an enormous capacity of 64 GB, or even 128 GB.

Finally, you may want to consider getting an Eye-Fi card. This special type of device looks very much like an ordinary SDHC card, but it includes a tiny transmitter that lets it connect to a wireless (WiFi) network and send your images to your computer on that network as soon as the images have been recorded by the camera. You also may be able to use Direct Mode, which lets the Eye-Fi card send your images directly to a computer, smart phone, tablet, or other device without needing a network, though Direct Mode can be tricky to set up.

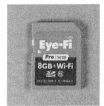

Fig 1-8:   Eye-Fi Card

I have tested an 8 GB Eye-Fi card, the Pro X2 model, with the RX100, and it works well. Within a few seconds after I snap a picture with this card installed in the camera, a little thumb-nail image appears in the upper right corner of my computer's screen showing the progress of the upload. When all images are uploaded, they are available in the Pictures/Eye-Fi folder on my computer. The Pro X2 model, pictured in Figure 1-8, can handle RAW files and video files as well as the smaller JPEG files. (At the time of this writing, the Pro X2 is the only variety of Eye-Fi card that can handle RAW files. A newer model with 16 GB capacity was announced in October 2012.) An Eye-Fi card is not a necessity, but I enjoy the convenience of having my images sent straight to my computer without having to put the card into a card reader or to connect the camera to the computer with a USB cable. I should note that the Eye-Fi card does not always work perfectly with my wireless network at home, probably because my computer is located on a different floor from the wireless router. In order to get the images to upload, I had to walk downstairs close to the router so the card could connect to the network. Once it connected, though, the uploading proceeded with no problems.

If you decide to use a Memory Stick card, be sure that you have a card reader that can accept those cards, which, as noted above, are not the same shape as SD cards and require readers with compatible slots.

In summary, you have several options for choosing a memory card. I like to use a high-speed 16 GB SDHC card, just to have extra capacity and speed in case they are needed. I enjoy the convenience of the Eye-Fi card also, but, unless you do a lot of photography within range of a wireless network or you are willing and able to configure Direct Mode to work properly, it may not be worth your while to get that type of card.

Once you have chosen a card, open the same door on the bottom of the camera that covers the battery compartment, and slide the card in until it catches. An SD card is inserted with its label pointing toward the back of the camera, as shown in Figure 1-9; a Memory Stick card is inserted with its label facing in the other direction. Once the card has been pushed down until it catches, close the compartment door and slide the latch to the outside position. To remove the card, you push down on its edge until it releases and springs up so you can grab it.

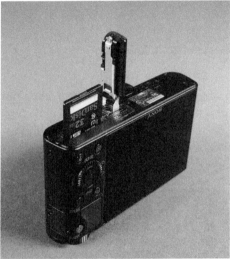

Figure 1-9:   Inserting SD Card into RX100

Although the card may work fine when newly inserted in the camera, it's always a good idea to format a card when first using it in a camera, so it will be set up with the correct file structure and will have any bad areas blocked off from use. To do this, turn on the camera by pressing the power button (marked On/Off, on top of the camera), then press the Menu button at the center right of the camera's back. Next, press the right direction button (right edge of the control wheel on the camera's back) multiple times, until the small orange line near the top of the screen is positioned under the number 1, next to an icon representing a memory card, as shown in Figure 1-10. That icon indicates the Memory Card Tool menu. The orange highlight rectangle should already be positioned on the top line of the menu, on the Format command; if not, press the top or bottom edge of the control wheel, or turn the wheel, until the Format command is highlighted.

27

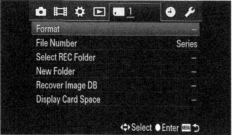

Figure 1-10:   Memory Card Tool Menu

Press the button in the center of the control wheel (called the "center button" throughout this book) when the Format command is highlighted. Then, on the next screen, shown in Figure 1-11, highlight Enter, and press the center button again to carry out the command.

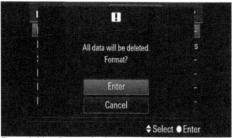

Figure 1-11:   Format Confirmation Screen

Setting the Language, Date, and Time

You need to make sure the date and time are set correctly before you start taking pictures, because the camera records that information (sometimes known as "metadata," meaning data beyond the information in the picture itself) invisibly with each image, and displays it later if you want. Someday you may be very glad to have the date (and the time of day) correctly recorded with your archives of digital images.

To get these basic items set correctly, press down on the power switch to turn the camera on. Then press the Menu button at the center right of the camera's back. Press the right side of the control wheel, marked with a lightning bolt, to move the orange line so it is underneath the number 1 next to a clock icon, representing the Clock Setup menu, as shown in Figure 1-12.

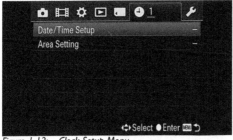

Figure 1-12:   Clock Setup Menu

Press the upper edge of the control wheel, if necessary, to move the orange highlight rectangle to the Date/Time Setup line at the top of the menu screen, and press the center button in the control wheel to activate the date and time settings, as shown in Figure 1-13.

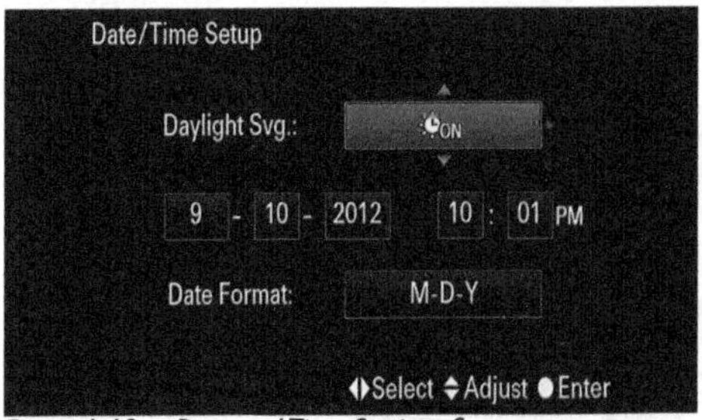

Figure 1-13:   Date and Time Settings Screen

By pressing the left and right edges of the control wheel or by turning the control wheel, move left and right through the Daylight Savings Time, month, date, year, time, and date format settings, and change the settings by pressing the up and down buttons (top and bottom edges of the control wheel). When everything is set correctly, press the center button to confirm. Then press the Menu button to exit from the menu system.

If you need to change the language that the camera uses for menus and other messages, press the Menu button as discussed above to enter the menu system, and navigate to screen number 3 of the Setup menu, which is marked by a wrench icon, as shown in Figure 1-14.

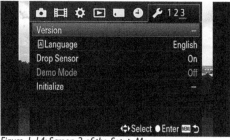

Figure 1-14: Screen 3 of the Setup Menu

Then navigate with the direction buttons, if necessary, to the Language item on the screen and press the center button to select it. You then can select from the available languages on the menu, as shown in Figure 1-15.

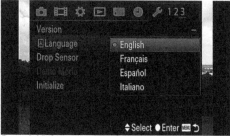

Figure 1-15: Setup Menu Language Selection Screen

Chapter 2: Basic Operations

Overview of Shooting Still Images

Now that the RX100 has the correct time and date set and has a fully charged battery inserted along with a memory card, let's explore some scenarios for basic picture-taking. For now, I won't get into discussions of what the various options are and why you might choose one over another. I'll just lay out a reasonable set of steps that will get you and your camera into action and will deposit a decent image on your memory card.

Introduction to Main Controls

Before I discuss some of the basic options for setting up the camera using the menu system and controls, it may be helpful to introduce the main controls, so you'll have a better idea of which button or dial is which. I won't discuss all of the controls here; they will all be covered in some detail in Chapter 5. For now, here is a series of images that show the major controls. As I come to each item for the first time in the text, I will describe its position and function; you may want to refer back to these images for a reminder about each control.

Top of Camera

On top of the camera are some of the more important controls and dials, as well as the two openings for the stereo microphone, as shown in Figure 2-1.

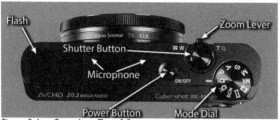

Figure 2-1:   Controls on Top of Camera

Back of Camera

Figure 2-2 shows the major controls on the camera's back.

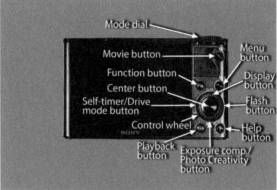

Figure 2-2:   Controls on Back of Camera

Front of Camera

There are only a few items to point out on the camera's front, shown in Figure 2-3.

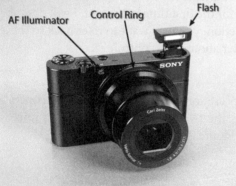

Figure 2-3:   Items on Front of Camera

Right Side of Camera

Inside the door on the right side of the camera is the micro-USB port, as seen in Figure 2-4.

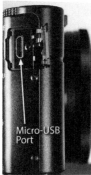

Fig 2-4: USB Port

That is where you connect the USB cable that is supplied with the camera in order to charge the battery, to connect the RX100 to a computer to manage images, or to connect to a printer to print images directly from the camera.

Bottom of Camera

Finally, as shown in Figure 2-5, on the bottom of the camera are the tripod socket, the door for the battery and memory card compartment, and the port for inserting an HDMI cable that connects the camera to an HDTV. In Appendix A, I will discuss a problem that comes up when you attach the RX100 to a tripod: The tripod's plate can make it very hard to turn the control ring. I offer some solutions to that problem in Appendix A.

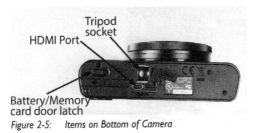

Figure 2-5:   Items on Bottom of Camera

Fully Automatic: Intelligent Auto Mode

Now I'll discuss how to use these controls to start taking pictures and videos. Here's a set of steps to follow if you want to set the camera to one of its most automatic modes and let it make (almost) all of the decisions for you. This is a good way to go if you need to grab a quick shot without fiddling with settings, or if you're new at this and would rather let the camera work its magic without having to provide much input.

1. Turn on the power by pressing the On/Off button on top of the camera. The LCD screen will illuminate to show that the camera has turned on.

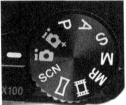

Figure 2-6: Intelligent Auto Mode

2. Find the mode dial on top of the camera at the right, and turn it so the green camera icon with a letter "i" is next to the white indicator line, as shown in Figure 2-6. This sets the camera to the Intelligent Auto shooting mode. If you see the help screen that describes the mode (called the Mode Dial Guide by Sony), as seen in Figure 2-7, press the center button (in the center of the control wheel on the back of the camera) to dismiss it. (I'll explain how to dispense with that help screen altogether in Chapter 7.)

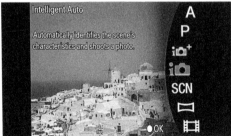

Figure 2-7: Mode Dial Guide

34

3. Press the Menu button in the right center of the camera's back to activate the menu system. As I discussed in Chapter 1, navigate through the various numbered screens of the menus by pressing the right and left edges of the control wheel on the back of the camera. You can tell which menu screen is currently active by looking at the small orange line (cursor) beneath the numbers. When a given screen is selected, navigate up and down through the various options on that screen by pressing the up and down direction buttons or by turning the control wheel right or left. When the orange selection bar is highlighting the option you want, press the center button to select that item. Then, pressing the up and down direction buttons or turning the control wheel, highlight the value you want to set for that option, and press the center button to confirm it. You can then continue making menu settings; when you are finished with the menu system, press the Menu button to exit back to the live view so you can take pictures.

4. Using the procedure described in step 3, make the following settings through the menu system:

Suggested Settings for Intelligent Auto Mode	
Image Size	L:20M
Aspect Ratio	3:2
Quality	Fine
Drive Mode	Single shooting
Flash Mode	Autoflash
Focus Mode	Single-shot AF
Soft Skin Effect	Off
Smile/Face Detect.	Off
Clear Image Zoom	Off
Digital Zoom	Off
AF Illuminator	Auto
SteadyShot	On
Color Space	sRGB

Suggested Settings for Intelligent Auto Mode	
Shooting Tip List	Use as needed
Write Date	Off
Memory	No setting needed

If you don't want to go through the steps to make all of these settings, don't worry; you are likely to get very usable images even if you don't adjust most of these settings at this point.

5. Press the Menu button again to make the menu disappear, if it hasn't done so already.

6. Press the right button on the control wheel, marked with a lightning bolt. A vertical menu will appear at the left side of the screen, as shown in Figure 2-8.

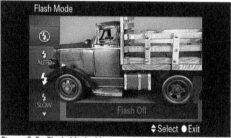

Figure 2-8: Flash Mode Menu

Make sure the Auto selection is highlighted with the orange selection block. If it is not, press the direction buttons or turn the control wheel to highlight it, so the Flash Mode is set to Auto. Press the center button to dismiss this menu.

7. Using a procedure similar to that in step 6, press the left button, marked with a timer dial and an icon showing a stack of images, and make sure the top selection, showing a single rectangular frame, is selected. This sets the camera to take single shots, rather than bursts of continuous shooting.

8. Aim the camera toward the subject and look at the LCD screen to compose the picture. Locate the zoom lever on the ring that surrounds the shutter button on the top right of the

camera. Push that lever to the left, toward the letter W on the camera body, to get a wider-angle shot (including more of the scene in the picture), or to the right, toward the letter T, to get a telephoto, zoomed-in shot.

9. If you're indoors or in an area with low light, be careful not to hold your finger on top of the flash at the top left of the camera. The camera may try to pop the flash up, but it can't if your finger is blocking it.

10. Once the picture looks good on the LCD screen, gently squeeze the shutter button halfway down and pause in that position. You should hear a little beep and see one or more sets of green focus brackets on the LCD screen, indicating that the subject will be in focus. You also can look for a green disc in the extreme lower left corner of the screen. If that green disc lights up steadily, the image is in focus; if it flashes, the camera was unable to focus. In that case, you can re-aim and see if the autofocus system does better from a different distance or angle.

11. After you have made sure the focus is sharp in the previous step, push the shutter button all the way down to take the picture.

Variations from Fully Automatic

Although the RX100 takes care of the basic settings for you when it's set to Intelligent Auto mode, this camera, unlike some other compact models, still lets you make a number of adjustments to fine-tune the shooting process. The procedure for making these settings is different depending on the shooting mode that is currently selected. In this chapter, we are using the Intelligent Auto mode, so I will discuss the method for making adjustments in that mode. The same method applies when the camera is set to the Superior Auto shooting mode (designated on the mode dial by the tan-colored camera icon with a plus sign). In all other shooting modes, these adjustments, to the extent they can be made, are made using different controls. I will discuss those adjustments in later chapters.

With that introduction, the following discussion will explain several features you can use to fine-tune the appearance of your images, use the self-timer or flash, and adjust other settings, when using the Intelligent Auto or Superior Auto shooting mode.

The Photo Creativity Feature

The Sony DSC-RX100 camera comes equipped with an interesting feature that Sony calls "Photo Creativity." This feature, which is available only in the Intelligent Auto and Superior Auto shooting modes, gives you a simple way to dial in certain adjustments to the appearance of your still images and videos. I can understand why Sony presents these adjustments in this way, making them easy to use and giving them non-technical names such as "Background Defocus" and "Brightness," rather than "aperture control" and "exposure compensation." However, it is somewhat confusing (to me, at least) that you have to remember to make these adjustments using different controls, depending on what shooting mode is in effect.

In any event, for now I will discuss how to make adjustments in the Intelligent Auto mode. In Chapter 3, I will discuss all of the shooting modes, and in Chapters 4 and 5 I will discuss how to make settings in other modes. For example, I will discuss aperture control in Chapter 3 in connection with the Aperture Priority shooting mode, and I will discuss exposure compensation in Chapter 5, in connection with the button that controls that function (the down direction button, in the bottom position on the control wheel).

With that introduction and with the knowledge that I will discuss different ways to make all of these settings in later chapters, the following discussion will cover how to make various settings in the most automatic shooting modes, using the Photo Creativity feature.

As a preliminary matter, it's important to note that the Photo

Creativity feature is not available if the Quality option on the Shooting menu is set to RAW or RAW & JPEG. So, you should make sure that Quality is set to Fine. (If you try to use Photo Creativity with RAW in effect, you will get an error message.) To use the Photo Creativity feature, press the down direction button on the control wheel—the button that is marked with the plus and minus icon and the camera icon with three plus signs at its right side, as shown in Figure 2-2. When you press that button, you will see some new icons and virtual controls appear on the LCD screen, as shown in Figure 2-9.

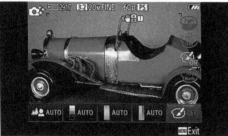

Figure 2-9: Photo Creativity - Initial Screen

At the bottom of the screen you will see a series of five blocks, each with an icon that represents a particular setting or effect you can change. When this group of blocks first appears, each of the first four blocks at the left should contain the word AUTO, and the block at the far right, with an icon of an artist's palette and brush, should show the word OFF. Use the right and left direction buttons on the control wheel to move through these five blocks; each one will be highlighted in orange when it is selected. You can keep pressing the right or left button to wrap around to the other side of the group of icons if you want. So, for example, when the artist's palette is highlighted, you can press the right button one more time to move directly to the block at the far left of the screen.

When one of the blocks is highlighted in orange, you can change the value for that particular setting or effect by turning the control wheel or by pressing the up or down direction button to move the indicator disc along a curved scale that will appear at the right side of the display.

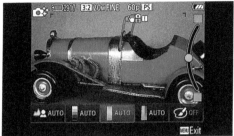

Figure 2-10: Photo Creativity Adjustment Screen

With the first four blocks, as you turn the wheel, a virtual disc will move along a scale at the right of the screen, and the appearance of the icon for that block will change to show how the setting is changing, as seen in Figure 2-10. When the block is first selected, a word or phrase describing the setting for that block will appear briefly on the screen and then disappear. The settings that are controlled by the first four blocks are as follows, from left to right:

Background Defocus. This first setting on the left is used to achieve the effect by which a photograph's foreground subject is sharply focused, while the background is defocused, or fuzzy. This effect, sometimes called "bokeh," can be used to separate the subject from a background that otherwise might be distracting or unpleasant. In more technical terms, what happens is that the camera's aperture (its opening to let in light) is opened up wider, which causes the depth of field to be shallower, allowing the background to go out of focus. When the indicator disc is at the bottom of the scale, the aperture is opened as much as possible, resulting in a more defocused background; as the disc approaches the top of the scale, the background should become sharper as the aperture is narrowed and the depth of field is increased. I will discuss this effect again in Chapter 3, in connection with the discussion of the Aperture Priority shooting mode. Figure 2-11 provides an example of an image with a defocused background.

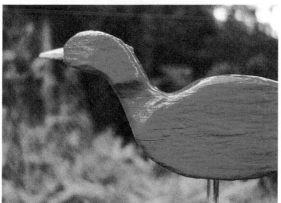

Figure 2-11: Example of Defocused Background

Brightness. The next setting from the left controls the brightness of your images. The indicator disc for this setting starts in the middle of the scale, with normal brightness. As you turn the control wheel to move the disc higher on the scale, the image gets brighter; as the disc moves below the mid-point, the image becomes darker. In technical terms, this setting controls exposure compensation, which can be used in situations when the normal exposure calculated by the camera would not be ideal. For example, if a dark object is photographed against a white background, the camera's automatic exposure control is likely to under-expose the subject, because the camera takes into account the broad expanse of white in the background and reduces the exposure level. With the Brightness control, you can increase the brightness level so the subject will appear properly exposed, as shown in Figure 2-12.

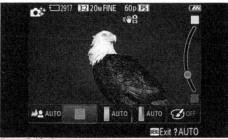

Figure 2-12: Brightness Adjustment

41

Color. The third setting from the left lets you adjust the white balance of your images, though Sony simply uses the term "Color" to simplify things. As I will discuss in Chapter 4, white balance is a setting that adjusts the camera's processing of colors according to the "color temperature" of a given light source. In general, light from sources such as incandescent bulbs is at a lower color temperature than light from the sun. The lower color temperatures are considered "warmer," with a reddish or brownish cast, and the higher ones yield color temperatures that are considered "cooler," with a more bluish appearance. (In this case, "warm" and "cool" have to do with the appearance, rather than the actual temperature, of the subjects.)

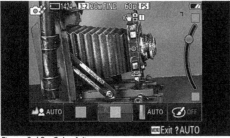

Figure 2-13: Color Adjustment

With this setting, again, the normal value is in the center of the curved scale. To make the colors of the scene appear cooler, or more bluish, turn the control wheel to the left to move the indicator disc toward the bottom of the scale; reverse that process to make the colors warmer, or more reddish. Figure 2-13 shows the Color setting adjusted to the reddish side.

Note that this adjustment does not change the actual White Balance setting; that setting is fixed at Auto White Balance for the automatic shooting modes; this adjustment merely tweaks that setting toward the warm or cool end of the scale. In the more advanced shooting modes, as discussed in Chapter 4, you can make more precise adjustments to the camera's white balance through the White Balance menu option.

Vividness. The fourth setting from the left gives you a way to adjust the intensity, or saturation, of the colors in your images.

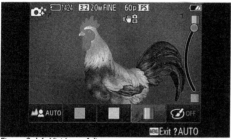

Figure 2-14: Vividness Adjustment

Here, again, the standard setting is in the middle of the curved scale; move the indicator upward for more intense colors and downward for softer, or less-saturated colors. In the more advanced shooting modes, you can adjust saturation in finer detail, along with contrast and sharpness, using the Creative Style menu option, as discussed in Chapter 4. Figure 2-14 shows Vividness set to its maximum.

Picture Effect. The final setting at the right of the screen, marked with the artist's palette, gives you access to the settings from the Picture Effect menu option, which is available through the Shooting menu in the more advanced shooting modes. When the Picture Effect block is highlighted, you can select from the following settings by moving the indicator along the scale: Toy Camera, Pop Color, Posterization Color, Posterization B/W, Retro Photo, Soft High-key, Partial Color: Red, Partial Color: Green, Partial Color: Blue, Partial Color: Yellow, and High Contrast Mono. These settings can yield fairly dramatic effects for your images, as is indicated by their labels. These are the same settings as those available through the Picture Effect item on the Shooting menu, although there are some settings and adjustments that are available through that menu item that cannot be made from the Photo Creativity system, such as selecting different varieties of the Toy Camera setting. I will discuss those settings and provide some examples in Chapter 4.

You can combine more than one Photo Creativity setting to achieve various effects. For example, if you activate the Partial Color effect using the rightmost block at the bottom of the screen, you can then move the highlight to the Color or Vividness block and change the color tint or the saturation of the color that you selected for the Partial Color effect. Or, you can decrease the exposure of the image and also decrease the intensity of the colors by using the Brightness and Vividness controls together.

To reset any one of the five settings to its default value, highlight its block and press the In-Camera Guide/Delete button (marked with a question mark). For the first four blocks, this action will reset the indicator to its default value (bottom of the scale for Background Defocus; middle of the scale for the other three). For the Picture Effect setting, this action will turn the selected effect off, leaving no effect active. If you want to reset all of the blocks at once, you can do so by turning the mode dial to another shooting mode (such as Superior Auto or Program) and then back to Intelligent Auto. To exit from the Photo Creativity screen altogether, press the Menu button.

The Photo Creativity settings are a very useful feature of the RX100, and it is quite convenient to be able to select one or more of them while the camera is in this automatic mode, so you don't have to invest too much effort into figuring out what settings to use. However, if you want to exercise more control over the settings, you will probably want to use one of the more advanced shooting modes and use the menu options and controls that allow you to make more detailed settings.

Flash

Now I'll go into a bit more detail about using the RX100's built-in flash unit, because that is something you may need to use on a regular basis. In Chapter 4 I'll provide more details about the Flash Mode settings and Flash Compensation, and

I'll discuss prevention of "red-eye" in Chapter 7. In Appendix A, I'll discuss using external flash units.

The built-in flash on the RX100 is not especially powerful, but it can provide enough illumination to let you take pictures in dark areas and to brighten up subjects that would otherwise be lost in shadows, even outdoors on a sunny day. After you have used the flash once or twice, the procedure should seem quite simple.

The flash unit will pop up on its own in certain situations, or you can force it to pop up. However, you should never try to force the flash to pop up manually; the key to controlling the behavior of the flash is to use the right direction button at the right edge of the control wheel on back of the camera. That button has a lightning bolt icon on it to announce its identity as the Flash button.

For this discussion, I'm assuming the camera is set to Intelligent Auto mode; in some other situations, including some of the Scene mode settings, the Flash button will not operate. In Intelligent Auto mode, press the right direction button once to summon the Flash Mode menu, and then press the up and down buttons or turn the control wheel to select the flash mode you want from that list. (You also can summon the Flash Mode menu from the Shooting menu; Flash Mode is the second item down on the second screen of the Shooting menu. See Chapter 4 for a discussion of all items on those menu screens.)

The vertical menu at the left of the screen, shown in Figure 2.8, contains icons representing the five flash mode options—a lightning bolt with the universal "no" sign crossing it out, for Flash Off; a lightning bolt with the word Auto, for Autoflash; a lightning bolt alone, for Fill-flash (meaning the flash will always fire); a lightning bolt with the word Slow, for Slow Sync; and a lightning bolt with the word Rear, for Rear Sync. When the camera is set to Intelligent Auto mode, the last two choices will appear grayed-out; if you highlight one of those and press the center button to select it, the camera will display a message saying you cannot make that selection in this shooting mode.

I discussed earlier how to set the flash unit to the Autoflash mode. If, instead of Autoflash, you choose Fill-flash, you will see the lightning bolt icon on the screen at all times, and the flash will fire regardless of whether the camera's exposure system believes flash is needed. This setting can be of use in some outdoor settings, such as when you need to reduce the shadows on your subject's face. The image of a small statue in Figure 2-15 was taken with Fill-flash to reduce shadows.

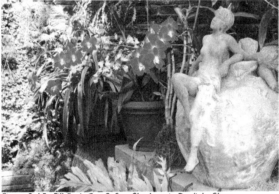

Figure 2-15: Fill-flash Can Soften Shadows in Daylight Shots

When the camera is set for certain types of shooting, such as using the self-timer with continuous shooting, the flash is forced off and cannot be turned on. With some other settings, such as continuous shooting, the flash will fire if you set it to do so, but the use of flash will limit the use of the other setting. In other words, instead of doing rapid continuous shooting, the camera will take multiple images, but at a very slow rate, because the flash cannot recycle quickly enough to fire multiple times. In some shooting modes, such as the Night Scene setting of Scene mode, you cannot even get the Flash Mode menu to appear; if you press the Flash button, the camera will display a message saying the flash is not available in that shooting mode, as shown in Figure 2-16.

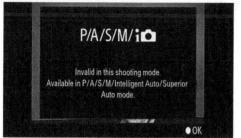

Figure 2-16: Error Message for Pressing Flash Button

If you set the mode dial to P, for Program mode, and then press the Flash button to select a flash mode, you will see the same five options for Flash Mode on the menu, but this time the Autoflash option will be grayed-out, because that selection is available only in the more automatic modes.

In summary, when using Intelligent Auto mode, if you don't want the flash ever to fire, because you are in a museum or similar location, you can select the Flash Off mode. If you want to leave the decision whether to use flash up to the camera, you can select Autoflash mode. If you want to make sure that the flash will fire no matter what, you can select Fill-flash mode. In Chapter 4, I'll talk about the other flash options, Slow Sync and Rear Sync, and how they work, and I'll discuss some other flash-related topics. For now, you have the basic information you need to select a flash mode when the camera is set to the Intelligent Auto shooting mode.

Drive Mode: Self-timer and Continuous Shooting

Finally, there is one more set of adjustments you can make when using Intelligent Auto mode that is worth discussing here. If you press the control wheel's left direction button, which is marked with a timer dial and an icon that looks like a stack of images, the camera will display a vertical menu for Drive Mode, as shown in Figure 2-17.

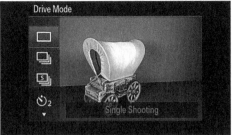

Figure 2-17: Drive Mode Menu

You navigate through the options on this menu by pressing the up and down direction buttons or by turning the control wheel.

I will discuss the Drive Mode menu options more fully in Chapter 4. For now, you should be aware of a few of the options. (I will skip over some others.) First, if you select the top option on the menu, represented by a single rectangular frame, the camera is set for single shooting mode; when you press the shutter button, a single image is captured. If you choose the second option, whose icon looks like a stack of images, the camera is set for continuous shooting, in which it takes a rapid burst of images while you hold down the shutter button.

If you select the fourth option, whose icon is a timer dial with a number beside it, the camera uses the self-timer. Use the left and right direction buttons to choose either 2 or 10 seconds for the timer delay. Once the timer is set, place the camera on a tripod, or just hold it in your hands, depending on the situation, and press the shutter button. The shutter will be released after the specified number of seconds. The 10-second delay is useful when you need to place the camera on a tripod and then join a group of people for a group photo; the 2-second delay is useful when you just want to make sure the camera is not jiggled by the action of pressing the shutter button. This option helps greatly when you are taking a picture for which focusing is critical, such as an extreme close-up. I will discuss the use of the self-timer and other Drive Mode options in more detail in Chapter 4.

Note that the Drive Mode menu also can be reached through the normal menu system. Drive Mode is the top option on the second screen of the Shooting menu.

Tracking Focus

Finally, there is one more setting that is available in Intelligent Auto mode that I will discuss in this chapter. This is Tracking Focus, which sets the camera to maintain its focus on a moving object. When the camera is using its normal display screen, you will see a prompt for Tracking Focus at the bottom of the display, as shown in Figure 2-18, indicating that you press the center button to turn on this feature. (If this prompt does not appear, that probably means that you have assigned a different function to the center button using the Function of Center Button option on the Custom menu. See Chapter 7 for a discussion of that option. To use Tracking Focus, reset that menu option to Standard.)

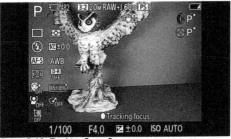

Figure 2-18: Tracking Focus Prompt

When you press the center button, a focus frame will appear in the center of the screen. Move the camera so that frame is over the item you want to track, such as a child or a pet. Then, with that subject in the frame, press the center button again, and the camera will try to keep that item centered in the focus frame, which will change to a double frame, as shown in Figure 2-19.

49

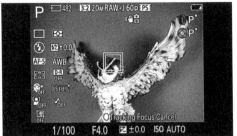

Figure 2-19: Tracking Focus in Use

As long as the subject stays within that double frame, the camera will attempt to keep it in focus. When you are ready, press the shutter button to take the picture.

There are other settings that can be made when the camera is set to Intelligent Auto mode, including Focus Mode, Face Detection, Digital Zoom, and others. I have included suggested settings for those items in a table earlier in this chapter, and I will discuss the details of those settings later, in Chapter 4.

Overview of Movie Recording

Now let's take a look at recording a short movie sequence with the RX100. Once the camera is turned on, turn the mode dial on the top of the camera to select the green camera icon, for Intelligent Auto mode. There is a special Movie mode setting marked by the movie-frame icon on the mode dial, but you don't have to use that mode for shooting movies; I'll discuss the use of that option and provide more details about movie-recording options in Chapter 8.

For now, press the Menu button to get access to the menu system, and press the right direction button enough times to move the small orange cursor underneath the number 1 next to the movie-frame icon, which represents the Movie menu, as shown in Figure 2-20. There is only one screen with seven items on that menu, because there are few options that can be controlled just for shooting movies. On the top line of the Movie menu, with File Format highlighted, press the center button to go to the sub-menu with the two choices for the format of movie recording. For now, be sure the top option, AVCHD, is highlighted; that format provides the highest quality for your videos.

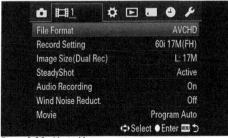

Figure 2-20: Movie Menu

For the rest of the settings, I will provide a table like the one included earlier in this chapter for shooting still images. The settings shown below are standard ones for shooting high-quality movies.

Suggested Movie Menu Settings for Shooting Movies in Intelligent Auto Mode	
File Format	AVCHD
Record Setting	60p 28M (PS)
Image Size (Dual Rec)	L:17M
SteadyShot	Active
Audio Recording	On
Wind Noise Reduction	Off

There are some other settings you can make on the Shooting menu for still images that will affect your movie recording; I will discuss that topic in Chapter 8. For now, if you are going to be shooting a movie that shows people's faces, you may want to go back to the Shooting menu and set the Face Detection item to On. You can leave the other items set as they were for shooting still images, as set forth in the earlier table for still shooting.

51

Now you have all of the necessary settings made for recording a movie. Just aim the camera at your subject, and, when you are ready to start recording the movie, press and release the red Movie button at the upper right corner of the camera's back. The screen will display a flashing red REC icon in the lower left corner of the display, next to a counter showing the elapsed time in the recording, as shown in Figure 2-21.

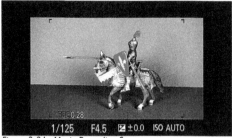
Figure 2-21: Movie Recording Screen

Hold the camera as steady as possible (or use a tripod), and pan (move side to side) slowly if you need to.

The camera will keep shooting until it reaches a recording limit, or until you press the red Movie button again to stop the recording. (The maximum time for continuous recording of any one scene is about 29 minutes.) Don't be concerned about the level of the sound that is being recorded, because you have no control over the audio volume while recording.

The camera will automatically adjust exposure as lighting conditions change. You can zoom the lens in and out as needed, but you should do so sparingly if at all, to avoid distracting the audience and to avoid putting the sounds of zooming the lens on the sound track. When you are finished, press the red Movie button again, and the camera will take a while to save the footage, displaying the "Recording . . ." message for a time on the screen.

Here is one point that's not specific to the RX100: Unless you have a good reason to do otherwise, hold the camera as steady as possible (using a tripod if possible), and don't move the camera except in very smooth, slow motions, such as a smooth pan to take in a wide scene gradually. Video from a jerkily moving camera can be very disconcerting to the viewer.

Those are the basics for recording video clips with the RX100. I'll discuss the movie options in more detail in Chapter 8.

Viewing Pictures

Before I delve into more advanced settings for taking still pictures and movies, as well as other matters of interest, I will discuss the basics of viewing your images in the camera.

Review While in Shooting Mode

Every time you take a still picture, the image will show up on the LCD for a short time, if you have the Custom menu's Auto Review option set to turn on this function. I'll discuss the details of that setting in Chapter 7. By default, your image will stay on the screen for 2 seconds after you take a new picture. If you prefer, you can set that display to last for 5 or 10 seconds, or to be off altogether.

Reviewing Images in Playback Mode

If you want to review images that were taken previously, you enter playback mode by pressing the Playback button—the one with the small triangle inside a rectangle to the lower left of the control wheel on the camera's back. One possibly confusing feature of the RX100 is that you can review only still images or movies at any one time. In other words, you will not be able to scroll through both movies and still images; you have to select one or the other. To do that, you can use the Still/Movie Select option on the Playback menu. I discuss that and other options for selecting stills or movies in Chapter 6.

Once you have selected still images or movies, you can scroll through the recorded images (or the first frames of the movies) by pressing the left and right direction buttons or by turning the control wheel. Hold down the left or right button to move more quickly through the images. You can enlarge the view of any still image by moving the zoom lever on top of the camera toward the T position, and you can scroll around in the enlarged image using the four direction buttons. If you press the zoom lever in the other direction, towards the wide-angle setting, you will see index screens with increasing numbers of thumbnail images; you can select any image from those screens by pressing the center button. I'll discuss more of your playback options in Chapter 6.

Playing Movies

To play movies in the camera, you first need to set the camera to play movies as opposed to stills. To do this, go to the Playback menu and select the top item, Still/Movie Select, and select either MP4 or AVCHD files for playback. The RX100 will then display only files from that category when you press the Playback button.

Move through the recorded images by the methods described above until you find the movie you want to play. You should see the word Play next to a white disc in the lower right corner of the screen, as shown in Figure 2-22.

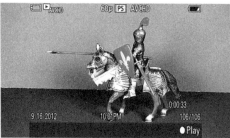
Figure 2-22: A Movie Ready to Play

(If you don't see that icon, press the Display button to display the detailed information screen.) Press the center button to start the movie playing. Then, as shown in Figure 2-23, you will see prompts at the bottom of the screen setting forth the controls you can use, including the center button to pause. To change the volume, press the down direction button and then use the up and down buttons or the control wheel to make the adjustments. To exit from playing the movie, press the Playback button. (I'll discuss other movie playback options in Chapter 8.)

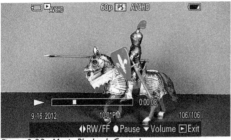

Figure 2-23: Movie Playback Controls

If you want to play the movies on a computer or edit them with video-editing software, you can use the PlayMemories Home software that comes with the camera, for use with a Windows computer. If you are using a Macintosh computer, you can use the iMovie program or some other program that can deal with AVCHD and MP4 video files, such as Adobe Premiere Elements or Premiere Pro.

Chapter 3: The Shooting Modes

Until now I have discussed the basics of setting up the camera for quick shots, relying heavily on features such as those available in Intelligent Auto mode to take pictures with settings controlled mostly by the camera's automation. As with other sophisticated digital cameras, though, with the Sony RX100 there is a large range of options available for setting the camera, particularly for taking still images. One of the main goals of this book is to explain the broad range of features available. To do this, I need to turn my attention to two subjects—shooting modes and the Shooting menu options. In this chapter, I'll discuss the shooting modes; in Chapter 4, I will discuss the Shooting menu.

Whenever you set out to record still images, you need to select one of the available shooting modes: Intelligent Auto, Superior Auto, Program, Aperture Priority, Shutter Priority, Manual, Memory Recall, Sweep Shooting, and Scene. (The only other mode available is for movies.) So far, we have worked primarily with the Intelligent Auto mode. Now I will discuss the others, after some review of the first one.

Intelligent Auto Mode

I've already discussed this shooting mode in some detail. This is the one you probably want to select if you just need to have the camera ready for a quick shot, maybe in an environment with fast-paced events when you won't have much time to fuss with settings of things such as ISO, white balance, aperture, focus, or shutter speed.

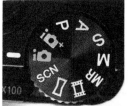

Figure 3-1: Intelligent,Auto Mode

To set this mode, turn the mode dial, on top of the camera to the right of the shutter button, to the icon of a green camera with the letter "i" (for "intelligent") next to it, as shown in Figure 3-1. When you select this mode, the camera makes quite a few decisions for you and limits your options in several ways. For example, you can't set ISO or White Balance to any value other than Auto, and you can't choose the metering method or use exposure bracketing. You can, however, use quite a few features, as discussed in Chapter 2, including the Photo Creativity options, Drive Mode, Flash Mode, Tracking Focus, and others. You also can use sophisticated options such as the RAW format, which I will discuss in Chapter 4 when I discuss the various other Shooting menu options.

One interesting aspect of the Intelligent Auto setting is that, in this mode (and also in Superior Auto mode, discussed next), the camera uses its built-in programming to attempt to figure out what sort of subject or scene you are shooting. Some of the subjects the camera will attempt to detect are Baby, Portrait, Night Portrait, Night Scene, Landscape, Backlight, Low Brightness, and Macro. It also will try to detect certain conditions, such as whether a tripod is in use or whether the subject is walking, and it will display appropriate icons for those conditions. So, if you see different icons when you aim at various subjects in this shooting mode, that means that the camera is evaluating the scene for factors such as brightness, backlighting, the presence of human subjects, and the like, so it can use the best possible settings for the situation.

For Figure 3-2, the camera evaluated a scene with bushes and flowers and varying distances and appropriately used its Landscape setting.

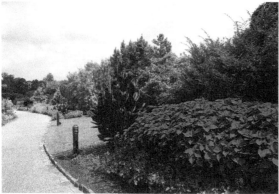

Figure 3-2: Scene Detection Example - Landscape

Figure 3-3 shows the use of this automatic detection as viewed on the LCD in Shooting mode.

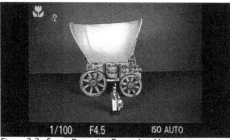

Figure 3-3: Scene Detection Example - Macro

In this case, where the subject was closer to the lens, the camera interpreted the scene as a macro, or closeup shot, and switched automatically into Macro mode, indicated by the flower icon. In addition, the camera correctly detected that it was attached to a tripod, as indicated by the tripod icon to the lower right of the macro symbol.

Of course, this system of scene detection depends on the electronic circuitry of the camera, which may not interpret every scene in the same way that you would. If that becomes a problem, you may want to make individual settings using one of the more advanced shooting modes, such as Program, Aperture Priority, Shutter Priority, or Manual. Or, you can use the SCN setting on the mode dial, and select the Scene setting that most closely fits the current situation.

Superior Auto Mode

With many compact cameras, there is only one largely automatic shooting mode. The RX100, however, provides you with two choices, both of which provide high degrees of automation but which have significant differences. The second automatic mode, called Superior Auto, is designated on the mode dial by the icon of a tan-colored camera with the letter "i" and a plus sign next to it, as shown in Figure 3-4.

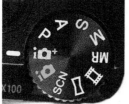

Figure 3-4: Superior Auto Mode

The Superior Auto mode includes all of the features and functions of Intelligent Auto mode, but it adds an extra level of sophistication. In Superior Auto mode, as in Intelligent Auto mode, the camera uses its scene recognition capability to try to determine what sort of subject matter and conditions are present, such as a portrait, a dimly-lit scene, and the like. For many of these scenes, the camera will function just as it does in Intelligent Auto mode. However, in a few specific situations, the camera will take a different approach: It will take a rapid burst of multiple shots, then process them internally and combine them digitally into a single composite image that has higher quality than would be possible with a single shot. The higher quality can be achieved because the camera generally has to raise the ISO setting to a fairly high level, which introduces visual "noise" into the image. By taking multiple shots and then combining them, the camera can average out and cancel some of the noise, thereby increasing the quality of the resulting image.

One problem with this system is that you, the photographer, have no control over when or whether the camera decides to use this burst shooting technique. There are only three situations in which the camera will do this: when it detects scenes that call for settings called Anti Motion Blur, Backlight Correction HDR, or Hand-held Twilight. When the camera believes this multiple-shooting method is appropriate, it fires several shots in a quick burst; you will hear the rapid firing of the shutter several times. Then, it will take longer than usual for the camera to process the multiple shots into a single composite image; you will likely see a message saying "Processing…" on the screen for several seconds. When the camera is using this mode, which Sony calls "overlay," you will see a small white icon in the upper left corner of the display that looks like a small stack of frames with a plus sign at its upper right corner, as shown in Figure 3-5.

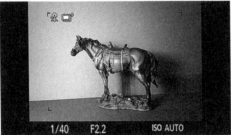

Figure 3-5: Superior Auto Mode - Overlay Icon in Corner

You should note that two of these shooting scenarios—Anti Motion Blur and Hand-held Twilight—are available as selections in Scene mode, discussed later in this chapter. The third, Backlight Correction HDR, is available only when the camera decides to use it. Also, you should note that none of the three multiple-shot settings will function when the Quality is set to RAW or RAW & JPEG on the Shooting menu.

Personally, I have not found much advantage from using the Superior Auto setting. However, it is similar to Intelligent

Auto, which is a very useful shooting mode, and there may be some cases in which the burst-shooting feature will improve the quality of an image, so it is not a bad idea to set the camera to the Superior Auto mode when you are shooting in low-light or backlit conditions. As a general rule, though, I prefer to use a mode such as Program, discussed below, and set my own values for items such as DRO, HDR, ISO, and metering mode.

Program Mode

Choose this mode by turning the mode dial to the P setting, as shown in Figure 3-6.

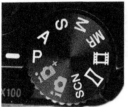

Figure 3-6: Program Mode

Program mode lets you control many of the settings available with the camera, apart from shutter speed and aperture. You still can override the camera's automatic exposure to a fair extent by using exposure compensation, as discussed in Chapter 5, as well as exposure bracketing, discussed in Chapter 4, and Program Shift, discussed later in this chapter. You don't have to make a lot of decisions if you don't want to, though, because the camera will make reasonable choices for you as defaults. However, you should note that, even though shutter speeds as long as 30 seconds are available in Shutter Priority and Manual exposure mode, the camera will never choose a shutter speed longer than one second in Program mode.

The Program Shift function is available only in Program mode; it works as follows. Once you have aimed the camera at your subject, the camera will display its chosen settings for shutter speed and aperture in the lower left corner of the display. At that point, you can turn the control wheel on the back of the camera, and the values for shutter speed and aperture will change, if possible under current conditions, so as to select different values for both settings while keeping the same overall exposure of the scene. You also can use the control ring (the large ring around the lens) to make this setting, if the Control Ring option is set to the Standard setting on the Custom menu, as discussed in Chapter 7.

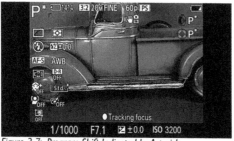

Figure 3-7: Program Shift Indicated by Asterisk

With this option, the camera "shifts" the original exposure to any of the matched pairs that appear as you turn the control wheel. For example, if the original exposure was f/2.0 at 1/30 second, you may see equivalent pairs of f/2.2 at 1/25, f/2.5 at 1/20, and f/2.8 at 1/15, among others. When Program Shift is in effect, the P icon in the upper left corner of the screen will have an asterisk to its right, as shown in Figure 3-7. To cancel Program Shift, you can turn the control wheel until the original settings are back in effect, or you can select any flash mode using the Flash button, which is also the right direction button. (Program Shift cannot function when the flash is in use.)

Why would you want to use the Program Shift feature? You might want a slightly faster shutter speed to stop action better, or a wider aperture to blur the background more, or you might have some other creative reason. Of course, if you really are interested in setting a particular shutter speed or aperture, you probably are better off using Aperture Priority mode or Shutter Priority mode. However, having the Program Shift capability available is a good thing for a situation in which you're taking pictures quickly using Program mode, and you want a fast way to tweak the settings somewhat.

Another important aspect of Program mode is that it greatly expands the choices available through the Shooting menu, which controls many of the camera's settings. You will be able to make choices involving ISO sensitivity, metering method, DRO/HDR, white balance, Creative Style, and others that are not available in the Auto modes. I won't discuss those settings here; if you want to explore that topic, see the discussion of the Shooting menu in Chapter 4 and check out all of the different selections that are available.

Aperture Priority Mode

You set the camera to the Aperture Priority shooting mode by turning the mode dial to the A setting, as shown in Figure 3-8.

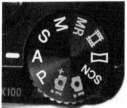

Figure 3-8: Aperture Priority Mode

Before discussing the nuts and bolts of the settings for this mode, let's talk about what aperture is and why you would want to control it. The camera's aperture is a measure of the width of its opening that lets in light. The aperture's width is measured numerically in f-stops. For the RX100, the range of f-stops is from f/1.8 (wide open) to f/11.0 (most narrow). The amount of light that is let into the camera to create an image on the camera's sensor is controlled by the combination of aperture (how wide open the lens is) and shutter speed (how long the shutter remains open to let in the light).

For some purposes, you may want to control the width of the aperture but still let the camera choose the corresponding shutter speed. Here are a couple of examples involving depth of field. Depth of field is a measure of how well a camera is able to keep multiple objects or subjects in focus at different distances. For example, say you have three of your friends lined up so you can see all of them, but they are standing at different distances—five, seven, and nine feet (1.5, 2.1, and 2.7 meters) from the camera. If the camera's depth of field is quite shallow at a particular focal length, such as five feet (1.5 meters), then, in this case, if you focus on the friend at that distance, the other two will be out of focus and blurry. But if the camera's depth of field when focused at five feet is broad, then it may be possible for all three friends to be in sharp focus in your photograph, even if the focus is set for the friend at five feet.

What does all of that have to do with aperture? One of the rules of photographic optics is that the wider open the camera's aperture is, the smaller its depth of field is at a given focal length. So in our example above, if you have the camera's aperture set to its widest opening, f/1.8, the depth of field will be relatively shallow, and it will be difficult to keep several items in focus at varying distances from the camera. If the aperture is set to the narrowest opening, f/11.0, the depth of field will be greater, and it will be possible to have more items in focus at varying distances.

With a camera like the RX100, with its relatively small sensor and wide-angle lens, the effects of aperture on depth of field are not as pronounced as with some other cameras. However, the following images generally illustrate the effects of aperture settings on depth of field, using an eagle figurine and a background of trees some distance away.

In these photos, the eagle figurine was quite close to the RX100's lens—within about 6 to 8 inches (15 to 20 cm). I focused on the eagle's eye in each case, using manual focus to get the focus as accurate as possible. For Figure 3-9, the aperture of the RX100 was f/1.8, the widest possible. With this setting, because the depth of field at this aperture was quite shallow, the background is quite blurry, and therefore less distracting than it otherwise would be. In fact, as you may be able to see, even some parts of the eagle are slightly blurry, because the depth of field is very shallow, and only the eye and some of the feathers are in the sharpest focus.

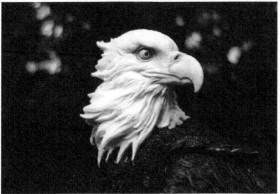

Figure 3-9: Aperture Set to f/1.8

Figure 3-10 was taken with the aperture set to f/5.6, about the halfway point for the aperture setting, resulting in a broader depth of field, and consequently keeping more of the eagle in focus and making the background sharper.

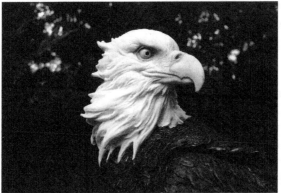

Figure 3-10: Aperture Set to f/5.6

Finally, in Figure 3-11, the aperture was set at f/11.0, the most narrow possible setting.

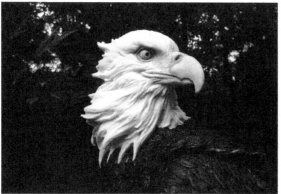

Figure 3-11: Aperture Set to f/11.0

With this aperture, the eagle is in sharp focus, and the back-ground is considerably less blurry than in the other two im-ages. These photos illustrate the effects of varying your aper-ture by setting it wide (low numbers) when you want to blur the background and narrow (high numbers) when you want to enjoy a broad depth of field and keep subjects at varying distances in sharp focus.

This situation arises often in the case of outdoor portraits. For example, you may want to take a photo of a subject outdoors with a background of trees and bushes, and possibly some other, more distracting objects, such as a swing set or a tool shed. If you can achieve a shallow depth of field by using a wide aperture, you can keep your subject in sharp focus, but leave the background quite blurry and indistinct. As was dis-cussed in Chapter 2, this effect is sometimes called "bokeh," a Japanese term describing an aesthetically pleasing blurriness of the background. In this situation, the blurriness of the back-ground can be a great asset, reducing the distraction from un-wanted objects and highlighting the sharply focused portrait of your subject.

In Figure 3-12 I took a close-up shot of a bright red flower, blurring the background by having the aperture set to f/1.8, the widest possible.

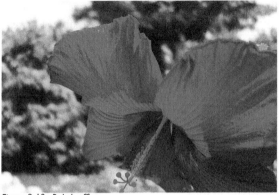

Figure 3-12: Bokeh effect

Now that we have considered some good reasons for selecting a specific aperture, here are the technical steps involved. Once you have moved the mode dial to the A setting, the next step is quite simple. Use either the control ring (the large, ridged ring around the lens) or the control wheel to change the aperture. (If the control ring does not change the aperture, check the setting for the Control Ring item on the Custom menu, as discussed in Chapter 7; that menu option should be set to Standard.)

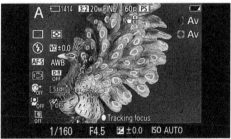

Figure 3-13: Shooting Screen in Aperture Priority Mode

As shown in Figure 3-13, the number of the f-stop (f/4.5 in this case) will appear in the bottom center of the screen next to the shutter speed. The camera will select a shutter speed that will result in a proper exposure given the aperture you have set. Although, in most cases, the camera will be able to select a corresponding shutter speed that results in a normal exposure, there may be instances in which this is not possible. For example, if you are taking pictures in a very bright location and have set the aperture to f/1.8, the camera may not be able to set a shutter speed fast enough to yield a proper exposure. In that case, the designation of the fastest possible shutter speed (1/2000) will flash on the camera's display to show that the exposure cannot be set using that aperture. The camera will still let you take the exposure, but it may be too bright to be usable. Similarly, if conditions are too dark for a good exposure at the aperture you have selected, the slowest shutter speed (8", meaning 8 seconds) will flash.

One more note on Aperture Priority mode that might not be immediately obvious and could easily lead to confusion: Not all apertures are available at all times. In particular, the widest-open aperture, f/1.8, is available only when the lens is zoomed out to its wide-angle setting (zoom lever moved toward the W). At the highest zoom levels, the widest aperture available is f/4.9.

To see an illustration of this point, here is a quick test. Zoom the lens out by moving the zoom lever all the way to the left, toward the W label. Then select Aperture Priority mode and select an aperture of f/1.8 by turning the control wheel or the control ring all the way in the direction for lower numbers. Now zoom the lens in by moving the zoom lever to the right, toward the T setting. After the zoom action is finished, you will see that the aperture has been changed to f/4.9, because that is the limit for the aperture at the telephoto zoom level. (The aperture will change back to f/1.8 if you move the zoom back to the wide-angle setting.) Also, as with Program mode, the full range of the camera's shutter speeds is not available. When set to Aperture Priority mode, the RX100 can select shutter speeds from 1/2000 second to 8 seconds.

Shutter Priority Mode

In Shutter Priority mode, you choose whatever shutter speed you want, and the camera will set the corresponding aperture in order to achieve a proper exposure of the image.

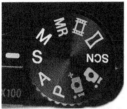

Figure 3-14: Shutter Priority Mode

In this mode, designated by the S position on the mode dial, as shown in Figure 3-14, you can set the shutter to be open for a variety of intervals ranging from 30 seconds to 1/2000 of a second. If you are photographing fast action, such as a baseball swing or a hurdles event at a track meet, and you want to stop the motion with a minimum of blur, you should select a fast shutter speed, such as 1/1000 of a second. The image shown in Figure 3-15 was taken with the shutter speed set at 1/800 second in order to freeze the bike rider in mid-air.

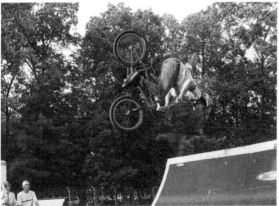

Figure 3-15: Shutter Priority, f/8.0, 1/800 Second, ISO 3200

Figures 3-16 through 3-18 are shots of a model Ferris wheel that show the effects of different shutter speeds. This wheel was turning at a steady rate, with a lighted blue bar rotating more rapidly inside the wheel.

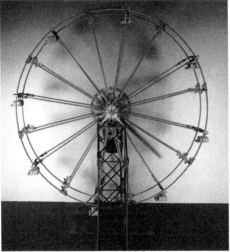

Figure 3-16: Shutter Priority, 1/500 Second

In Figure 3-16, taken at 1/500 second, the action is frozen and you can see the blue bar clearly in the lower right quadrant.

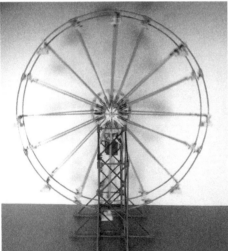

Figure 3-17: Shutter Priority, 1/20 Second

In Figure 3-17, taken at 1/20 second, you can see a good deal of blurring at the slower speed.

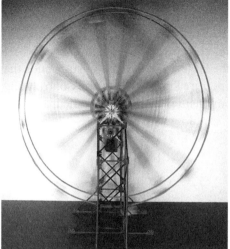

Figure 3-18: Shutter Priority, ¼ Second

In Figure 3-18, taken at 1/4 second, the wheel and bar are even more blurred by the motion.

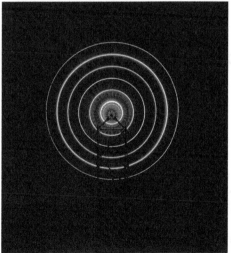

Figure 3-19: Shutter Priority, 2 Seconds

In Figure 3-19, I turned out the lights in the room and exposed the image for 2 seconds. In this case, the interior bar traced its

71

colored lights in complete circles, essentially transforming the image into a different scene.

You select this shooting mode by turning the mode dial on top of the camera to the S indicator, as shown in Figure 3-14. Then you select the shutter speed by turning the control wheel or the control ring—the large, ridged ring that surrounds the lens. (Again, as with Aperture Priority mode, the Control Ring function on the Custom menu must be set to Standard for the ring to control shutter speed.)

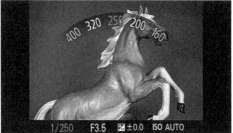

Figure 3-20: Control Ring Display Showing Shutter Speed

If you use the control ring, the LCD will display a circular scale showing the changing shutter speeds, as shown in Figure 3-20, and the selected speed will then appear on the left side of the screen, next to the aperture setting. (You can turn off the circular display on the Custom menu, as discussed in Chapter 7.)

If you use the control wheel, the shutter speed will just change in place at the lower left of the display as you turn the wheel. Note that there is one possibly confusing aspect of the camera's display for Shutter Priority mode. Although the mode dial uses the letter S to stand for Shutter Priority, on the detailed display screen, the camera's screen uses the notation Tv in the upper right corner, which stands for Time value, a notation often used for this shooting mode.

As you cycle through various shutter speeds, the camera will select the appropriate aperture to achieve a proper exposure, if possible. As I discussed in connection with Aperture Priority mode, if you select a shutter speed for which the camera cannot select an aperture that will yield a normal exposure, the LCD will change appearance to indicate how dark or light the resulting shot will be, and the aperture reading at the bottom of the display will flash. The flashing aperture means that proper exposure at that shutter speed is not possible at any available aperture, according to the camera's calculations. For example, if you set the shutter speed to 1/320 of a second in a fairly dark indoor environment, the aperture number (which will be f/1.8, the widest setting, if the zoom is set to wide angle) will flash, indicating that proper exposure is not possible, and the display will be quite dark. As I discussed for Aperture Priority, you can still take the picture if you want to, though it may not be usable. A similar situation may take place if you select a slow shutter speed (such as 4 seconds) in a relatively bright location.

When setting the shutter speed, note that the fractions of a second are easy to interpret, because they are displayed as standard fractions, such as 1/5 or 1/200. A few values are displayed as decimals, including 0.4, 0.5 and 0.8 second.

Manual Exposure Mode

One of the many features of the RX100 that distinguish it from the average run of compact cameras is that it has a fully manual exposure mode, a tremendous tool for serious photographers who want to exert full creative control over exposure decisions.

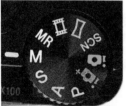

Figure 3-21: Manual Exposure Mode

The technique for using this mode is not too far removed from what I discussed in connection with the Aperture Priority and Shutter Priority modes. To control exposure manually, set the mode dial to the M indicator, as shown in Figure 3-21. You now have to control both shutter speed and aperture by setting them yourself. To set the aperture, turn the control ring around the lens (assuming the control ring is set for this function through the Custom menu, as discussed in Chapter 7); to set the shutter speed, turn the control wheel on the back of the camera.

If the control ring is not set to control aperture, or if you prefer not to use the ring for that purpose, you can use the control wheel to control both aperture and shutter speed. To do that, just press the down direction button on the control wheel to switch between those two selections. When you press that button, either the shutter speed number or the aperture number on the display will turn orange for about ten seconds to indicate that that value is currently being controlled by the control wheel.

As you adjust the shutter speed and aperture, a third value, to the right of the aperture value, will also change. That value is shown by a positive, negative, or zero number next to a box containing the letters "M.M.", which stand for "metered manual," as shown in Figure 3-22.

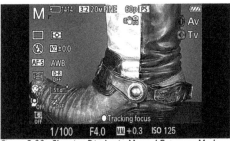

Figure 3-22: Shooting Display in Manual Exposure Mode

That figure represents any deviation from what the camera's metering system considers to be a normal exposure. So, even though you are setting the exposure manually, the camera will still let you know whether the selected aperture and shutter speed will produce a standard exposure.

For example, if the values you have selected will result in a dark exposure, the M.M. value will be negative, and the LCD display will appear dark; with a positive value, it will be unusually bright. The M.M. value can go up or down only to +2.0 or -2.0 EV (exposure value) units; after that point, the value will flash, indicating that the camera considers the exposure to be excessively abnormal.

Of course, you can ignore the M.M. indicator; it is there only to give you an idea of how the camera would meter the scene. You very well may want part or all of the scene to be darker or lighter than the metering would indicate to be "correct."

With Manual exposure mode, the settings for aperture and shutter speed are independent of each other. When you change one, the other one stays unchanged until you adjust it manually. The camera is leaving the creative decision about exposure entirely up to you, even if the resulting photograph would be washed out by excessive exposure or under-exposed to the point of near-blackness.

The range of apertures you can set in this mode is the same as for Aperture Priority mode: f/1.8 to f/11.0. The range of shutter speeds is the same as for Shutter Priority, with one important addition: In Manual mode, you can set the shutter speed to the BULB setting, just beyond the 30-second mark. With this setting, you have to press and hold the shutter button; as long as it is held down, the shutter will stay open. You can use this special setting to take photos in almost-complete darkness by holding the shutter open for a minute or even longer. One problem with doing so is that it is very difficult to avoid jiggling the camera and thereby causing blur to the image. In Appendix A, I will discuss an accessory to help with this issue.

Finally, you should be aware of the procedure for setting the camera's ISO in Manual mode. In Chapter 4, I'll talk more about the ISO setting, which controls how sensitive the camera's sensor is to light. With a higher ISO number, the sensor is more sensitive and the image is exposed more quickly, so the shutter speed can be faster or the aperture more narrow, or both, depending on conditions. In other shooting modes, the camera can set ISO automatically, but in Manual mode you have to set the ISO value yourself. If you try to select Auto ISO while in Manual mode, the camera will display an error message. If you have selected Auto ISO while in another shooting mode and then switch to Manual mode, the camera will set the ISO to 125.

To set the ISO value, press the Menu button to get access to the Shooting menu, go to the third screen, and highlight the ISO item at the top of that screen. Press the center button to bring up the ISO menu, and scroll through the selections using the up and down direction buttons or turning the control wheel. Use a low number like 80 or 100 to emphasize image quality when there is plenty of light; use a higher number in dim light.

You also need to realize that higher ISO settings are likely to cause visual "noise," or graininess, in your images, so you need to weigh the advantages of being able to take pictures in dim light against the risk of having images that are excessively coarse in appearance. Generally speaking, you should try to set the ISO no higher than 800 if you need to ensure the highest quality for your images. You can still get quite acceptable results with ISO 1600 or higher, though, unless you need to make very large prints.

Scene Mode

Scene mode, represented by the SCN setting on the mode dial, as shown in Figure 3-23, is a different animal from the other shooting modes we have discussed. This mode does not have a single defining feature, such as permitting control over one or more aspects of exposure. Instead, when you select Scene mode and then choose a particular Scene type within that mode, you are in effect telling the camera what sort of environment the picture is being taken in, and what type of image you are looking for, and letting the camera make the decision as to what settings to use to produce that result.

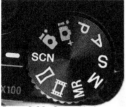
Figure 3-23: Scene Mode

One aspect of using Scene mode is that, with most of its settings, you cannot select many of the options that are available in Program, Aperture Priority, and Manual exposure mode, such as Creative Style, Picture Effect, Metering Mode, White Balance, Autofocus Area, and ISO. There also are some menu settings and control settings that are available with certain Scene settings but not others, as discussed later in this chapter.

Although some photographers may not like Scene mode because it seems to take creative decisions away from you, I have found that it can be quite useful in certain situations. Remember that you don't have to use the various settings only for their labeled purposes; you may find that some of them offer a group of settings that is well-suited for some shooting scenarios that you regularly encounter. I'll discuss how Scene mode works and you can decide for yourself whether you might take advantage of it on some occasions.

You enter Scene mode by turning the mode dial to the SCN indicator. Now, unless you want to settle for whatever type of Scene setting is already in place, you need to pick one from the fairly impressive list of 13 Scene settings. There are several ways to do this, depending on current settings.

If the Mode Dial Guide is turned on through the Setup menu, then, whenever you turn the mode dial to the SCN setting, the Scene Selection menu, shown in Figure 3-24, will appear.

If the Mode Dial Guide is not turned on, then you need to use the Shooting menu to call up the Scene Selection screen. Press the Menu button, navigate to the 5th screen, and choose the Scene Selection item. Once you have the orange highlight on that icon, press the center button and then scroll through the 13 selections on the vertical Scene Selection menu using the up and down direction buttons or the control wheel.

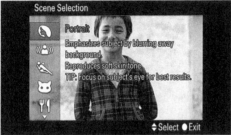

Figure 3-24: Scene Selection Menu Screen

Press the center button again to select one of the settings and return to the shooting screen. You will then see an icon representing that setting, in the upper left corner of the LCD display. For example, Figure 3-25 shows the display when the Anti Motion Blur setting is selected.

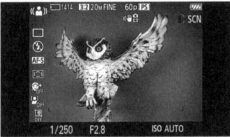

Figure 3-25: Shooting Display with Anti Motion Blur Setting

One helpful point about the Scene menu system is that each Scene setting has a main screen with a brief description of the setting's uses as you move the selector over it, as shown in Figure 3-26, so you are not left trying to puzzle out what each icon represents. As you keep pushing the up or down button or moving the control wheel to move the selector over the other Scene types, when you reach the bottom or top edge of the screen, the selector wraps around to the first or last setting and continues going.

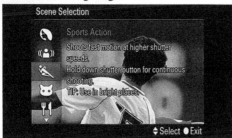

Figure 3-26: Help Screen for Scene Mode Setting

Finally, there is one more way to select a Scene type. If the control ring is set to its Standard setting, then, when the camera is in Scene mode you can just turn the control ring to cycle through the various Scene types; the icon for each type will appear in the upper left corner of the screen. (If you are using manual focus or DMF this will not work, because the control ring will adjust focus.)

That's all there is to do to select a Scene type. But there are numerous choices, and you need to know something about each choice to know whether it's one you would want to select. In general, each different Scene setting carries with it a variety of values, including things like focus mode, flash status, range of shutter speeds, sensitivity to various colors, and others.

It's also helpful to note that some of the settings are designed for certain types of shooting rather than particular environments such as sunset or fireworks. For example, the Anti Motion Blur and High Sensitivity settings are designed for difficult shooting environments, such as dimly lighted areas.

With that introduction, I will discuss the main features of each of the 13 choices, with sample images for some of the settings.

Portrait

The Portrait setting is designed to produce flesh tones with a softening effect, as shown in Figure 3-27. You should stand fairly close to the subject and set the zoom to some degree of telephoto, so as to blur the background if possible; the camera will try to use a wide aperture to assist in this blurring. The flash mode is initially set to Flash Off, but you can set the mode to Autoflash or Fill-flash if you want to even out the lighting or reduce shadows on your subject's face.

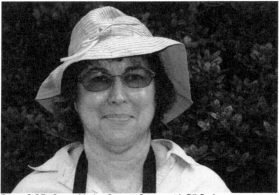

Figure 3-27: Scene Mode - Portrait Setting with Fill-flash

You can use the self-timer or the self-portrait settings of Drive Mode, but you cannot use bracketing or continuous shooting.

Anti Motion Blur

As noted earlier, this Scene mode setting is not meant for a particular subject, but for a certain type of situation. This option is useful when you are shooting in an area with dim lighting or with the lens zoomed in to a telephoto setting. In either of those situations, the image is subject to blurring because of camera motion. In dim lighting, this blurring can happen because the camera is likely to use a slow shutter speed to expose the image properly, and it is hard to hold the camera perfectly steady for more than about 1/30 second. In the telephoto case, any camera motion is exaggerated because of the magnification of the image.

To counter the effects of this blurring, with Anti Motion Blur the camera raises the ISO to a higher than normal level so the camera can use a fast shutter speed and still let in enough light to expose the image properly. Because higher ISO settings result in increased visual noise, the camera takes a rapid burst of multiple shots and combines them through its internal processing into a single composite image with reduced noise. What is particularly remarkable about this setting, though, is that the camera also counteracts blur from motion of the subject to a fair extent, by analyzing the shots and rejecting those with motion blur as much as possible.

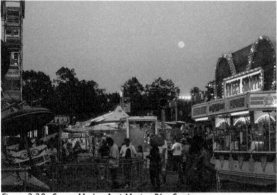

Figure 3-28: Scene Mode - Anti Motion Blur Setting

Anti Motion Blur is useful for shots taken after sunset as the light is fading if you don't want to use flash, as shown in Figure 3-28. You should not expect good results if you use this setting with fast-moving subjects, because the camera would not be able to eliminate the motion blur. With slower-moving subjects, though, the RX100 can do a good job of reducing the blur. With this setting, you cannot set the Drive Mode or the Flash Mode.

Sports Action

The Sports Action mode is for use when lighting is bright and you need to freeze the action of your subjects, such as athletes, children at play, pets, or other objects in motion. Depending on conditions, the camera may set a high ISO value so it can use a fast shutter speed to stop action. The flash is initially forced off, but you can turn on Fill-flash if you want. The camera sets itself for continuous shooting, so you can hold down the shutter button and capture a burst of images. In that way, you should increase your chances of capturing the action at a perfect moment. You can switch to the fastest level of continuous shooting if you want, but you cannot set Drive Mode to single shooting. Somewhat oddly, though, you can set Drive Mode to use the self-timer, which can result in a single shot or multiple shots, depending on how you set it. (I'll discuss the self-timer options in Chapter 4).

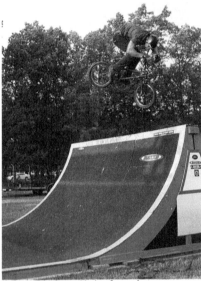

Figure 3-29: Scene Mode - Sports Action

For the shot in Figure 3-29, the camera set itself to f/5.0 at 1/250 second to stop the motion of the bike rider.

Pet

The Pet setting is designed to let you shoot photos of cats, dogs, and other animals in motion. It is similar to Sports Action to some extent, in that the flash is off but can be set to Fill-flash. The Pet setting is different, though, because it lets you use the Soft Skin Effect setting on the Shooting menu, and does not let you use continuous shooting. I would recommend that you use this setting when you are shooting a relatively posed or calm shot of your dog, cat, or other pet; if the animal is running around, you might be better off with the Sports Action selection.

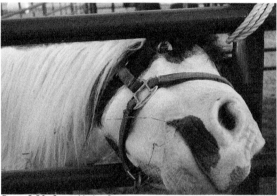

Figure 3-30: Scene Mode - Pet

I used this setting at a county fair recently, and snapped the picture in Figure 3-30 of a friendly pony who was looking for a handout.

Gourmet

The Gourmet setting, according to Sony, is meant to let you shoot food so that it looks "delicious." In more ordinary terms, with this setting, the RX100 boosts the brightness and vividness of the colors in the scene to enhance the appearance of a prepared dish of food. This setting is useful for people who write food blogs, or who just like to record all of their meals for posterity. The camera lets you have the flash either forced off or set for Fill-flash. Continuous shooting is not available, but you can use the self-timer. Figure 3-31 is an example of using this setting to record the "meal" being enjoyed by a butterfly at an indoor exhibit with fruits and flowers designed to attract butterflies. The color enhancement of the gourmet setting lent itself to showing off the coloring of the butterfly as well as the plate of attractive foods.

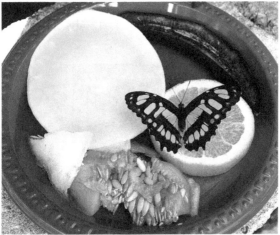

Figure 3-31: Scene Mode - Gourmet

Macro

With the Macro setting, the RX100 sets itself up to take close-ups. Although you can focus at close range in other shooting modes, it is convenient to be able to use this single setting to call up a group of options that are well-suited for taking extreme close-ups of flowers, insects, or other small objects.

When you select the Macro option, the camera will let you set the flash to Forced Off, Fill-flash, or Autoflash. You cannot use continuous shooting, but you can use the self-timer.

With the RX100, there is no special setting for macro focus; in any focus mode, the camera can focus as close as about 2 inches (5 cm) when the lens is zoomed out to its wide-angle setting. When the lens is zoomed in all the way to its telephoto setting, it can focus as close as about 22 inches (55 cm). One important point to note about macro focusing, though, is that, even when the camera is set to the Macro setting in Scene mode, you can use the manual focus option. This can be an excellent option when using Macro, because you can fine-tune the focus, which becomes critical and hard to measure precisely when you are taking pictures of insects or other objects in extreme close-ups. To use manual focus, select Focus Mode from the second screen of the Shooting menu and select the bottom option, Manual Focus. Then, use the control ring to adjust the focus. I will discuss the use of manual focus further in Chapter 4.

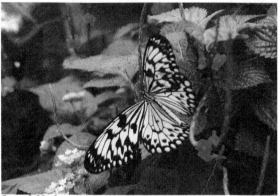

Figure 3-32: Scene Mode - Macro

The image in Figure 3-32 was taken using the Macro setting, with autofocus. I will discuss other aspects of macro shooting in Chapter 9.

Landscape

Landscape is one of the Scene mode settings that I tend to use a great deal. It is very convenient to spin the mode dial to the SCN slot and then just pull up the Landscape setting when I'm taking pictures at a scenic location outdoors. The camera lets you use Fill-flash in case you want to shoot an image of a person in front of a scenic vista or other attraction, and it boosts the brightness and intensity of the colors somewhat. Otherwise, it limits your choices; you cannot use continuous shooting, but you can use the self-timer. Figure 3-33 is an example taken using the Landscape setting at the local botanical gardens.

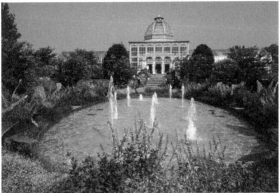

Figure 3-33: Scene Mode - Landscape

Sunset

This setting is a good one to choose if you are trying to capture the rich, reddish hues of the sky when the sun is rising or setting. The camera will let you use the Fill-flash setting if you want to, presumably to take a portrait of a person with the sunset or sunrise in the background. You cannot use continuous shooting, though you can use the self-timer. The main feature of this setting is that the camera dramatically boosts the intensity of the reddish hues in the scene.

Of course, as I have mentioned earlier, you don't have to confine the use of this, or any Scene setting, to the particular subject its name implies. For example, if you are photographing red and orange leaves of trees that are changing colors in autumn, you might want to try the Sunset option as one way to create an enhanced view of the brightly-colored foliage.

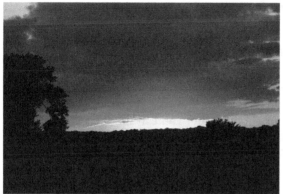

Figure 3-34: Scene Mode - Sunset

In Figure 3-34, I used the Sunset option to photograph a traditional scene of the setting sun.

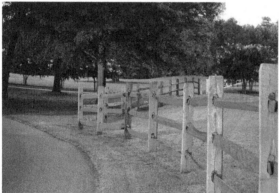

Figure 3-35: Creative Style - Sunset

In Figure 3-35, in the same location at the same time, I turned the camera in the other direction to capture the effect of the sun's slanted rays on trees and a fence. (For this shot, I used the Sunset setting of the Creative Style feature, rather than the Scene mode's Sunset option, but the effect is the same.)

Night Scene

The Night Scene setting is intended for use when you want to preserve the natural darkness of a night-time setting. The camera disables the use of the flash completely; if the scene is quite dark, you should use a tripod to avoid camera motion during the long exposure that may be required. You cannot use continuous shooting, but you can use the self-timer. This setting is good for photographing landscapes and other out-door scenes at night or in the late evening, without disrupting the natural scene with the camera's flash. The camera does not raise the ISO level or use multiple shots, as it does with other modes used in dim lighting, such as Anti Motion Blur and Hand-held Twilight.

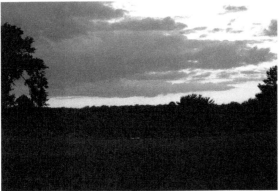

Figure 3-36: Scene Mode - Night Scene

In Figure 3-36, I used the Night Scene setting to photograph the sky shortly after sunset, showing how the RX100 deals with a scene of this type when not using either of its Sunset settings.

Hand-held Twilight

This Scene mode setting gives you another option for taking pictures in low light without a flash or tripod. With this special setting, as with Anti Motion Blur, the camera boosts the ISO to a fairly high level so it can use a fast shutter speed, and takes multiple images in rapid succession. The camera then combines these shots internally into one composite image in order to counteract the effects of high ISO, which often causes visible "noise" or grain in an image.

However, the Hand-held Twilight setting is likely to use a lower ISO setting than Anti Motion Blur would, in order to minimize noise and emphasize image quality. Although the camera will attempt to select frames with minimal motion blur, the final result with this setting is more likely to show motion blur than a shot made with the Anti Motion Blur setting.

Hand-held Twilight is a great option if you are shooting a landscape or other static subject when you cannot use a tripod or flash and the light is dim. If you can use a tripod, you might be better off using the Night Scene setting, discussed above. Or, if you don't mind using flash, you could just use Intelligent Auto, Program, or one of the more ordinary shooting modes. Hand-held Twilight is a very useful option when it's needed, but it will not yield the same overall quality as a shot at a lower ISO with the camera on a steady support.

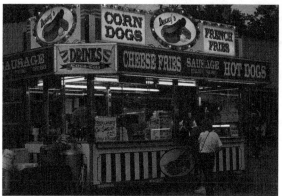

Figure 3-37: Scene Mode - Hand-held Twilight

In Figure 3-37, I made use of this setting at the county fair as it was starting to get dark.

Night Portrait

This is another night-oriented setting, intended for situations in which you are taking a portrait of a person and are willing to use the camera's built-in flash. The main factor that distinguishes this option from those discussed above is that, with Night Portrait, the camera activates the flash, in Slow Sync mode. You cannot turn the flash off. I will discuss Slow Sync and provide an example in Chapter 4, but basically, with this setting the camera uses a slow shutter speed, so that, as the flash illuminates the portrait subject in the foreground, there is enough time for the ambient light from the background to register on the sensor, so the final image will show both the flash-lit foreground subject and the naturally-lit background. You can use the self-timer, but not continuous shooting. You also can use RAW quality if you wish, so this setting is a good choice for a high-quality portrait outdoors at night. Because of the slow shutter speed, it's a good idea to use a tripod if possible to avoid motion blur from any camera movement during the longer-than-usual exposure.

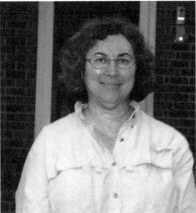

Figure 3-38: Scene Mode - Night Portrait

In Figure 3-38 the house behind the subject is able to show up clearly because the camera uses a fairly slow shutter speed.

Fireworks

This Scene type sets the camera to capture vivid images of fireworks bursts. It sets the camera to a 2-second shutter speed and intensifies the colors. If you can, you should set the camera on a tripod or other sturdy support and turn off the SteadyShot image stabilization option on the Shooting menu. The camera disables the flash and continuous shooting.

High Sensitivity

With this setting, you have one more option for shooting in low-light environments. In this case, the camera disables the flash and continuous shooting, but allows use of the self-timer. The camera is likely to set a high ISO, in the range of 3200 or higher, if the lighting is sufficiently dim to call for that high a setting. However, unlike the case with Hand-held Twilight, the camera takes only a single shot. As a result, there is no special processing of multiple images to reduce visual noise, and the image may be rather grainy.

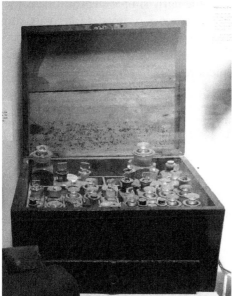

Figure 3-39: Scene Mode - High Sensitivity - ISO 3200

91

So, if you need to produce an image that is smooth and as noise-free as possible, you probably should use Hand-held Twilight or Anti Motion Blur instead of High Sensitivity. However, there might be occasions when you don't mind the grainy, noisy appearance that a high ISO can bring. It's very good to have these various choices available when you are confronted with a dimly lit location.

In Figure 3-39, I used this setting to photograph some Civil War-era medicine bottles in a dimly lighted museum display. The camera set the ISO to 3200 and exposed the image for 1/60 second at its maximum aperture of f/1.8.

Sweep Shooting Mode

Now it's time to consider the next setting that is available on the mode dial. This shooting mode is designed for a very specific purpose—the shooting of panoramic images. The RX100, like several other Sony cameras, including the NEX series, includes an excellent capability for automating the capture of panoramas. If you follow the fairly simple steps involved, the camera will stitch together a series of images internally and produce a high-quality final result that sets forth a dramatic, wide (or tall) view of a scenic vista or other subject that lends itself to panoramic depiction.

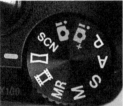

Figure 3-40: Sweep Shooting Mode

It is significant that Sony has given this shooting mode its own spot on the mode dial, indicating the importance of this type of photography nowadays. (Some other cameras include the panorama setting as a Scene mode type that has to be selected from a menu.) Because of this placement on the dial, you can very quickly set the camera up to take panoramas. Just turn the dial to select the icon that looks like a long, squeezed rectangle, as shown in Figure 3-40. You will then immediately see a message telling you to press the shutter button and move the camera in the direction of the arrow that appears on the screen, as shown, in Figure 3-41.

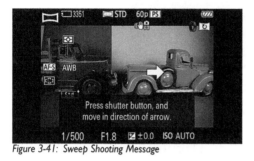
Figure 3-41: Sweep Shooting Message

At that point, you can follow those directions and likely get excellent results. However, because the RX100 is designed for the more advanced photographer, the camera allows you to make a number of choices for your panoramic images using the Shooting menu. Just press the Menu button, and you will go to the menu screen that is currently being displayed.

Navigate to the Shooting menu, which displays fewer options than in most other shooting modes, because several options are not appropriate for panoramas. For example, the Image Size, Aspect Ratio, and Quality settings are grayed-out and unavailable. Also, options such as Drive Mode and Autofocus Area are of no use in this situation and cannot be selected. In addition, you will not be able to zoom the lens in; it will stay fixed at its wide-angle position. (If the lens was zoomed in previously, you will see it zoom back out automatically when you switch the mode dial to the Sweep Shooting selection.)

You will, however, see two options on the first screen of the Shooting menu that are not available in any other shooting mode: Panorama Size and Panorama Direction, as shown in Figure 3-42. If you select Panorama Size, you will see two options, Standard and Wide.

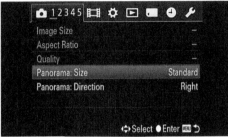
Figure 3-42: Panorama Options on Shooting Menu

With Standard, a horizontal panorama will have a size of 8192 by 1856 pixels, which is a resolution of about 15 megapixels (MP). If you choose Wide, a horizontal panorama will have a size of 12416 by 1856 pixels, resulting in a resolution of about 23 MP. (This figure is larger than the camera's maximum resolution of 20 MP, because, with the panorama settings, the camera is taking multiple images and stitching them together.)

A vertical panorama at the Standard setting is 3872 by 2160 pixels, or about 8.3 MP; a vertical panorama at the Wide setting is 5536 by 2160 pixels, or about 12 MP.

The Panorama Direction option lets you choose Right, Left, Up, or Down for the direction in which you will sweep the camera to create the panorama. If you have the control ring set to use its Standard settings through the Custom menu and you are not using manual focus or DMF, you can just turn the control ring and the camera will cycle through the four arrows for the four panorama directions, so you will not have to use the Shooting menu for that purpose.

Also, it's worth noting that you can use the Direction settings with different orientations of the camera to achieve different results than usual. For example, if you set the direction to Up and then hold the camera sideways while you sweep it to the right, you will create a horizontal panorama that has 2160 pixels in its vertical dimension rather than the standard 1856.

Those are the most important settings for most panoramas. There are a few other options you can select for panoramas on the Shooting menu, including Focus Mode, Metering Mode, White Balance, Creative Style, and SteadyShot. I will discuss all of these menu options in Chapter 4. In my opinion, the best options for these settings for shooting panoramas are the following, at least as a starting point:

Suggested Settings for Shooting Panoramas	
Focus Mode	Single-shot AF
Metering Mode	Multi
White Balance	Auto White Balance
Creative Style	Standard
SteadyShot	On (unless using a tripod)

One other setting you can make when shooting panoramas is exposure compensation, which is set using the down direction button on the control wheel. I will discuss that function in Chapter 5. Based on my experience, it is fairly unlikely that you would need to use exposure compensation when shooting a panorama, but you might want to use it for a creative effect, so it is useful to have it available.

Once you have made all of the settings you want for your panorama, just follow the directions on the screen. Press and release the shutter button, and start moving the camera at a steady rate in the direction you have chosen for your panorama. I tend to shoot my panoramas moving the camera from left to right, but you may have a different preference. You will hear a steady clicking as the camera takes multiple shots during the sweep of the panorama. A white box and arrow will proceed across the screen; your task is to finish the camera's sweep at the same moment that the box and arrow finish their travel across the scene. If you move the camera either too quickly or too slowly, the panorama will not succeed; if that happens, just try again.

Generally speaking, panoramas work best when the scene does not contain moving objects such as cars or pedestrians, because, when items are in motion, the multiple shots are likely to pick up the same object more than once, in different positions.

It is advisable to use a tripod if possible, so you can keep the camera steady in a single plane as it moves. If you don't have a tripod available, you might try using the excellent electronic level that Sony provides with the RX100. You first have to make sure the level is activated through the DISP button (Monitor) option on the first screen of the Custom menu, as discussed in Chapter 7. Then press the Display button until the screen with the electronic level appears. Make sure the outer tips of the level stay green as much as possible, and the resulting panorama should benefit from the level shooting.

Note that focus, exposure, and white balance are fixed as soon as the first image is taken for the panorama.

When a panoramic shot is played back in the camera, it is initially displayed at a small size so the whole image can fit on the display screen. You can then press the center button to make the panorama scroll across the display at a larger size, using the full height of the screen.

The next page has two sample panoramas, Figures 3-43 and 3-44, both shot from left to right using the Standard setting, hand-held.

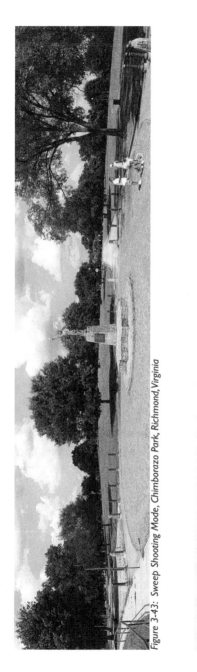

Figure 3-43: Sweep Shooting Mode, Chimborazo Park, Richmond, Virginia

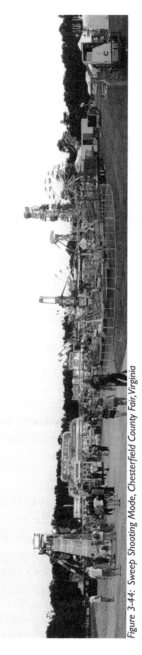

Figure 3-44: Sweep Shooting Mode, Chesterfield County Fair, Virginia

Memory Recall Mode

There is just one more shooting mode left to discuss, apart from Movie mode, which I will discuss in Chapter 8. This last mode, called Memory Recall, is an extremely convenient and powerful tool that gives you expanded options for your photography.

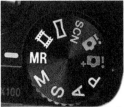

Figure 3-45: Memory Recall Mode

When you turn the mode dial to the MR position (shown in Figure 3-45) and then select one of the 3 groups of settings that can be stored there, you are, in effect, selecting a custom-made shooting mode that you have created yourself using your own favorite settings. You can set up the camera exactly as you want it, with stored values for items such as shooting mode, shutter speed, aperture, zoom amount, white balance, ISO, and other menu settings, and then recall all of those values instantly just by turning the mode dial to the MR slot and selecting option 1, 2, or 3 on the Memory Recall screen. And, with the RX100, unlike some other camera models, you can store settings for any shooting mode, including the Auto and Scene modes.

Here is how this works. First, take your time and set up the camera with all of the settings you want to be able to recall. For example, suppose you are going to do street photography. You may want to use a fast shutter speed, say 1/250 second, in black and white, at ISO 1600, using continuous shooting with autofocus, using Large and Fine JPEG images, and shooting in the 4:3 aspect ratio.

The first step is to make all of these settings. Set the mode dial to Shutter Priority and use the control wheel to set a shutter speed of 1/250 second. Then press the Menu button to call up the Shooting menu, and, on the first screen, select L for the image size, 4:3 for Aspect Ratio, and Fine for Quality. Then move to the second screen and choose Continuous Shooting for Drive Mode and Continuous AF for Focus Mode. On the third screen, set ISO to 1600, then scroll down three items to White Balance and select Daylight. Next, scroll down two more positions to the Creative Style option, and select the B/W setting for black and white. You also may want to push the zoom lever all the way to the left, for wide-angle shooting. You can set any other available menu options as you wish, but the ones listed above are the ones I will consider for now.

Once all of these settings are made, press the Menu button (if the menu isn't still on the screen) to call up the Shooting menu, and navigate to the Memory item, which is the final item on the last screen of the Shooting menu.

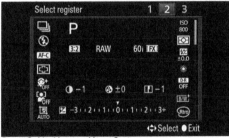

Figure 3-46: Memory Menu Option

After you press the center button, you will see a screen like the one in Figure 3-46, showing icons and values for all of the settings currently in effect and the numbers 1, 2, and 3 at the upper right corner of the display. The message Select Register appears at the upper left of the screen, indicating that you can now assign all of the settings shown on the display to register number 1, 2, or 3 of the Memory Recall mode. In the example shown here, the number 2 is highlighted. Now press the center button, and you will have selected register 2 to store all of the settings you just made.

Next, to check how this worked, try making some very different settings, such as setting the camera for Manual exposure with a shutter speed of 1 second, Creative Style set to Vivid, continuous shooting turned off, the zoom lever moved all the way to the right for telephoto, and Quality set to RAW. Then turn the mode dial back to the MR slot, make sure the number 2 for register 2 is highlighted, and press the center button to exit back to the shooting display. You will see that all of the custom settings you made have instantly returned, including the zoom position, shutter speed, and everything else.

This is really a wonderful feature, and more powerful than similar features on some other cameras, which can save menu settings but not settings such as shutter speed and zoom position, or can save settings only for the less-automatic shooting modes, but not the Scene and Auto modes. What is also quite amazing is that, if you now switch back to Manual exposure mode, the camera will restore the settings that you had in that mode before you turned to the MR mode. (The position of the zoom lens will not revert to where it was, though.)

Note that this mode is very versatile, because you can store settings for any shooting mode, including Program, Aperture Priority, Shutter Priority, Manual exposure, and even the Scene, Auto, Sweep Shooting, and Movie modes. You also can store settings from the Shooting menu and the Movie menu, as well as the aperture, shutter speed, exposure compensation, and optical zoom setting. So, for example, you could set up one of the 3 memory registers to recall Scene mode, set to the Macro setting, with the lens zoomed back to its wide-angle position. In that way, you could be ready for close-up shooting on a moment's notice.

The Memory Recall feature is especially useful with a camera as small as the RX100, because there are not many physical controls and it can be cumbersome to change settings when you have to dig into the menu system to make settings for ISO, white balance, focus mode, and other basic items. With one twist of the mode dial and the press of a button, you can call up a complete group of settings that is tailored for a particular type of shooting. It is really worth your while to experiment with this option and develop a set of three groups of settings that works well for your shooting needs.

Chapter 4: The Shooting Menu

Much of the power of the RX100 resides in the many options included in the Shooting menu, which provides the user with numerous areas of control over the appearance of the images and how they are captured. Depending on your own preferences, you may not have to use this menu too much. You may prefer to use the camera's physical controls, with which you can make many settings, or you may prefer to take advantage of the camera's various Scene mode or Auto mode settings, which choose many options for you. However, it's nice to know that you have this degree of control over many functions available if you want it, and it is very useful to understand what types of settings you can make. In addition, with the RX100, more than with many other compact cameras, you can control a fair number of settings on the Shooting menu even when the camera is set to one of the Scene or Auto modes. Therefore, you will be giving up a lot of potential control over your photographic results if you avoid using this powerful menu.

The Shooting menu is easy to use once you have played with it a bit. The available menu options can change depending on the setting of the shooting mode dial on top of the camera. For example, if the camera is set to Intelligent Auto mode, the Shooting menu options are fairly limited because that mode is for a user who wants the camera to make many of the decisions without input. If the camera is set to Sweep Shooting mode, the available Shooting menu options also are quite limited, because of the specialized nature of that mode, which is designed for creating panoramas. For the following discussion, I'm assuming you have the camera set to Program mode, because in that setting you have access to most of the options on the Shooting menu.

Turn the mode dial on top of the camera to P, which represents Program mode, as shown in Figure 4-1.

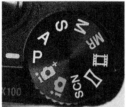

Figure 4-1: Program Mode

Enter the menu system by pressing the Menu button, on the camera's back to the upper right of the control wheel. Move through the numbered screens of the menu system by pressing the right direction button on the control wheel. With each press of that button, the small orange line (cursor) at the top of the screen moves underneath a number beside an icon.

📷 1 2 3 4 5	🎞	⚙	▶	▣	🕐	🔧
Image Size						L: 20M
Aspect Ratio						3:2
Quality						RAW & JPEG
Panorama: Size						Standard
Panorama: Direction						Right

↔ Select ● Enter 📖 ↩

Figure 4-2: Shooting Menu

When the menu system first appears on the screen, the cursor should sit beneath the number 1 beside the camera icon, which represents the Shooting menu, as shown in Figure 4-2. As you keep pressing the right direction button, the cursor will move through all 5 screens of the Shooting menu.

As you continue to move the cursor through the menu screens

103

with the RX100 set to shooting mode, after the Shooting menu comes the Movie menu, marked at the top by a movie-frame icon. Then comes the Custom menu, marked by a gear icon, followed by the Playback menu, headed by an icon with a playback triangle. The last three menus are the Memory Card Tool, Clock Setup, and, finally, the Setup menu, marked by a wrench icon. In this chapter, I am going to discuss only the Shooting menu; the other menu systems will be discussed in Chapters 6 (Playback), 7 (Custom, Memory Card Tool, Clock Setup, and Setup), and 8 (Movie).

On the Shooting menu, you'll see a fairly long list of options divided into 5 numbered screens. In most cases, each option (such as Image Size) occupies one line, with its name on the left and its current setting (such as L:20M) on the right. In other cases (such as Shooting Tip List, Scene Selection, and Memory), there may be only a small dash on the right side of the screen, meaning that you have to press the center button (middle of the control wheel) to get access to further options, or that the selection is not currently applicable. For example, if the camera is set to Program mode, the Scene Selection item on screen 5 of the Shooting menu will be followed by a dash, because no Scene type can be selected when the camera is set to Program mode.

You also will see that some items on the menu's screens are "grayed-out," as the Panorama Size and Panorama Direction options are in Figure 4-2, for example. This means that those options are not available for selection in the current context. In this case, the camera was set to Program mode; the Panorama menu options are available for use only when the camera is set to Sweep Shooting mode.

If you want to follow along with the discussion below of the options on the Shooting menu, leave the shooting mode set to Program, which gives you access to all but a few options on the Shooting menu. (I'll also discuss the options that are available in other modes as I come to them.) I'll start at the top of screen

1, and discuss each option on the way down the list for each of the 5 screens.

Image Size

This first option on the Shooting menu lets you select the resolution, or pixel count, of your still images. The Image Size setting is related to the next two entries on the menu, Aspect Ratio and Quality, to control the overall appearance and "quality" of your images, in a broad sense.

The Image Size setting itself controls only the size in pixels of the image that is recorded by the camera. The Sony RX100 has an unusually large digital sensor for a camera of its size, and that sensor has a high maximum resolution, or pixel count. That is, the sensor is capable of recording a still image with 5742 pixels, or individual points of light, in the horizontal direction and 3648 pixels vertically. When you multiply those two numbers together, the result is about 20.9 million pixels, often referred to as megapixels, or MP, or M. (Not all of those pixels are used to create the image, so the effective MP count for the RX100 is slightly lower, at 20.2 M.)

The pixel count or resolution of the still images is important mainly when it comes time to enlarge or print your images. If you need to produce large prints (say, 8 by 10 inches or 20 by 25 cm), then you should select a high-resolution setting for Image Size. You also should choose the largest Image Size setting if you believe you may need to crop out a small portion of the image and enlarge it for closer viewing. For example, if you are shooting photos of wildlife and an animal or bird you are interested in is in the distance, you may need to enlarge the image digitally to see that subject in detail. In that case, also, you should choose the highest setting for Image Size.

The available settings for Image Size with the RX100 are L, M, S, and VGA, for Large, Medium, Small, and VGA, as shown in Figure 4-3.

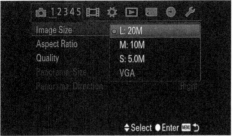

Figure 4-3: Image Size Menu Option

When you select one of the first three of these options from the Shooting menu, the camera will display a setting such as L:20M, meaning Large: 20 megapixels. The number of megapixels will change depending on the setting for Aspect Ratio, discussed below. This change occurs because, when the shape of the image changes, the number of horizontal pixels or the number of vertical pixels changes also, in order to form the new shape. For example, if the Aspect Ratio setting is 3:2, the maximum number of pixels is used, because 3:2 is the aspect ratio of the camera's sensor. However, if you set Aspect Ratio to 16:9, the number of horizontal pixels (5742) stays the same, but the number of vertical pixels is reduced from 3648 to 3080, in order to form the 16:9 ratio of horizontal to vertical pixels. When you multiply those two numbers (5742 and 3080) together, the result is about 17.7 million pixels, which the camera states as 17M, as shown in Figure 4-4.

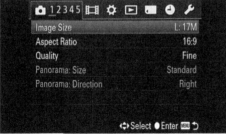

Figure 4-4: Image Size with 16:9 Aspect Ratio

The VGA option, the smallest size possible, is available only if the Aspect Ratio is set to 4:3. Otherwise, this option is grayed-out and cannot be selected. VGA stands for Video Graphics Array, the designation used for old-style computer screens, which have a 4:3 aspect ratio. The pixel count for this setting is very low—just 640 by 480 pixels, yielding a resolution of 0.3 M, much less than one megapixel. This very small size is suitable if you need to send images by e-mail or need to store a great many images on a memory card.

In my view, one of the few reasons to choose an Image Size smaller than L would be if you were running out of space on your memory card and had to keep taking pictures in an important situation. Here are some figures that show approximately how many images can be stored on a memory card.

Number of Images That Fit on 8GB Card			
	Large	Medium	Small
RAW & JPEG	243	284	309
RAW	368	-----	-----
Fine	719	1257	1937
Standard	1238	1969	2793

As you can see, if you are using an 8GB memory card, which is a fairly reasonable size nowadays, you can fit 243 images on the card even at the maximum settings of 3:2 for Aspect Ratio, Large for Image Size, and RAW & JPEG for quality. If you limit the image quality to Fine, with no RAW images, you can fit 719 images on the card. If you reduce the Image Size setting to Small, you can then store 1937 images. In my experience, I am unlikely ever to need more than about 200 or 300 images in any one session. And, of course, I can use a larger memory card or multiple memory cards.

If space on your memory card is not a consideration, then I recommend you go ahead and use the L setting at all times. You never know when you might need the larger-sized image, so you might as well use the L setting and be safe. Your situation might be different, of course. If you were taking photos purely for a business purpose, such as making photo identification cards, you might want to use the Small setting in order to store the maximum number of images on a memory card and reduce expense. For general photography, though, I rarely use any setting other than L for Image Size. (One exception could be when I want to increase the range of the optical zoom lens without losing image quality; see the discussion of Clear Image Zoom and related topics later in this chapter.)

One more note: When Quality, discussed later in this chapter, is set to RAW, the Image Size option is grayed out and unavailable for selection, because you cannot select an image size for RAW images; they are always at the maximum size, as is reflected on the table of images that can fit on a memory card.

Aspect Ratio

This second option on the Shooting menu lets you choose the proportions of the images that you record with the camera.

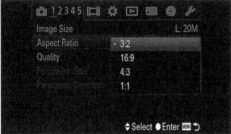

Figure 4-5: Aspect Ratio Menu Option

The choices are the default of 3:2, as well as 16:9, 4:3, and 1:1, as shown in Figure 4-5. As I discussed briefly in connection with Image Size, above, these numbers represent the ratio of the units of width to the units of height. So, for example, with the 16:9 setting, the image is 16 units wide for every 9 units of height. The aspect ratio that uses all pixels on the image sensor is 3:2; with any other aspect ratio, some of the pixels are cropped out. So, if it matters to you to record every possible pixel, you should use the 3:2 setting. If you shoot using the 3:2 aspect ratio, you can always alter the aspect ratio of the image later in editing software such as Photoshop, by cropping away parts of the image. However, if you want to have your images in a certain shape and don't plan to do post-processing in software, the aspect ratio settings of this menu item may be just what you want. The RX100 is notable for providing more options in this area than many other cameras do, so let's go through the list of possibilities. After each of the aspect ratios discussed below, I am including an image I took at that setting from the same location at the same time, to give a general idea of what the different aspect ratios look like.

The default 3:2 setting, which was used for Figure 4-6, includes the maximum number of pixels, and is the same ratio used by traditional 35mm film. This aspect ratio can be used without cropping to make prints in the common U.S. size of 6 inches by 4 inches (15 cm by 10 cm).

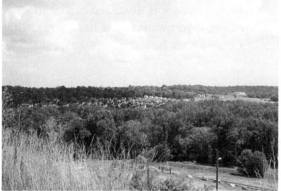

Figure 4-6: Aspect Ratio 3:2

The 16:9 setting, illustrated by Figure 4-7, is normally considered to be the "widescreen" mode, like that found on many modern HD television sets. You might use that setting when you plan to show your images on an HDTV set. Or, you might just like the appearance of this particular shape of image; or it might be suitable for a particular composition in which the important subject matter is stretched out in a horizontal arrangement.

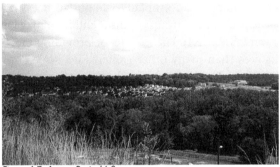

Figure 4-7: Aspect Ratio 16:9

The 4:3 setting, shown in Figure 4-8, is in the shape of a traditional (non-widescreen) computer screen, so, if you want to view your images on that sort of display, this may be your preferred aspect ratio. Also, as was discussed earlier in connection with Image Size, if you want to use the VGA setting for Image Size, the camera must be set to the 4:3 aspect ratio.

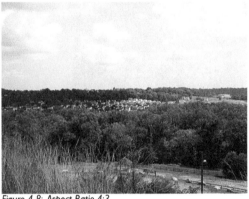

Figure 4-8: Aspect Ratio 4:3

The 1:1 ratio, illustrated in Figure 4-9, represents a square shape, which some photographers prefer because of its symmetry and because the neutrality of the shape leaves open many possibilities for using the images.

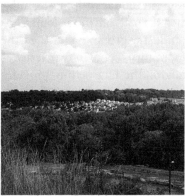

Figure 4-9: Aspect Ratio 1:1

The Aspect Ratio setting is available in all shooting modes except for Sweep Shooting. However, although you can set Aspect Ratio when the camera is in Movie mode (mode dial turned to movie-film icon), that aspect ratio will not take effect until you switch to another mode, such as Program, in which that setting can be made. This is because, when the mode dial is set to the Movie position, you cannot take still images except during the recording of a movie, and those images will have the same aspect ratio as the movie.

Quality

The Quality setting, just below Aspect Ratio on the Shooting menu, is one of the most important ones you can make. The choices are RAW, RAW & JPEG, Fine, and Standard, as shown in Figure 4-10. The term "quality" in this context has a specific meaning that concerns the way in which digital images are processed. In particular, the images are digitally "compressed" in a way that reduces their size without losing too much information or detail from the picture. However, the more an image is compressed, and the smaller the file size becomes, the greater the loss of detail and clarity in the image. RAW files, which are really in a class by themselves, are the least compressed of all, and have the greatest level of quality, though they also come with some complications, as discussed below. All other

111

(non-RAW) formats used by the RX100 (as with most similar cameras) are called JPEG, which is an acronym for Joint Photographic Experts Group, an industry group that created the JPEG standard. The JPEG files, in turn, come in two varieties on the RX100: Fine and Standard. The Fine setting provides the least compression; images captured with the Standard setting undergo more compression, resulting in smaller files with somewhat reduced quality.

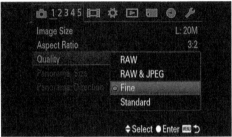

Figure 4-10: Shooting Menu - Quality Setting

Here are some guidelines about using these settings. First, you need to choose between RAW and JPEG images. RAW files are larger than other files, so they take up more space on your memory card, and on your computer, than JPEG files. But RAW files offer some great advantages over JPEG files. When you shoot in the RAW format, the camera records as much information as it can about the scene before it, and preserves that information in the file that it saves to the memory card. Then, when you open the RAW file later on your computer, you will have the ability to extract that information in various ways. What this means, for example, is that you can actually change the exposure or white balance of the image when you edit it on the computer, just as if you had changed your settings while shooting. In effect, the RAW format gives you what almost amounts to a chance to travel back in time to improve some of the settings that you didn't get quite right when you pressed the shutter button.

RAW is not a cure-all; you can't fix bad focusing or really excessive underexposure or overexposure. But you can improve exposure-related issues such as brightness and white balance very nicely with your RAW-processing software. You can use the Image Data Converter software that comes with the RX100 in order to view or edit RAW files, and you also can use other programs, such as Adobe Camera Raw, that have been updated to handle RAW files from this camera.

Using RAW can have some disadvantages, depending on your needs. As noted above, the files take up a lot of storage space on your memory card or computer; RAW images taken with the RX100 are about 20 megabytes (MB) in size, while Large JPEG images I have taken have been between about 4 and 10 MB, depending on the settings used. Also, RAW files have to be processed on a computer; you can't take a RAW file and immediately send it by e-mail or print it on photo paper; you first have to use RAW-processing software to convert it to JPEG, TIFF, PSD or some other standard format for printing and manipulating digital photographs. If you are pressed for time, you may not want to take that extra step. Finally, some features of the RX100 are not available when you are using the RAW format, such as the Auto HDR, Digital Zoom, and Picture Effect settings on the Shooting menu.

If you're undecided as to whether to use RAW or JPEG, you have the option of selecting RAW & JPEG, the second choice for the Quality menu item. With that setting, the camera records both a RAW and a JPEG image when you press the shutter button. The advantage with that system is that you have a RAW image with the highest quality and with the ability to do extensive post-processing manipulation, and you also have a JPEG image that you can use more quickly for viewing, e-mailing, printing, and the like. The disadvantages are that this setting consumes your storage space more quickly than saving your images in just RAW or JPEG format, and that it can take the camera longer to store the images, so there may be a short delay before you can take your next shot.

When you select RAW & JPEG, you can still select an Image Size setting, which will apply only to the JPEG image; the RAW image, as noted earlier, is always of the maximum size. You cannot select a Quality setting for the JPEG image with the RAW & JPEG selection; the JPEG image will always be fixed at the Fine setting for Quality.

In short, your best bet for preserving the quality of your images and your options for post-processing and fixing exposure mistakes later is to choose RAW files. However, if you would prefer to use features such as Sweep Shooting mode, some Scene mode types such as Anti Motion Blur, the Picture Effect menu option, and others, which are not available with RAW files, then choose JPEG. If you do choose JPEG, I strongly recommend that you choose the Large size and Fine quality, unless you have an urgent need to conserve storage space on your memory card or on your computer. If you want RAW quality and are not concerned about storage space or speed of shooting, choose RAW & JPEG. However, you will still not be able to use Picture Effect and some other options.

Panorama Size and Panorama Direction

The next two commands on the Shooting menu are available only when the mode dial is set to the Sweep Shooting mode. I discussed these settings in Chapter 3, in connection with the discussion of that shooting mode. Note that, when the control ring is set to its Standard setting through the Custom menu, you can set the panorama direction by turning that ring (unless you are using manual focus or DMF, which use the ring).

Drive Mode

This first option on the second screen of the Shooting menu gives you access to the continuous-shooting features of the RX100, an extremely useful and powerful set of capabilities for shooting bursts of images, bracketing exposures, using the self-timer, and other functions. You can also get access to this menu option by pressing the Drive Mode button (left direction button), as discussed in Chapter 5.

When you highlight this menu option and press the center button, a vertical menu appears at the left of the screen as shown in Figure 4-11, with eight choices represented by icons: Single Shooting, Continuous Shooting, Speed Priority Continuous Shooting, Self-timer, Self-portrait, Self-timer (Continuous), Exposure Bracketing, and White Balance Bracketing. (You have to scroll down to see the last four choices.)

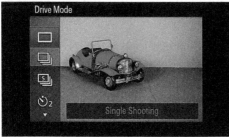

Figure 4-11: Drive Mode Menu Option - First Screen

The details for each of these drive mode settings are discussed below. Before discussing them, though, I will provide a brief introduction to the concept of continuous shooting.

With film cameras, continuous shooting involves the use of a special motor to advance the film rapidly, and often the use of an extra-large cassette to hold a large quantity of film. This sort of equipment is bulky and expensive, and, of course, shooting and developing large numbers of exposures is itself quite expensive. With digital cameras like the RX100, expense is no longer a factor. Continuous shooting is literally available at your fingertips whenever you want to take advantage of it.

The usefulness of shooting rapid bursts of exposures is more obvious in some contexts than in others. For example, when you're shooting sports events, it's clearly worthwhile to fire off a swift sequence of shots in order to catch the perfect instant when a baseball player tags a runner heading for home plate, or to catch a soccer ball as it bounces off a player's head toward the goal. But continuous shooting also can be helpful in more ordinary shooting, such as when you're taking pictures of children at play. You have a better chance of capturing a fleeting smile, laugh, or cute gesture if you keep the exposures rolling. And, even when your subject is not moving noticeably at all, it can be advantageous to take multiple shots. For example, when you're taking a portrait, there may be subtle changes in the subject's expression, or in the way sunlight falls on a cheek, or in the subject's posture. Taking a series of shots gives you some insurance against coming away from the photo session with no winning images.

With that introduction, let's take a look at the terrific assortment of continuous-shooting options that the RX100 provides. All of the settings (except the first one, for single shots, and some of the self-timer options) offer various ways to take multiple shots, with a press (or press and hold) of the shutter button. Neither of the burst-shooting options is available when the mode dial is set to the Movie or Sweep Shooting positions. Also, burst shooting is not available with any of the Scene mode settings except Sports Action. (With that setting, single shooting is not available.) Following are details for each of the options on the Drive menu.

Single Shooting

This is the normal mode for shooting images. Select this option, the top choice on the Drive Mode menu, when you want to turn off all continuous shooting. Note that, in some cases, having one of the continuous drive mode options selected will make it impossible to make other settings, such as Soft Skin Effect and Long Exposure Noise Reduction. Also, as noted above, this option is not available with the Sports Action setting of Scene mode.

Continuous Shooting

This second option on the Drive mode menu, highlighted in Figure 4-12, is a powerful setting, because it gives the RX100 the ability to shoot a continuous series of still images as you hold down the shutter button.

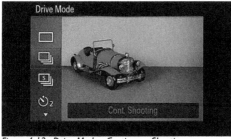

Figure 4-12: Drive Mode - Continuous Shooting

This capability is, of course, extremely useful in many contexts, from shooting an action sequence at a sports event to taking a series of shots of a portrait subject in order to capture his or her changing facial expressions.

The Continuous Shooting option is the first of two types of general burst shooting available with the RX100. When you select this choice, the camera will shoot continuously when you hold down the shutter button, and it will adjust its focus (but not the exposure) with each shot.

Depending on the conditions, including lighting and other settings on the camera and the speed of your memory card, the rate of burst shooting can vary markedly. When conditions are optimal, the camera can shoot at roughly 2 frames per second (fps) using this option. When I shot with a fast (UHS-1) SDHC card, with Quality set to Fine, after the first burst of about 14 shots at this speed the speed fell off to a more leisurely pace of about one fps. With Quality set to RAW & JPEG, the camera started shooting its burst at a slower pace and shooting slowed markedly after about 10 shots.

Although you can turn on the flash when Continuous Shooting is selected, and the camera will actually take a series of shots as you hold down the shutter button, the time between shots will be several seconds, because the flash cannot recycle

117

quickly enough to take a rapid series of shots. The Image Size setting does not appear to affect the shooting rate.

This speed is not very great compared to that of the Speed Priority option, discussed below. However, being able to take a relatively steady stream of shots with focus being adjusted for each one can be worth the reduction in speed, when your subject is moving or you need to focus on subjects at varying distances.

Speed Priority Continuous Shooting

If you need to shoot a series of images at the fastest rate possible, then the Speed Priority Continuous Shooting option, shown in Figure 4-13, is the one to choose.

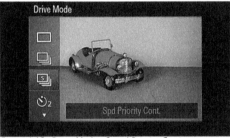

Figure 4-13: Drive Mode - Speed Priority Continuous

With this selection, the camera will capture images at a rate up to 10 fps. The trade-off for speed in this case is that the camera will not adjust its focus between shots (and, as with the first continuous-shooting mode, will not adjust exposure either).

Also, the Quality setting affects the efficiency of the Speed Priority setting. Again using my fastest memory card, when I set the camera to take RAW & JPEG or just RAW shots, the continuous shooting came to a complete stop after the first rapid burst of about 6 or 8 shots and then resumed at a slow pace. With Quality set to Fine, the camera took one rapid burst of about 10 shots and then eased off to a slower pace of about one shot per second. As with the standard Continuous Shooting option, using the flash slows the shooting down drastically.

Once you have finished shooting a burst of shots, you will notice that it can take the camera quite a while to record them all to the memory card; the LCD display will remain dark while the camera writes the images to the card.

Self-timer

The next icon down on the menu of Drive Mode options represents the self-timer, as shown in Figure 4-14.

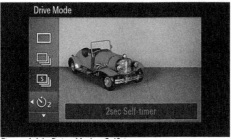

Figure 4-14: Drive Mode - Self-timer

The self-timer is useful for occasions when you need to be the photographer and also appear in a group photograph, because you can set the RX100 on a tripod, set the timer for 10 seconds, and then move around to place yourself in the group before the shutter clicks. The self-timer also is helpful in other situations, though, such as whenever you are taking a picture under conditions in which you don't want to cause blur by jiggling the camera as you press the shutter button. For example, when you're taking a macro shot very close to the subject, the focusing can be very critical, and any bump to the camera could throw off the focus. Using the self-timer means the camera has a chance to settle down after the shutter button is pressed, before the image is actually recorded.

Once you select the self-timer option, you are presented with two choices: ten seconds and two seconds. When the self-timer option is highlighted, just press the left or right direction button on the control wheel to choose between these options. Once you have made this selection, the self-timer icon will appear in the upper left corner of the display, with the chosen number of seconds (10 or 2) displayed next to the icon, as shown in Figure 4-15.

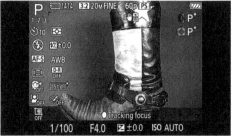

Figure 4-15: Self-timer Icon on Shooting Mode Display Screen

(If you don't see the icon, press the Display button—up direction button—until the screen with the various shooting icons appears.)

Once the self-timer is set, when you press the shutter button to take a picture the timer will count down for the specified number of seconds and then take the picture. The reddish lamp on the front of the camera will blink, and the camera will beep during the countdown.

Also, don't forget that the camera has several other potentially very useful timer functions, besides this traditional self-timer. Those features are discussed next.

Self-portrait Timer

The next option on the Drive Mode menu, Self-portrait timer, as shown in Figure 4-16, is another variety of self-timer. In this case, instead of choosing a time interval of 10 seconds or 2 seconds, you have the choice of setting the Self-portrait timer to take a picture of one person or two people. As was the case with the self-timer, you use the left and right direction buttons to make this selection. Once the selection is made, the camera

120

will wait until it detects the chosen number of human faces, and then it will fire the shutter.

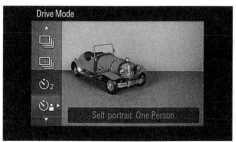

Figure 4-16: Drive Mode - Self-portrait Timer

For example, you can set the Self-portrait timer to look for one person, then point the camera at yourself. Once the camera detects your face, it will initiate the 2-second self-timer operation. The lamp on the front of the camera will blink, and the camera will beep as it counts down and snaps an image of your face. Similarly, if you have set the camera to look for two people, it will take the picture after detecting two faces. In my experience, you need to have the lens zoomed back to its wide-angle position for this feature to work.

The idea with this option is that it is difficult to take a self-portrait otherwise, because you cannot see when your face is properly framed in the display. With this feature, the camera verifies that your face (with or without a companion face) is in the picture, and then captures the image. I don't have much interest in taking self-portraits, so I haven't found that much use for this capability. However, it could be useful when you are photographing children, by setting the camera on a tripod, and telling the child that the camera will automatically take picture when he or she walks up to a certain point and looks toward the camera. This operation might win the child's interest and result in an interesting shot. You may find other uses for the feature as well, so don't consider it to be solely a way to take your self-portrait.

Self-timer (Continuous)

The next item down on the Drive Mode menu, shown in Figure 4-17, gives you another variation on the self-timer.

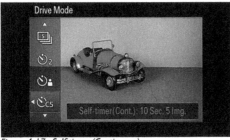

Figure 4-17: Self-timer (Continuous)

In this case, the menu option lets you set the timer to take multiple shots after the timer counts down. The time delay for this timer is set at 10 seconds and cannot be changed. Using the left and right direction buttons, you can set the camera to take either 3 or 5 shots after the delay. This option can be of great use when you are taking a group photo; when a series of shots is taken, you are increasing your chances of getting at least one shot in which no one's eyes are closed and everyone is looking at the camera and smiling. You can choose any settings you want to for Image Size and Quality, including RAW & JPEG, and you will still get three rapidly-fired shots, though the speed of the shooting will decrease slightly at the highest Quality settings.

Exposure Bracketing

This next option on the Drive Mode menu, shown in Figure 4-18, lets you set up the camera to take three images continuously with one press of the shutter button, but with different exposure levels for each image, thereby giving you a greater chance of having one image that is properly exposed. This feature also can be used for taking three exposures at different values that you can later combine in editing software to create a composite HDR image.

122

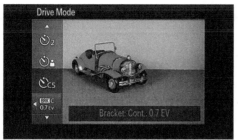

Figure 4-18: Drive Mode - Exposure Bracketing

Once you highlight this option, you will see a horizontal triangle, indicating that you can select either 0.3 EV or 0.7 EV using the left and right direction buttons, as with the self-timer options discussed above. These numbers represent the difference in EV, or exposure value, between the three exposures that the camera will take. For example, if you select 0.7 EV as the interval, the camera will take 3 shots, one at the metered exposure level, one at a level 0.7 EV (or stop) below that, resulting in a darker image, and one at a level of 0.7 EV above that, resulting in a brighter image.

Once you have set this option as you want it and composed your shot, press the shutter button and the camera will take three shots in rapid succession. In this case, unlike the situation with burst shooting, you do not have to hold down the shutter button, because the camera is programmed to make three exposures no matter how long the button is held down.

The first exposure will be taken at the metered value, the second one underexposed by the selected interval, and the third one overexposed to the same extent. You cannot turn on the flash when using this option. You can use exposure compensation, in which case the camera will use the image with exposure compensation as the base level, and then take exposures that deviate under and over the exposure of the image with exposure compensation.

Neither of the bracketing options—exposure or white balance—is available in the Intelligent Auto or Superior Auto shooting modes.

White Balance Bracketing

The final option at the bottom of the Drive Mode menu, White Balance Bracketing, seen in Figure 4-19, works in the same way as Exposure Bracketing, except that the value that is varied for the three shots is white balance rather than exposure.

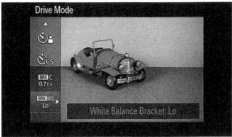

Figure 4-19: Drive Mode - White Balance Bracketing

Using the left and right direction buttons, you first select either Lo or Hi for the amount of deviation from the normal white balance setting. The camera will then take a series of three shots, one at the normal setting, the next one deviating by setting a lower color temperature, resulting in a "cooler," more bluish image, and the last one deviating by setting a higher color temperature, resulting in a "warmer," more reddish image. See the discussion of the White Balance setting later in this chapter for more information about color temperature. Note that, when you use this form of bracketing, unlike Exposure Bracketing, you will hear only one shutter sound, because the camera takes just one image and then electronically creates the other two exposures with the different white balance values.

Flash Mode

In Chapter 2, I discussed the use of the RX100's built-in flash, which is controlled with the Flash Mode menu option. As I discussed earlier, that menu option can be reached by pressing the Flash button, which is the right button on the control wheel. Flash Mode also is the second option on the second screen of the Shooting menu.

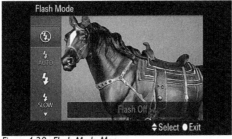

Figure 4-20: Flash Mode Menu

As I noted earlier, there are five options on the Flash Mode menu: Flash Off, Autoflash, Fill-flash, Slow Sync, and Rear Sync, the first four of which are shown in Figure 4-20. There is no single shooting mode in which all five of the options are available. I will provide here a brief summary of the options I discussed in Chapter 2, followed by a discussion of the options I did not discuss there.

Flash Off

If you want to make sure the flash will not fire, choose Flash Off. This is a good choice when you are in a museum or other location where it would be inappropriate or embarrassing for the flash to fire, or when you know you will not want to use the flash. It also could be helpful to avoid depleting a battery that is running low. This option is available in all shooting modes except for the Night Portrait setting of Scene mode.

Autoflash

When you select the Autoflash option, you are leaving it up to the camera's programming to determine whether or not the flash should be fired. The camera will analyze the lighting and other aspects of the scene, and decide whether to use the flash

125

without any further input from you. This selection is available only in the Intelligent Auto and Superior Auto modes, and with the Macro and Portrait settings of Scene mode.

Fill-flash

With the Fill-flash option, you are making a definite decision to use flash. No matter what the lighting conditions are, if you choose Fill-flash, the flash will fire. This is the option to use when the sun is shining and you need to soften shadows on a subject's face, or to correct the lighting when a subject is back-lit. Note that, with this option, the camera uses what could be called "Front Sync," as opposed to Rear Sync, the final option on the Flash Mode menu, which is discussed below. The Fill-flash option is available for selection in all shooting modes except Movie and Sweep Shooting, and some Scene settings.

Slow Sync

Slow Sync is one of the options I did not discuss in detail in Chapter 2. This option is designed for use in a situation in which you are taking a photograph of a subject at night or in dim lighting, and are using flash. With this option, the camera sets a relatively slow shutter speed so that the ambient (natural) lighting will have time to register on the image. In other words, if you're in a fairly dark environment and fire the flash normally, it will likely light up the subject (say a person), but because the exposure time is short, the surrounding scene may be black. If you use the Slow Sync setting, the slower shutter speed allows the surrounding scene to be visible also.

The two images shown here were taken by the RX100 with identical room lighting and camera settings, except that Figure 4-21 was taken with the flash set to Fill-flash, resulting in an exposure at f/4.5 at 1/30 second, while Figure 4-22 was taken with the flash set to Slow Sync, resulting in an exposure at f/4.5 for 1.0 second. In the first image, the flash illuminated the kettle in the foreground, but the background, consisting of furniture in the next room, is dark. In the second image, the furniture in the farther room is illuminated by ambient light, because of the much slower shutter speed.

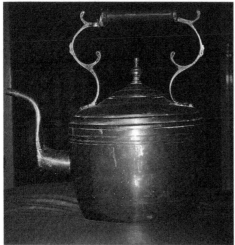

Figure 4-21: Fill-flash, f/4.5, 1/30 Second

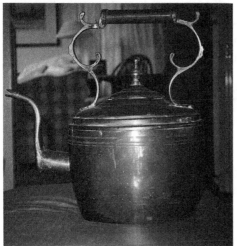

Figure 4-22: Slow Sync, f/4.5, 1 Second

When you are using the Slow Sync setting, you should plan to use a tripod, because, in many cases, the camera will choose a very slow shutter speed, in the range of 3 seconds or even

127

longer. Also, note that you can choose Slow Sync even when the camera is set to Shutter Priority mode. If you do so, you should make sure to select a slow shutter speed, because the whole point of this setting is to use a slow shutter speed in order to light the background with ambient light. If you set the camera to Shutter Priority mode, you can decide precisely which shutter speed to use, but it would not make sense to select a relatively fast speed, such as, say, 1/30 second. The same considerations apply for Manual exposure mode; the camera also will let you select Slow Sync for the Flash Mode setting in that shooting mode.

Rear Sync

The last setting on the Flash Mode menu is Rear Sync. This option is one you should not often need unless you encounter the particular situation it is designed for. If you don't activate this setting (that is, if you select any other flash mode in which the flash fires), the camera uses the unnamed default setting, which could be called "Front Sync." In that case, the flash fires very soon after the shutter opens to expose the image. If you choose the Rear Sync setting instead, the flash fires later, just before the shutter closes.

The reason for using Rear Sync is to help you avoid a strange-looking result in some situations. This issue arises, for example, with a relatively long exposure, say one-half second, of a subject with lights, such as a car or motorcycle at night, moving across your field of view. With normal (Front) sync, the flash will fire early in the process, freezing the vehicle in a clear image. However, as the shutter remains open while the vehicle keeps going, the camera will capture the moving lights in a stream extending in front of the vehicle. If, instead, you use Rear Sync, the initial part of the exposure will capture the lights in a trail that will appear behind the vehicle, while the vehicle itself is not frozen by the flash until later in the exposure. With Rear Sync in this particular situation, if the lights in question are taillights that look more natural behind the vehicle, the final image is likely to look more natural than with the Front Sync (default) setting.

The images in Figures 4-23 and 4-24 illustrate this concept using a remote-controlled model car with a flashlight shining out of its tail end.

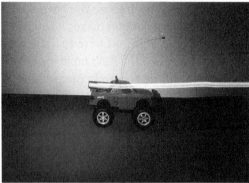

Figure 4-23: Fill-flash or Front Sync

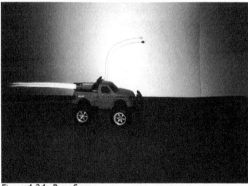

Figure 4-24: Rear Sync

Both pictures were shot with the RX100's flash, using an exposure of 0.5 second in Shutter Priority mode. In Figure 4-23, using the normal (Fill-flash) setting, the flash fired quickly, and the light beam continued on during the long exposure to make the streaks of bright light appear in front of the car.

In Figure 4-24, using Rear Sync, the flash did not fire until the car had traveled to the right, overtaking the place where the light had made its streaks visible. If you are trying to convey a sense of natural motion, the Rear Sync setting, as seen here, is likely to give you better results than the default setting.

To sum up the situation with the Rear Sync setting, a good general rule is not to use it unless you are sure you have a definite need for it. Using the Rear Sync option makes it harder to compose and set up the shot, because you have to anticipate where the main subject will be when the flash finally fires late in the exposure process. But, in the relatively rare situations when it is useful, Rear Sync can make a dramatic difference. Rear Sync is available in the more advanced shooting modes: Program, Aperture Priority, Shutter Priority, and Manual.

Focus Mode

The Focus Mode option gives you four choices for the method the RX100 uses for focusing on your subject. This is one of the more important choices you can make for your photography.

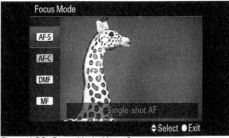

Figure 4-25: Focus Mode Menu Screen

Following are details about each of the four selections, which are shown in Figure 4-25.

Single-shot AF

The first option on the vertical menu that appears when you select this option is called Single-shot AF, designated by the AF-S icon on the menu. With this option, the camera does its best to focus automatically on the scene the camera is aimed at, using the focus area that is selected using the AF Area menu option, discussed below. The RX100 continuously adjusts its focus; you may hear the sounds of the autofocus mechanism adjusting and you may see the image waver as the focus changes, when you move the camera over subjects at differing distances.

With the Single-shot AF setting, the focus will be locked in when you press the shutter button halfway down.

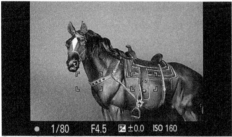

Figure 4-26: Single-shot Autofocus Screen with Focus Frames

At that point, you will see green focus brackets on the screen indicating the point or points where the camera achieved sharp focus, as shown in Figure 4-26, and you will hear a beep. In addition, a green disc in the lower left corner of the display will light up steadily, indicating that focus is confirmed. If focus cannot be achieved, the green disc will blink and no focus brackets will appear on the screen.

Once you have pressed the shutter button down halfway to lock focus (and exposure), you can use that locked focus on a different subject, as long as the subject is at the same distance as the one the camera originally locked its focus on. For example, if you have focused on a person at a distance of 15 feet (4.6 m), and then you decide you want to include another person or object in the scene, once you have locked the focus on the first person by pressing the shutter button halfway down, you can move the camera to include the other person or object in the scene, as long as you keep the camera at about the same

131

distance from the subject. The focus will remain locked at that distance until you press the shutter button the rest of the way down to take the picture.

Continuous AF

The next option for Focus Mode, Continuous AF, is designated by the AF-C icon on the menu. With this option, as with Single-shot AF, the RX100 focuses continuously until you press the shutter button. The difference with this mode is that the camera does not lock in the focus when you press the shutter button down halfway. At that point, the exposure will be locked while you hold the shutter button down halfway. However, the focus will continue to be adjusted if the subject moves or the distance to the subject changes through camera motion. You will not hear a beep or see any focus brackets to confirm focus. Instead, the green indicator in the lower left corner of the display will change its appearance to show the focus status.

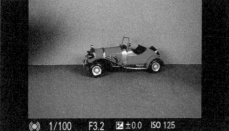

Figure 4-27: Continuous AF Screen Showing Focus Indicator

If the green disc is surrounded by curved lines, as shown in Figure 4-27, that means focus is currently sharp but is subject to adjustment if needed. If only the curved lines appear, that means the camera is still trying to achieve focus. If the green disc flashes, that means the camera is having trouble focusing.

This focusing mode can be useful when you are shooting a moving subject. With this option, you can get the RX100 to fix its focus on the subject, but you won't have to let up the shutter button to re-focus; instead, you can keep holding the shutter button down halfway until the instant when you want to take the picture; in this way, you may save some time, rather than having to keep starting the focus and exposure process over by pressing the shutter button halfway again. However, this focus mode is by no means perfect on the RX100. The lens has a tendency to pulsate as it seeks focus, and it can take a long time to lock focus, especially at wider apertures. I generally prefer using AF-S or DMF.

DMF

The third option for Focus Mode is DMF, which stands for Direct Manual Focus. This feature lets you use a combination of autofocus and manual focus, and can be very useful in some situations. One area in which DMF can be helpful is when you are shooting an extreme close-up of a small object, when focusing can be critical and hard to achieve. You can choose the DMF feature, and then start the focusing process by pressing the shutter button halfway down. The camera will make its best attempt to focus sharply using the autofocus mechanism. Then you can use the camera's manual focusing mechanism (turning the control ring, as discussed below in this chapter) to fine-tune the focus, concentrating on the parts of the subject that you want to be most sharply focused.

Another time DMF can be of considerable assistance is when you are shooting a scene that contains objects at varying distances, and you want to focus on one of the more distant ones. In this case, you can start out using manual focus, to get an approximate focus on the object you want to focus on, thereby letting the camera know which item to focus on. Then you can press the shutter button halfway down to let the camera take over and use autofocus to improve the sharpness of the focus.

If you have used DMF on other cameras, you may not expect to be able to start with either manual focus or autofocus. With some other systems, you were required to start with the camera's autofocus, and then use manual focus afterwards. With the RX100, you can start with either manual focus or autofocus, whichever is best for the situation at hand.

Finally, you may find that you actually prefer DMF to the standard option of AF-S. I have increasingly been using DMF as my main focusing method, because I can cause the camera to autofocus whenever I want to by pressing the shutter button halfway, but the RX100 doesn't use up its battery with constant focus adjustments, as is the case with AF-S. One drawback is that, with DMF, the control ring is dedicated to use for manual focus adjustment, so it cannot be used for any other function.

Manual Focus

The final selection on the Focus Mode menu, Manual Focus, is another very important option to have available. As I indicated in the discussion of DMF, above, there are various situations in which you may achieve sharper focus by adjusting it according to your own judgment rather than by relying on the camera's autofocus system. Those situations include shooting extreme close-ups, when focus is critical; shooting a group of objects at differing distances, when the camera will not know which one to focus on; or shooting through a barrier such as a wire fence, which may interfere with focusing.

Also, manual focus gives you the freedom to use a soft focus effect purposely. As I will discuss later in this chapter, the RX100 actually includes a setting on the Picture Effect menu option called "Soft Focus," which imparts a pleasing softness to your image. If you would rather achieve this sort of effect on your own by controlling the focusing more directly, you can set the camera for manual focus and de-focus all or part of the subject in precisely the way you want.

Using manual focus with the RX100 is a pleasure, because of the way the controls are set up. All you have to do is turn the control ring—the large ring around the lens, next to the camera's body. This action is quite intuitive, and is similar to the way most lenses were focused in the days before autofocus existed. Depending on the settings you have made on the Custom menu, there may be several functions available to assist with your focusing. I will discuss those menu options in Chapter 7, but I will briefly describe these focus aids here, because you very well may need them when focusing manually.

The first option, MF Assist, is turned on or off through the first option on the third screen of the Custom menu. When MF Assist is turned on, then, whenever you start turning the control ring to adjust focus in Manual Focus mode, the image on the display is automatically magnified 8.6 times, as shown in Figure 4-28, so you can more clearly check the focus.

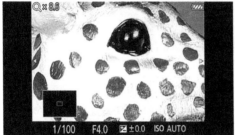

Figure 4-28: Manual Focus Screen with 8.6X Magnification

Once the magnified image is displayed, if you press the center button the image is magnified further, to 17.1 times normal. Press the center button again to return to the 8.6-times view. You can adjust how long the magnified display stays on the screen using the Focus Magnifier Time option, which is directly below MF Assist on the Custom menu. I prefer to set the time to No Limit, so the magnification does not disappear just as I am getting the focus adjusted as I want it. With the No Limit setting, the magnification remains on the screen until you dismiss it by pressing the shutter button halfway down.

If you don't want the camera to enlarge the image as soon as you start focusing, you can use the Focus Magnifier option instead of MF Assist. The Focus Magnifier option is not turned on by default; to make it available you need to assign it to a control button using the second screen of the Custom menu. With the Function of Center Button and similar menu options, you can set either the center, left, or right button on the control wheel to activate the Focus Magnifier option.

Once the Focus Magnifier option is assigned to a button, when you press that button a small orange frame appears on the screen, as shown in Figure 4-29.

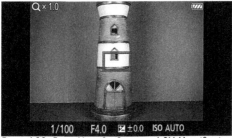

Figure 4-29: Focus Magnifier Screen at 1.0X Magnification

You can then move that frame around the screen using the control wheel or the direction buttons. That frame represents the area of the scene that will be magnified when you press the center button. If you want, you can use both the MF Assist and Focus Magnifier options, though I see no need to do so. In most cases, my preference is to use only the MF Assist option, which is sufficient for my needs. I prefer not to give up the function of a control button to the Focus Magnifier option, which does not add that much to your focusing options. However, as discussed in Chapter 9, when shooting with the RX100 through a telescope, I used the Focus Magnifier option, because it was easier to deal with that tricky focusing situation by being able to control when the magnification was used.

The RX100 provides one more aid to manual focusing, called Peaking, which is available as the next-to-last item on the first screen of the Custom menu. The Peaking Level option can be left turned off, or it can be set to Low, Mid, or High. When Peaking is turned on, then, when you are using manual focus, the camera places bright lines around the areas of the image that it judges to be in focus, as shown in Figures 4-30 (without Peaking) and 4-31 (with Peaking set to Mid).

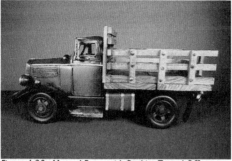

Figure 4-30: Manual Focus with Peaking Turned Off

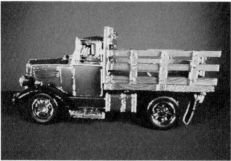

Figure 4-31: Manual Focus with Peaking Set to Mid

Besides setting the intensity of this display, as discussed above, you can set the color the camera uses—either white, red, or yellow—using the Peaking Color option on the Custom menu. My personal preference is not to use Peaking, because the MF Assist and Focus Magnifier options provide me plenty of information to achieve good focus, but you might want to experiment to see if Peaking is useful to you.

Finally, there is one more way to customize the use of manual focus with the RX100 that is worth mentioning here. On the second screen of the Custom menu, as noted above, you can assign the center, left, or right direction button to control any one of a long list of functions. One of these functions, called AF/MF Control Toggle, is especially useful if you anticipate a need to switch back and forth between autofocus and manual focus on frequent occasions. When this function is assigned to a button (the center button probably is the most convenient choice, at least for me), you can press the button whenever you want to switch instantly between these two focus modes. This is so much more convenient than going back to the Shooting menu and using the Focus Mode menu option, that it may be worthwhile giving up a button to this use.

In summary, the RX100 has a truly amazing array of assistance to offer when you are focusing manually. With some other compact cameras, manual focus is very difficult to use, because you have to turn a very small dial or the magnification options are not helpful. I find that, with the RX100, I actually prefer using manual focus to autofocus in some situations, because it is so powerful and easy to use.

Autofocus Area

The fourth option on the second screen of the Shooting menu, Autofocus Area, lets you choose what area of the image the camera focuses on using its autofocus mechanism.

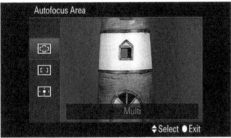

Figure 4-32: Autofocus Area Menu Option

There are three choices, shown in Figure 4-32, which I will describe in turn.

Multi

With the Multi option, which is the default choice, the RX100 activates 25 focusing zones over the full expanse of its display and tries to detect one or more areas within the scene to focus

138

on, based on their location. When it has achieved sharp focus on one or more of those areas, the camera displays a green frame indicating the locations of those areas. You may see one or several green frames on the screen, as shown in Figure 4-33.

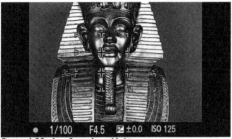

Figure 4-33: Autofocus Area Multi

The Multi option is an excellent one to use for general photography when you are sightseeing or taking shots of landscapes and the like.

Center

If you select Center for the Autofocus Area setting, the camera places a small black focus frame in the center of the display and it will focus on whatever object it finds within that frame.

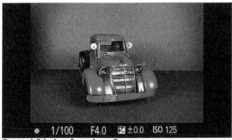

Figure 4-34: Autofocus Area Center

If the camera is able to focus there, it will beep and the frame will turn green, as shown in Figure 4-34. This focus method is useful if you are certain that you will be focusing on an object in the center of the scene. Even if you need to focus on an off-

139

center object, though, you can still make use of this focusing method. For example, if you need to focus on an object at the right side of the scene, you can aim the camera so as to place that object within the center focus frame, and press the shutter button down halfway to lock in the focus. Then, while keeping the shutter button pressed halfway down, move the camera back to the position where you want it, with that object on the right side of the scene, and press the shutter button all the way down to take the picture.

Flexible Spot

The third and final Autofocus Area option, Flexible Spot, gives you the most control over where the camera directs its autofocus operation.

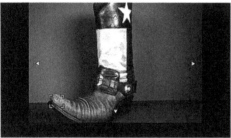

Figure 4-35: AF Area Flexible Spot Adjustment Screen

When you select this option from the Shooting menu, the camera places a small orange focus frame in the center of the image. You can move this frame around to any part of the display by pressing any of the four direction buttons on the control wheel. In Figure 4-35, the frame has been moved to the toe of the cowboy boot. When the focus frame is located where you want it, press the center button to fix it in place and return to the shooting screen. If you want to move the frame again, press the center button again to activate it.

This option is an excellent one to use if you are trying to focus on a specific area in a scene, especially if the camera might have difficulty in determining where to direct its focus, because of the placement of multiple objects in the same general area.

Soft Skin Effect

This menu option is designed to soften skin tones in the faces of your subjects. The option is grayed out and unavailable in some situations, such as when one of the Drive Mode options is selected. I have not found much difference in images taken with or without this setting in effect, but it may be worth a try to see if it produces any results.

Smile/Face Detection

This menu option gives you access to two separate functions with fairly different features.

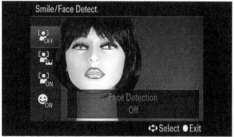

Figure 4-36: Smile/Face Detection Menu Option

There are four separate entries on the vertical menu that pops up when this menu item is selected, shown in Figure 4-36. You can select the top option, Off, which leaves all options turned off, or you can select one of the other three, which operate as follows:

Face Detection On (Registered Faces)

This option is designated on the menu screen by an icon of a person's head and a crown. When you select this choice, the camera supposedly searches for faces that you have previously registered using the Face Registration option on the Custom menu, as discussed in Chapter 7. If it detects a registered face,

141

it should consider that face to have priority, in which case it will adjust the Autofocus Area, Flash Mode, exposure compensation, white balance, and Red Eye Reduction values automatically to produce optimum exposure for that particular face.

In daily shooting, I do not use this feature. I guess it could be useful if you are taking pictures of children in a group setting and you want to make sure your own child is in focus and has his or her face properly exposed. I tried this feature out by registering one face and then aiming the camera at that face along with an unregistered face. In some cases, the camera picked the registered one as the priority face, but at other times it chose the unregistered one. Other users have reported good results with this feature, though, so, if it would be useful to you, by all means explore it further.

Face Detection On

This setting is similar to the previous one, except that it does not involve registered faces.

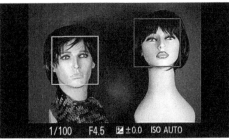

Figure 4-37: Face Detection Feature in Use

As shown in Figure 4-37, the camera will detect any human faces, up to eight in total, and select one as the main face to concentrate its settings on. Before you press the shutter button, the camera will display white or gray frames around any faces it finds. When you press the shutter button down halfway to lock focus and exposure, the frame over the face the camera has selected as the main face will turn green.

142

Smile Shutter

The final option for this menu item is the Smile Shutter, which is a sort of self-timer that is activated when the subject smiles.

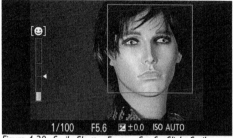

Figure 4-38: Smile Shutter Feature Set for Slight Smile

After highlighting this option, you can use the left and right buttons to choose the level of smile that is needed to trigger the camera—Slight Smile, Normal Smile, or Big Smile. Then press the center button to exit back to the shooting screen, and aim the camera at the subject or subjects. (You can, of course, put the camera on a tripod and aim it at yourself, if you want.)

As shown in Figure 4-38, the camera will then show a scale on the screen with a pointer to indicate how large a smile is needed in order to trigger a shot. As soon as the camera detects a smile of that magnitude from any person, the shutter will fire. The reddish self-timer lamp will illuminate, and you will hear the click of the shutter activating. If a person smiles again, the camera will be triggered again, with no limit on the number of shots that can be taken. So, in effect, this feature acts as a limited kind of remote control, with one specific function. Here again, as with the Self-portrait self-timer, I consider this option to be something of a novelty, which can be entertaining but is not necessary for everyday photography.

Auto Portrait Framing

This menu option provides a function that is somewhat unusual for any camera—it rearranges the composition of your shot based on its own electronic judgment. This function is available only when you have Face Detection turned on. Then, when the camera detects a face and you take a picture of that face, the camera may, if it finds it possible, crop the image and produce a new version of the image with the frame trimmed to emphasize the face in a more pleasing way. For an example of what the camera does, see Figures 4-39 and 4-40, which show the uncropped and cropped versions, respectively.

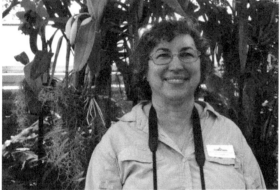

Figure 4-39: Auto Portrait Frame Example - Before Cropping

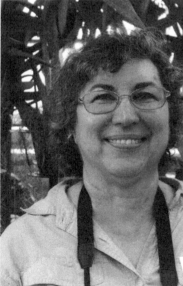

Figure 4-40: Auto Portrait Framing - Cropped

The camera saves both versions, so there is no harm in using this feature. It could be useful if you are pressed for time or are unable to get into position to take the shot you want. If you need a more nicely cropped version of the image quickly for a slide show, perhaps, this could be a good way to fill that need.

Auto Portrait Framing is available for selection only if the camera is set for autofocus with Autofocus Area set to Multi, and Quality set to Fine or Standard. (This option does not work with RAW images.)

ISO

The ISO acronym represents the International Organization for Standardization, which develops international standards for many areas of industry, science, and other fields. When I first started in film photography, the standard for the sensitivity of photographic film was labeled ASA, for American Standards Association. The ISO acronym reflects the more international nature of the modern photographic industry.

The original use of the ISO/ASA standard was to designate the "speed," or light sensitivity, of film. For example, a "slow" film might be rated ISO 64, or even ISO 25, meaning it takes a large amount of exposure to light to create a usable image on the film. Slow films yield higher-quality, less-grainy images than faster films. There are "fast" films available, some black-and-white and some color, with ISO ratings of 400 or even higher, that are designed to yield usable images in lower light. Such films can often be used indoors without flash, for example.

With digital technology, the industry has retained the ISO concept, though it applies not to film, but to the light sensitivity of the camera's sensor, because there is no film involved in a digital camera. The ISO ratings for digital cameras are supposed to be essentially equivalent to the ISO ratings for films. So if your camera is set to ISO 80, there will have to be a good deal of light to expose the image properly, but if the camera is set to ISO 1600, a reasonably good (but "noisier" or "grainier") image can be made in very low light.

The upshot of all of this is that, generally speaking, you should shoot your images with the camera set to the lowest ISO possible that will allow the image to be exposed properly. (One exception to this rule is if you want, for creative purposes, the grainy look that comes from shooting at a high ISO value.) For example, if you are shooting indoors in low light, you may need to set the ISO to a high value (say, ISO 800) so you can expose the image with a reasonably fast shutter speed. Otherwise, if the camera uses a slow shutter speed, the resulting image would likely be blurry and possibly unusable.

To summarize: Shoot with low ISO settings (around 125) when possible; shoot with high ISO settings (800 or higher) when necessary to allow a fast shutter speed to stop action and avoid blurriness, or when desired to achieve a creative effect with graininess.

With that background, here is how to set ISO on this camera. As is discussed in detail in Chapter 5, one good feature of the RX100 is that you can get quick access to certain important settings, such as ISO, using the Function button menu, or, if you want, using the left or right control button or the control ring. However, you can also set ISO from the Shooting menu, and this is not a bad way to make this setting. So, especially if you want to use the control ring and other buttons for other purposes, it's good to know how to get access to the ISO setting with this menu item.

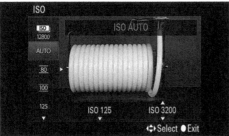

Figure 4-41: ISO Menu Option

ISO is the first item on the third screen of the Shooting menu. After you highlight it, press the center button to bring up the vertical ISO menu at the left of the screen, as shown in Figure 4-41. Then scroll through the various options by turning the control wheel or by pressing the up and down direction buttons to select a value ranging from one of the two Auto options at the top, through 80, 100, 125, 200, and other specific values, to a maximum of 6400 at the bottom of the scale. (If you want to set the ISO higher than 6400, you need to use the Multi Frame Noise Reduction feature, discussed below.)

If you choose Auto (the second option on the menu), the camera will select a value automatically, depending on the lighting conditions. However, one great feature of the RX100 that I have not seen on many compact cameras is that you can select both the minimum and maximum levels for the Auto ISO. In other words, you can set the camera to choose the ISO value automatically within a defined range such as, say, ISO 200 to ISO 1600. In that way, you can be assured that the camera will not select a value outside that range, but you will still leave some flexibility for the setting.

To set minimum and maximum values, while the orange highlight is on the Auto ISO option, press the right direction button to move the highlight to the right side of the screen, where there are two rectangles, labeled, when highlighted, ISO Auto Minimum and ISO Auto Maximum, as shown in Figure 4-42.

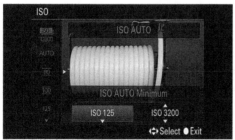

Figure 4-42: Setting ISO Minimum and Maximum Values

Move the highlight to each of these blocks in turn using the right direction button, and change the value as you wish, using the up and down direction buttons or turning the control wheel. You can set both the minimum and the maximum to values from 125 to 6400. When both values have been set, press the center button to exit back to the shooting screen.

Once those values are set, whenever you select Auto ISO, the camera will keep the ISO level within the range you have specified. Of course, you can always set a specific ISO value at any other level by selecting it from the ISO menu item.

Multi Frame Noise Reduction

Finally, I will discuss the top item on the ISO menu, whose icon is quite similar to the icon for the ISO Auto item that I just discussed. However, the top item is quite different. If you highlight the icon with the orange selection block, you will see that the name of this item is Multi Frame Noise Reduction.

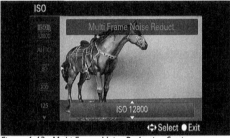

Figure 4-43: Multi Frame Noise Reduction Setting

This special setting lets you select an ISO value as high as 25600, considerably higher than the maximum value that you can set from the standard ISO menu. This value is an "expanded" setting, derived electronically from the camera's programming. When you select the Multi Frame Noise Reduction option, the camera will take multiple shots in a rapid burst, and then combine them internally into a composite image with reduced noise. This processing takes place in order to counteract the effects of using very high ISO values, which introduce considerable amounts of noise into the image. The camera also attempts to select frames with minimal motion blur.

After you have selected Multi Frame Noise Reduction, use the right direction button to move the selection highlight to the right side of the screen. The highlight will then be on the selection block for the ISO setting to be used, as shown in Figure 4-43. Use the up and down direction buttons or turn the control wheel to select a value, which can be set to ISO Auto, or to a specific value from 200 all the way up to 25600. If you choose ISO Auto for this setting, then the camera will select an ISO value up to 25600 according to the lighting conditions, and will take multiple shots using that value. You cannot use the flash when Multi Frame Noise Reduction is in effect. Also, you cannot use RAW quality with this setting.

Using the Multi Frame Noise Reduction setting is the only way to set the RX100 to the ISO levels above 6400. If you are faced with the prospect of taking pictures in an unusually dark environment, consider using this specialized setting, which really is more akin to a shooting mode than to an ISO setting.

Finally, here are some more notes on ISO: In Manual exposure mode, you cannot select Auto ISO; you have to select a numerical value. In the Auto shooting modes, Scene mode, and Sweep Shooting mode, Auto ISO is automatically set, and you cannot adjust the ISO setting. When Multi Frame Noise Reduction is selected, you cannot select continuous shooting from the Drive Mode menu. Also, note that the settings for ISO 80 and 100 are surrounded by lines on the menu. This indicates that those two settings are not "native" to the RX100's sensor, whose base ISO is 125. So, although using the two lower settings reduces exposure, it does not improve dynamic range or reduce noise in your images significantly.

Metering Mode

This option lets you choose among the three patterns of exposure metering offered by the RX100: Multi, Center, and Spot,

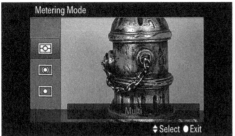

Figure 4-44: Metering Mode Menu Option

This choice tells the camera's automatic exposure system what part of the scene to consider when setting the exposure. With Multi, the camera uses the entire scene that is visible on the LCD. With Center, the camera still measures all of the light from the scene, but it gives additional weight to the center portion of the image, on the theory that your main subject is in or near the center. Finally, with Spot, the camera evaluates only the light that is found within the spot metering zone.

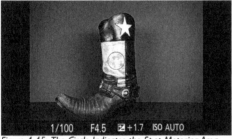

Figure 4-45: The Circle Indicates the Spot Metering Area

In Spot mode, the camera places a small circle in the center of the screen indicating the metered area, as seen in Figure 4-45. With this setting, you can see the effects of the exposure system clearly by selecting the Program exposure mode and aiming that small circle at various points, some bright and some dark, and seeing how sharply the brightness of the scene in the LCD changes. If you try the same experiment in Multi mode, you will still see changes, but more subtle and gradual ones.

150

Note, if you choose Spot metering, the circle you will see is different from the rectangular frames the camera uses to indicate the Center or Flexible Spot Autofocus Area mode settings. If you make either of those AF Area settings at the same time as the Spot metering setting, you will see both a spot-metering circle and an autofocus frame in the center of the LCD, as in Figure 4-46, showing the screen with the Spot metering and Center Autofocus Area settings in effect.

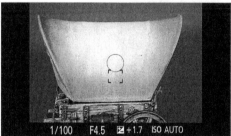

Figure 4-46: Circle for Spot Metering, Frame for Flexible Spot AF

Be aware which one of these settings is in effect, if either a circle or a frame is visible in the center of the screen. Remember that the circle is for spot metering, and the rectangular bracket is for center or spot focus.

Note, also, in the two Auto modes and all varieties of Scene mode, the only metering method available is Multi.

Flash Compensation

The Flash Compensation option lets you control the output of the camera's built-in flash unit. This function works similarly to exposure compensation, which is available by pressing the down direction button in the more advanced shooting modes. (Exposure compensation is discussed in Chapter 5.) The difference between the two options is that Flash Compensation varies only the brightness of the light emitted by the flash, whereas exposure compensation varies the overall exposure of a given shot, whether or not flash is used.

Flash Compensation is a good option to use when you want to use the flash but don't want the subject to be overwhelmed with light. One situation in which I like to use this setting is when I am shooting a portrait outdoors with the Fill-flash setting to reduce shadows on the subject. With a bit of negative Flash Compensation, I can keep the flash from overexposing the image.

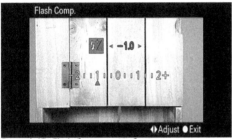

Figure 4-47: Flash Compensation Setting

This menu item is simple to use; just highlight it on the menu screen and press the center button, then, on the next screen, shown in Figure 4-47, press the left and right direction buttons or turn the control wheel to dial in the amount of positive or negative compensation you want. Be careful to set the value back to zero when you are done with the setting, because any setting you make will stay in place even after the camera has been powered off and back on again. Note, also, that Flash Compensation is not available with the Auto, Scene, or Sweep Shooting modes.

White Balance

One issue that arises in all photography is that film, or a digital camera's sensor, reacts differently to colors than the human eye does. When you or I see a scene in daylight or indoors under various types of artificial lighting, we generally do not notice a difference in the hues of the things we see depending on the light source. However, the camera does not inherently have this auto-correcting ability. The camera "sees" colors differently depending on the "color temperature" of the light that illuminates the object or scene in question. The color temperature of light is a numerical value expressed in a unit known as kelvins (K). A light source with a lower kelvin rating produces a "warmer" or more reddish light. A light source with a higher kelvin rating produces a "cooler" or more bluish light. For example, candlelight is rated at about 1,800 K; indoor tungsten light (ordinary light bulb) is rated at about 3,000 K; outdoor sunlight and electronic flash are rated at about 5,500 K; and outdoor shade is rated at about 7,000 K.

What does this mean in practice? If you are using a film camera, you may need a colored filter in front of the lens or light fixture to "correct" for the color temperature of the light source. Any given color film is rated to expose colors correctly at a particular color temperature (or, to put it another way, with a particular light source). So if you are using color film rated for daylight use, you can use it outdoors without a filter. But if you happen to be using that film indoors, you will need a color filter to correct the color temperature; otherwise, the resulting picture will look excessively reddish because of the imbalance between the film and the color temperature of the light source.

With a modern digital camera, you do not need to worry about filters, because the camera can adjust its electronic circuitry to correct the "white balance," which is the term used in the context of digital photography for balancing color temperature.

The RX100, like most current digital cameras, has a setting for Auto White Balance, which lets the camera choose the proper color correction to account for any given light source. The Auto White Balance setting works well, and it probably will do the job for you in many situations, especially if you are taking snapshots whose colors are not critical.

If you need more precision in the white balance of your shots, though, the RX100 also has fixed settings available for several common light sources, as well as options for setting the white balance by color temperature and for setting a custom white balance based on the light source currently in use.

Here is how to make the White Balance setting on the RX100 through the Shooting menu.

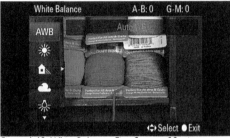

Figure 4-48: White Balance - First Screen of Settings

Once you have highlighted this menu option, press the center button to bring up the vertical menu at the left of the screen, shown in Figure 4-48. Then, by using the up and down direction buttons or by turning the control wheel, you can scroll through the icons on that menu, which correspond to the following choices, which take up more than a full screen. The choices on the first screen are the following: Auto White Balance (AWB); Daylight (sun icon); Shade (house icon); Cloudy (cloud icon); and Incandescent (round light bulb icon).

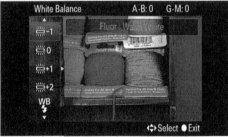

Figure 4-49: White Balance - Second Screen of Settings

The choices on the second screen, shown in Figure 4-49, are: Fluorescent Warm White (fluorescent bulb with -1); Fluorescent Cool White (same, with 0); Fluorescent Day White (same, with +1); Fluorescent Daylight (same, with +2); and Flash (WB with lightning bolt icon).

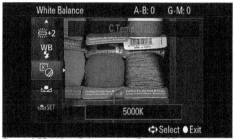

Figure 4-50: White Balance - Last Group of Settings

The last choices, shown in Figure 4-50, are: Color Temperature/Filter (K and filter icon); and Custom (special symbol). Below the Custom icon is one more icon with the word SET, which represents the option for setting the Custom value.

To select one of the settings on this list, just scroll to it and press the center button to select it. These settings should be largely self-explanatory, because most of them describe a particular light source in common use. As you can see, there are four different settings for fluorescent bulbs, so you should be able to find a setting that is appropriate for any such bulbs you encounter, though you may need to experiment a bit to find which setting is best for a given bulb. For settings such as Daylight, Shade, Cloudy, and Incandescent, just select the setting that matches the light that is dominant in your location. If you are indoors at night and using only incandescent lights, this decision will be easy. If you are indoors with a variety of electric lights turned on and sunlight coming in through the windows, the situation may be more uncertain. In that case, you may want to use either the Color Temperature/Filter setting or the Custom option.

The Color Temperature/Filter option lets you set the camera's white balance according to the numerical color temperature of the light source. One way to make that setting is to use a color temperature meter like the Sekonic Prodigi meter shown in Figure 4-51.

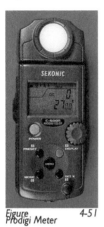

Figure 4-51
Prodigi Meter

That meter works well, and I find it quite convenient to use it when I'm striving for accuracy in my white balance settings. This device is fairly expensive, though, and you may not want to use that option. In that case, you can still use the Color Temperature/Filter option, but you will have to do some guesswork or use your own sense of color. For example, if you are shooting under lighting that is largely from incandescent bulbs, you can use the value of 3,000 K as a starting point, because, as noted earlier in this discussion, that is an approximate value for the color temperature of that light source. Then you can try setting the color temperature figure higher or lower, and watch the camera's display to see how natural the colors look. As you lower the color temperature, the image will become more "cool" or bluish; as you raise it, the image will appear more "warm" or reddish. Once you have found the best setting, leave it in place and take your shots.

To make this setting, after you highlight the icon for Color Temperature/Filter, press the right direction button to move the orange highlight to the right side of the camera's screen, so that it highlights the color temperature figure, as shown in

Figure 4-52.

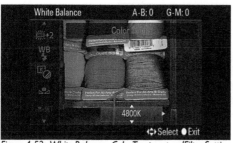

Figure 4-52: White Balance - Color Temperature/Filter Setting

Then raise or lower the number using the up and down direction buttons or by turning the control wheel.

If you don't want to work with numerical color temperatures, you can use the RX100's excellent ability to set a custom white balance. Using this setting can be a bit confusing with the RX100, because the Custom setting has two icons on the White Balance menu. The first Custom icon, located just below the Color Temperature/Filter icon, is the one to select when you want to set the camera to use the currently stored Custom White Balance setting. The second icon, below that one, with the word SET included, is the one to select when you want to obtain a new reading for the Custom White Balance setting, by using the camera's special procedure for setting that value. So, before you can use the upper Custom icon, you need to make sure that you have used the lower Custom icon to set the Custom White Balance value as you want it.

Here is the procedure for setting the Custom White Balance. First, highlight the Custom SET icon at the bottom of the White Balance menu. Press the center button to select this option, and the camera will display a message saying, "Use spot focus area data. Press shutter to load," as shown in Figure 4-53.

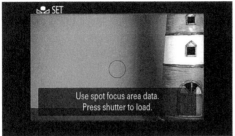

Figure 4-53: Setting Custom White Balance

At this point, aim the camera so the small spot circle in the center of the screen is filled with a solid white or gray color from a sheet of paper or a photographic gray card, like the one shown in Figure 4-54.

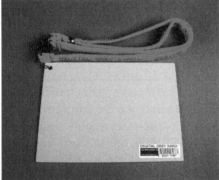

Figure 4-54: Photographic Gray Card

Then press the shutter button, and the camera will set the white balance according to the light source that was illuminating the surface you photographed. The display will show the measured color temperature along with values for variations along two color axes. You will see a number displayed next to the letters A-B, representing the amber-blue axis, and G-M, for green-magenta. If there is no variation along either of these axes, you will see the number 0 next to the pair of letters. If there is some variation, you will see an indication such as G-M: G1, meaning 1 degree of variation toward green along the green-magenta axis, as shown in Figure 4-55.

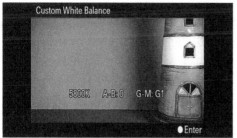

Figure 4-55: Results Screen for Custom WB Setting

Then, whenever you want to use the custom white balance you have just saved, you need to select the next-to-bottom icon on the White Balance menu, the one without the word SET next to it. Of course, you can change the custom setting whenever you want to, if you are shooting under different lighting conditions.

There is one more way in which you can adjust the White Balance setting, by taking advantage of the two color axes discussed above. If you really want to tweak the White Balance setting to the nth degree, after you have selected your desired setting (whether a preset or the Custom setting) press the right direction button, and you will be presented with a screen for fine adjustments, as shown in Figure 4-56.

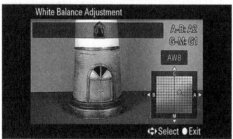

Figure 4-56: White Balance Adjustment Screen

You will see a pair of axes that intersect at a zero point, marked by an orange dot. The four axes are labeled G, B, M, and A for green, blue, magenta, and amber. You can now use all four di-

159

rection buttons to move the orange dot away from the center toward any of the axes, to adjust these four values until you have the color balance exactly how you want it. If you prefer, you can turn the control wheel to adjust the G-M axis, but you still need to press the left and right buttons to adjust the B-A axis. Be careful to undo any adjustments using these axes when they are no longer needed; otherwise, the adjustments will alter the colors of all of your images that are shot in a shooting mode for which White Balance can be adjusted, even after the camera has been powered off and then back on.

White Balance cannot be adjusted for the Scene or Auto modes, but it can be adjusted for the Movie and Sweep Shooting modes.

One final note about white balance: If you shoot using RAW quality, you can always correct the white balance setting after the fact, in your RAW software. So, if you are using RAW, you don't have to worry so much about what setting you are using for white balance. Still, it's a good idea always to check the setting before shooting, to avoid getting caught with incorrect white balance when you are not using the RAW format.

Before I leave the topic of white balance, I am going to include on the next page a chart in Figure 4-57 that shows how the different White Balance settings affect the images taken by the RX100. The images in this chart were taken under artificial light balanced for daylight, with the camera set for each available White Balance setting, as indicated on the chart. As you can see, you might as expected, the best results were obtained with the Auto White Balance, Daylight, Color Temperature, and Custom settings. The Fluorescent Day White setting also appeared to match the actual color temperature quite closely.

Sony RX100 White Balance Chart

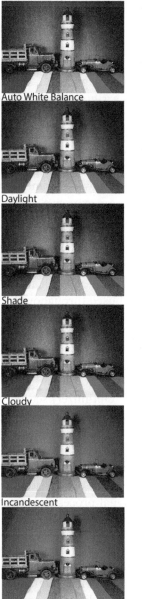

Auto White Balance

Daylight

Shade

Cloudy

Incandescent

Fluorescent Warm White

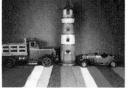

Fluorescent Cool White

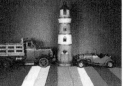

Fluorescent Day White

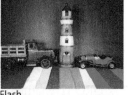

Fluorescent Daylight

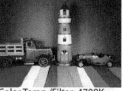

Flash

Color Temp./Filter: 4700K

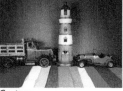

Custom

Figure 4-57: White Balance Chart for RX100

161

DRO/Auto HDR

The next setting down on the Shooting menu gives you several options for controlling the dynamic range of your shots and for using the in-camera HDR processing of the RX100. These are very useful settings that can help you avoid problems with excessive contrast in your images. Such problems arise because digital cameras cannot easily process a very wide range of dark and light areas in the same image—that is, their "dynamic range" is limited. So, if you are taking a picture in an area that is partly lit by bright sunlight and partly in deep shade, the resulting image is likely to have some dark areas in which the details are lost in the shadows, or some areas in which the highlights, or bright areas, are excessively bright, or "blown out," so, again, the details of the image are lost.

One approach to this problem is to use High Dynamic Range, or HDR, techniques, in which multiple photographs of the same scene with different exposures are combined into one composite image that is properly exposed throughout the entire scene. The RX100 can take HDR shots on its own, or you can take separate exposures and combine them in software on your computer into a composite HDR image. I will discuss the details of these HDR techniques a bit later in this chapter.

The RX100's DRO (Dynamic Range Optimizer) setting gives you another way to deal with the problem of uneven lighting, with special processing in the camera that can boost the details in the dark areas and reduce overexposure in the bright areas at the same time, resulting in a single image with better-balanced exposure than would be possible otherwise. In order to do this, the DRO setting uses digital processing to reduce highlight blowout and pull details out of the shadows.

To use the DRO feature, here are the steps. Press the Menu button and highlight this option, then press the center button to bring the DRO/Auto HDR menu up on the camera's display, as shown in Figure 4-58. Then scroll down through the options on that menu, using the up and direction buttons or turning the control wheel.

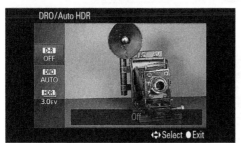

Figure 4-58: DRO/Auto HDR Menu Option

With the first option, D-R Off, no special processing is used at all. If you select the second choice, you can then press the right and left direction buttons to move through the various choices for the DRO setting: Auto, or Level 1 through Level 5. With the Auto setting, the camera will analyze the scene and attempt to pick an appropriate amount of DR processing. Otherwise, you can pick the level; the higher the number, the greater the degree of processing to even out the contrast between the light and dark parts of the image. In Figures 4-59 through 4-62, there are examples of the use of the various levels of DRO processing, ranging from Off to Level 5.

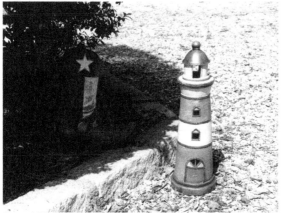

Figure 4-59: No DRO in Use

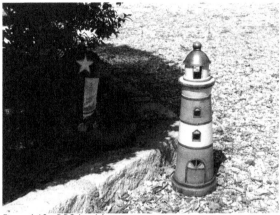

Figure 4-60: DRO Level 1

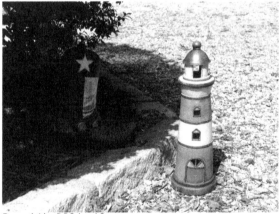

Figure 4-61: DRO Level 3

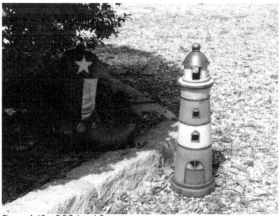

Figure 4-62: DRO Level 5

As you can see, the greater the level of DRO used, the more evenly the RX100 processed the lighting in the scene, primarily by selectively enhancing details in the shadowy areas. There is some risk of increasing visual noise in the dark areas with this sort of processing, but the RX100 does not seem to do badly in this respect; I have not seen increased noise levels in images processed with the DRO feature.

If you scroll to the bottom of the menu, you can choose an option that involves in-camera HDR processing. With this technique, the photographer takes two or more shots of a scene that has a wide dynamic range, some shots underexposed and others overexposed, and then merges them together using Photoshop or special HDR software to blend differently exposed portions from all of the images. The end result is a composite HDR image that can exhibit clear details throughout all parts of the image.

Because of the popularity of HDR, many camera makers have incorporated some degree of dynamic range processing into their cameras in an attempt to help the cameras even out areas of excessive brightness and darkness to preserve details. With the RX100, as with many modern cameras, Sony has provided an automatic method for taking multiple shots that the camera combines internally to achieve one HDR composite image

To use this feature, highlight the bottom option on the DRO/ Auto HDR menu, as shown in Figure 4-63, then press the right and left direction buttons to scroll through the various options for the HDR setting until you have highlighted the one you want, and then press the center button to select that option and exit back to the shooting screen. The available options are Auto HDR and HDR with EV settings from 1.0 through 6.0.

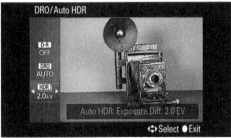

Figure 4-63: HDR Setting at Level 2.0 EV

If you select Auto HDR, the camera will analyze the scene and the lighting conditions and select a level of exposure difference on its own. If you select a specific level, the camera will use that level as the overall difference among the three shots it takes.

For example, if you select 1.0 EV for the exposure difference, the camera will take 3 shots in a rapid burst, each 1/3 of an EV level (f-stop) different in exposure from the next—one shot at the metered EV level, one shot at 1/3 EV lower, and one at 1/3 EV higher. If you choose the maximum exposure difference of 6.0 EV, then the shots will be 2.0 EV apart in their brightness levels.

When you press the shutter button, the camera will take 3 shots in a quick burst; you should either use a tripod or hold the camera very steady. When it has finished processing the shots internally, the camera will save the composite image as well as the single image that was taken at the metered exposure.

For Figures 4-64 and 4-65, I used the Auto HDR feature on the same subjects as in the earlier DRO examples.

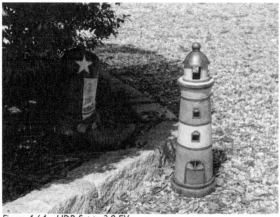

Figure 4-64: HDR Set to 3.0 EV

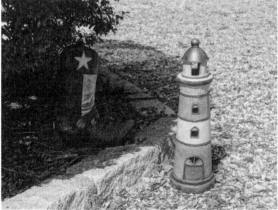

Figure 4-65: HDR Set to 6.0 EV

For Figure 4-64, Auto HDR was set to Level 3; for Figure 4-65, it was set to its highest value, Level 6. As you can see, neither of these levels was sufficient to eliminate the contrast between the lighting of the lighthouse and the boot, though HDR Level 6 came fairly close.

For comparison, I also took several shots of the same scene

167

using a wide range of exposure levels by varying the shutter speeds from 1/500 second to one full second. I merged those images together in Photomatix Pro software and tweaked the result until I got what seemed to be the optimal appearance of both boot and lighthouse.

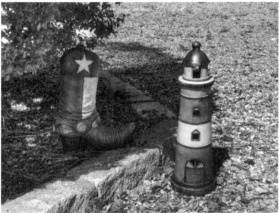

Figure 4-66: Composite HDR Image from Photomatix Pro Software

In my opinion, the HDR image done in software, shown in Figure 4-66, does a better job of evening out the dynamic range of the scene than either the DRO settings or the Auto HDR feature of the RX100.

The in-camera dynamic range options can be of use when you need to take pictures that are partly shaded and partly in bright sunlight and you don't have the time or the inclination to take multiple pictures and combine them later with HDR software into a composite HDR image.

My recommendation is to leave the DRO Auto setting turned on whenever you are taking general shots of a trip or for fun, especially if you don't plan to do any post-processing of the images using software. If you are planning to do post-processing, then you may want to shoot using the RAW quality setting so you can work with the shots later to achieve evenly exposed final images. You also might want to use Manual exposure mode or exposure bracketing to take a series of shots at different exposures, so you can blend them together using Photoshop, Photomatix, or some other HDR software. One great feature of the RX100 is that it provides unusually high levels of dynamic range in its RAW files, particularly if you shoot with low ISO settings.

Note that the Auto HDR setting cannot be set if you are using RAW quality for your images. The DRO settings do work with RAW images, but these settings will have no effect on the RAW images unless you process them with Sony's Image Data Converter software.

In addition, both the DRO and Auto HDR settings are unavailable when the camera is set to any of the Auto, Scene, or Sweep Shooting modes. You can use the flash with these settings, but it will fire only for the first HDR shot, and it defeats the purpose of the settings to use flash, so you probably should not do so.

Creative Style

The Creative Style setting offers excellent options for altering the appearance of your images by making in-camera adjustments to their contrast, saturation (color intensity), and sharpness. Using the fairly wide variety of settings available with this option, you can add or subtract intensity of color or work in subtle changes to the look of your images, as well as shooting in monochrome. Of course, if you plan to edit your images on a computer using software such as Photoshop, you can duplicate these effects readily at that stage. But, if you don't want to spend time processing your images in that way, having the ability to alter the look of your shots using this menu option can add a good deal to the enjoyment of your photos.

Using this feature is quite straightforward. First, highlight Creative Style, the next-to-last item on the third screen of the Shooting menu, and press the center button to move to the next screen, as shown in Figure 4-67.

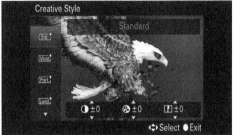

Figure 4-67: Creative Style Menu Option

Using the up and down direction buttons or turning the control wheel, scroll through the six major settings that are available: Standard, Vivid, Portrait, Landscape, Sunset, and Black and White. If you want to choose one of these settings with no further adjustment, just press the center button when your chosen option is highlighted.

If you want to fine-tune the contrast, saturation, and sharpness for one of these settings, here are the steps to take. Move the orange highlight bar onto the desired setting, such as Vivid or Portrait, and then press the right direction button to move a second orange highlight bar into the right side of the screen.

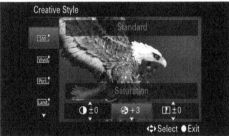

Figure 4-68: Creative Style Adjustments Screen

You will see a label above a line of three icons accompanied by numbers at the bottom of the screen, as shown in Figure 4-68. As you move the highlight left and right through those icons, the label will change to show which value is currently active and ready to be adjusted. When the chosen value (contrast, saturation, or sharpness) is highlighted, use the up and down buttons or turn the control wheel to adjust the value upward or downward by up to 3 units. When the Black and White setting is active, there are only two adjustments available—contrast and sharpness; saturation is not available, because it adjusts the intensity of colors, and there are no colors to adjust.

By varying the amounts of these three parameters, you can achieve a considerable range of different appearances for your images. For example, by increasing saturation, you can add punch and make colors stand out. By adding contrast and/or sharpness, you can impose a "harder" appearance on your images, making them look grittier and more realistic.

The Creative Style option works with all shooting modes except the Auto modes and Scene mode, and it works with RAW images as well. It is a valuable tool for refining and tweaking the appearance of your images.

In Figure 4-69, I provide comparison photos showing each setting as applied to the same scene under the same lighting conditions, to illustrate the different effects you can achieve with each variation. General descriptions of these effects are provided after the comparison chart.

Creative Style Comparison Chart

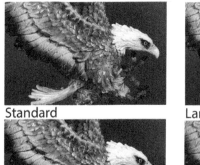

Standard

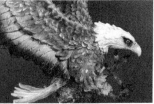

Landscape

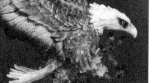

Vivid

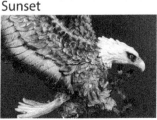

Sunset

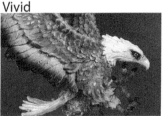

Portrait

Black and White

Figure 4-69: Creative Style Comparison Chart

Standard

The Standard setting is equivalent to having this feature turned off; no special processing is applied to your images.

Vivid

The Vivid setting increases the saturation, or intensity, of all of the colors in the image. As you can see from the samples, it calls attention to the scene, though it can easily seem excessive if used in the wrong context. The Vivid setting might work well if you want to emphasize the colors in a birthday party scene or a carnival.

Portrait

The main feature of this setting is a reduction in the saturation and sharpness of colors, in order to soften the appearance of skin tones. You might want to use this setting if you want to take portraits that are flattering rather than harsh and realistic.

Landscape

With the Landscape setting, the RX100 increases all three values—contrast, saturation, and sharpness—in order to make the features of a landscape, such as trees and mountains, stand out with clear, sharp outlines.

Sunset

With the Sunset option, the camera increases the saturation to emphasize the red hues of the sunset.

B/W

This setting removes all color, converting the scene to black and white. Some photographers use this setting to achieve a realistic look for their street photography.

Note that the RX100 also has specific settings for Portrait, Landscape, and Sunset in the Scene mode, discussed in Chapter 3. However, the similarly named settings of the Creative Style menu item have the advantage of being available in the more advanced shooting modes, including Program, Aperture Priority, Shutter Priority, and Manual, so you have access to other settings, such as ISO, Metering Mode, White Balance, DRO/Auto HDR, and others. In addition, as noted above, you can tweak the Creative Style settings by fine-tuning contrast, saturation, and sharpness. If you want to exercise full creative control over your photography, there are advantages to using the Creative Style settings, instead of the Scene mode settings, for those shots.

Picture Effect

The Picture Effect menu option provides a rich array of settings for shooting images with in-camera special effects. The Sony RX100 gives you a terrific variety of ways in which to add creative touches to your shots, and the Picture Effect settings are probably my favorites. Of course, there is a lot of competition in the arena of special-effects photography nowadays from apps for cameras that are built into cell phones (such as Instagram, Hipstamatic, and others), and there also is competition from the trend for using cameras like the Holga, film-based models whose images are purposely degraded to look old-fashioned, with low resolution, grain, and other attributes of images taken by cheap, plastic cameras.

The Picture Effect option lets you delve into this area and into numerous other types of creative photo-making, with considerable flexibility. The Picture Effect settings do not work with RAW images. If you set a Picture Effect option and then select RAW quality, the Picture Effect setting will be canceled. However, you still have control over many of the most important settings on the camera, including Image Size, White Balance, ISO, and even, in most cases, Drive Mode. So, unlike the situation with the Scene mode settings, when you select a Picture Effect option you are still free to control the means of taking your images as well as other aspects of their appearance.

To use any of these effects, select the Picture Effect menu option as shown in Figure 4-70 and, as with other menu screens, scroll down through the choices at the left of the screen.

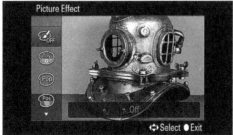

Figure 4-70: Picture Effect Menu Option

Some selections have no further options, and some have additional settings that you can make by pressing the left and right direction buttons.

I will discuss each option in turn. In Figure 4-71, I provide a chart with one example image taken with each effect, all taken of the same scene—a life-size fantasy cottage on display inside the conservatory at the local botanical gardens. Then, for some of the effects, I will include additional images of other scenes to provide larger illustrations.

Following are some details about each of the settings.

Off

The top setting on the Picture Effect menu is used to cancel all Picture Effect settings. When you are engaged in ordinary picture-taking, you should make sure the Off setting is selected so that no unwanted special effects interfere with your images.

Toy Camera

The Toy Camera menu gives you an alternative to using one of the popular models of "toy" film cameras such as the Holga, Diana, or Lomo, which are popular with hobbyists and artists who use them to take photos with grainy, low-resolution appearances. (There is a genre of photography called "Lomography," named for the Lomo camera.) With all of the Toy Camera settings, the RX100 processes the image so it looks as if it were taken by a camera with a cheap lens; the image is dark at the corners and somewhat blurry. The several individual settings, reached by pressing the right and left direction buttons, act as follows:

Normal: No additional processing.

Cool: Adjusts white balance to the "cool" side, resulting in a bluish tint.

Warm: Uses a "warm" white balance, giving a reddish hue.

Picture Effect Samples

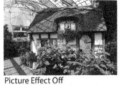

Picture Effect Off

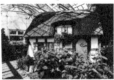

High Contrast Monochrome

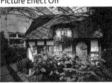

Toy Camera Cool

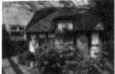

Soft Focus High

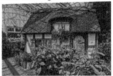

Pop Art

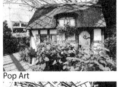

Posterization Color

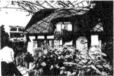

HDR Painting High

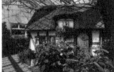

Rich-tone Monochrome

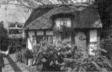

Retro Photo

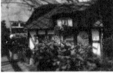

Miniature

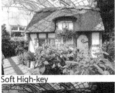

Soft High-key

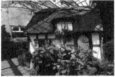

Watercolor

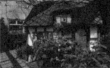

Partial Color Green

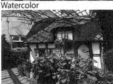

Illustration Mid

Figure 4-71: Picture Effect Chart

Green: Adds a green tint, similar to dialing in an adjustment on the green axis for white balance.

Magenta: Similar to the Green setting, but adjustment is along the magenta axis.

Figure 4-72 shows a fountain with the Toy Camera setting. Many people really enjoy the stylized, purposely cheapened look of images taken with the Holga and similar cameras. The RX100 comes with a built-in ability to let you experiment with this genre, so you might give it a try if you have any interest.

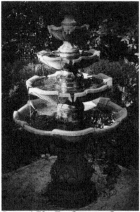

Figure 4-72: Toy Camera - Green

Pop Color

This next setting, according to Sony, is intended to give a "pop art" feel to your images through emphasis on bright colors. I don't have much background in art history, but I'm not sure that pop art is distinguished primarily by bright colors; I thought it had more to do with the subject matter, including images that originated from advertising and comic strips. Be that as it may, as you can see in Figure 4-71, what you get with this setting is another way to add "punch" and intensity, along with added brightness, to your color images. I have not found that this effect adds anything more to my images than the Vivid setting of the Creative Style option.

Posterization

The Posterization setting adds a fairly dramatic effect to your images. Using the right and left direction buttons, you can choose to apply this effect in color or in black and white. In either case, with this effect the camera applies a distinctive form of processing that results in heightened emphasis on colors (or dark and light areas if you select black and white) and imbues the image with a high-contrast, pastel-like look. It is somewhat like one of the more exotic types of HDR processing. The number of different colors (or shades of gray) used in the image is decreased to make it look as if the image were created from just a few poster paints; the result has an unrealistic but dramatic effect. It's a good idea to remember that, with all of the Picture Effect settings, you can still make additional settings, including White Balance, exposure compensation, and others. With Posterization, you might try using some positive or negative exposure compensation, which can change the appearance of this effect dramatically. For Figure 4-73, however, I did not use exposure compensation.

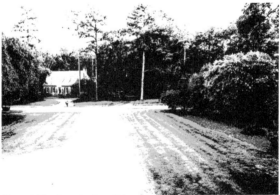

Figure 4-73: Posterization - Color

In general, I recommend using the Posterization setting only when you want to achieve a striking artistic effect, perhaps to create a distinctive-looking poster or greeting card.

Retro Photo

With the Retro Photo setting, the RX100 uses sepia coloring and reduced contrast in order to mimic the appearance of an aging photo. This effect is not as pronounced as the sepia effects I have seen on other cameras; with the RX100, a good deal of the image's original color still shows up, but there is a subtle softening of the image with the sepia coloration.

Soft High-key

The term "high key" refers to a technique in which the photographer uses bright lighting throughout the scene, striving for a very bright overall look with light colors and few shadows. This technique often is used in advertising photography. With the RX100, Sony has added softness, to give the image a bright, light appearance without the harshness that might otherwise result from the overexposed appearance. I enjoy the pleasant, relaxing look of images taken with this effect.

Partial Color

The Partial Color effect lets you choose a single color to retain in an image; the camera then reduces the saturation of all other colors to monochrome, so that only objects of that single color remain in color in the image. I really enjoy this setting, which can be used to isolate a particular object with great dramatic effect.

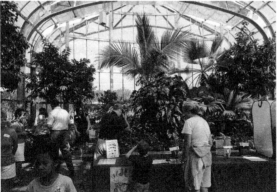

Figure 4-74: Partial Color - Green

179

In Figure 4-74, I used the Green setting to isolate the greenery inside the conservatory at the botanical gardens; in Figure 4-75, I used the Red setting to show the bricks of a house. As you can see, some of the earth around a tree was sufficiently red to show up in color as well.

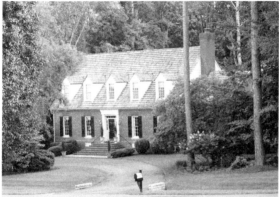

Figure 4-75: Partial Color - Red

The choices for the color to be retained are red, green, blue, and yellow; use the left and right direction buttons to select one of those colors. Then, just aim the camera at your subject; you will see on the LCD display what objects will show up in color. There is no direct way to adjust the color tolerance of this setting, so you cannot, for example, set the camera to accept a broad range of reds to be retained in the image. However, if you change the White Balance setting, the camera will perceive colors differently. So, if there is a particular object that you want to depict in color but the camera does not "see" it as red, green, blue, or yellow, you can try selecting a different White Balance setting and see if the color will be retained. You also can fine-tune the white balance using the color axes to add or subtract these hues, if you want to bring a particular object within the range of the color that will be retained. Also, by choosing a color that does not appear in the scene at all, you can take a straight monochrome photograph.

180

High Contrast Monochrome

This next setting is well explained by its label; it provides you with an easy way to take black and white photographs that have a stark, high-contrast appearance. You might want to consider this setting for street photography or any other situation in which you are not looking for a soft or flattering appearance. I used this setting for Figure 4-76, which provides an example of the extremes of black and white that are likely to appear with this effect.

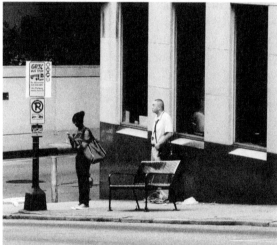

Figure 4-76: High Contrast Monochrome

Soft Focus

The Soft Focus effect is another setting that is variable; you can select either Low, Mid, or High by pressing the right and left direction buttons to scroll through those options. This effect is quite straightforward; the camera blurs the focus to achieve a dreamlike aura. Note that this is the first of several Picture Effect settings that cannot be previewed on the screen; you have to take the picture and then play it back in order to see the results of the Soft Focus setting. As I noted earlier in this chapter, you also have the option of selecting manual focus and de-focusing the image to your own taste to achieve a similar effect.

181

HDR Painting

The HDR Painting setting is similar to the HDR setting of the DRO/Auto HDR menu option. With this setting, the camera takes a burst of 3 shots at different exposure settings and combines them internally into a single image with HDR processing to achieve even exposure over a wide range of areas with respect to light and shadow. Unlike the more standard HDR setting, this one does not let you select the specific exposure differential for the 3 shots, but it lets you choose Low, Mid, or High for the intensity of the effect. Also, it adds stylized processing to give the final image a painterly appearance. I like this setting quite a bit; you can achieve some very clear, dramatic images with this option. For example, in Figure 4-77, I shot from inside the glass-walled conservatory building.

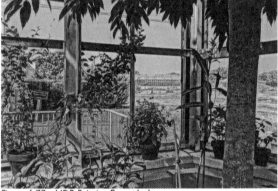

Figure 4-77: HDR Painting Example I

The effect, to me at least, is a somewhat fantastical view of the scenery outside. In Figure 4-78, I took a view from inside another building toward the conservatory. Here again, the result to me does seem somewhat like a painting, even though the objects in the image were all photographed; everything is real, but looks somewhat unreal.

Naturally, because of the use of multiple images, you can't preview the results on the screen before taking the picture. Because the camera takes multiple shots, using a tripod is advisable if you want to avoid blur from camera motion.

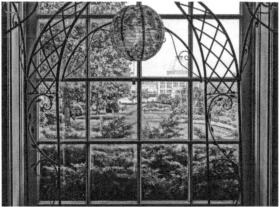

Figure 4-78: HDR Painting Example 2

Rich-tone Monochrome

The Rich-tone Monochrome setting can be considered as a black and white version of the HDR Painting setting. With this option, like that one, the RX100 takes a rapid burst of 3 shots at different exposures and combines them digitally into a single composite photo that has a broader dynamic range than would otherwise be possible. Unlike the color setting, though, this one does not let you select the intensity of the effect. I used it in Figure 4-79 for a downtown view. I like the clear, somewhat neutral but well-defined appearance of the cityscape with this setting. It can produce deep, rich grayscale tones.

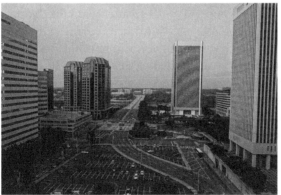

Figure 4-79: Rich-tone Monochrome

183

Miniature

The next Picture Effect setting is called the Miniature effect. When you apply this option to an image, the camera adds blurring at one or more sides of an image or at the image's top or bottom, to simulate the appearance of a photograph of a tabletop model or miniature. Such images often appear blurred in one area, either because of the narrow depth of field of these close-up photos, or because of the use of a tilt-and-shift lens, which causes blurring at the edges. This is a rather odd and specialized effect, but I have seen it show up on television commercials and elsewhere, so it evidently is becoming increasingly popular. For this feature to work well, you need to choose an appropriate subject. I have found that this effect looks interesting when applied to something like a street scene or a house, which might actually be reproduced in a tabletop model. For example, if you are able to get a high vantage point above a road intersection, you may be able to get a very effective photo of the traffic at the intersection, and then apply this processing to make it look as if you had photographed a high-quality mock-up of an intersection with model cars.

When you have highlighted this option on the Shooting menu, you can press the right and left direction buttons to choose either Top, Middle (Horizontal), Bottom, Right, Middle (Vertical), Left, or Auto for the configuration of the effect. If you choose a specific area, that is the area that will remain sharp. For example, if you choose Top, then, after you take the picture, the top area (roughly one-third) will remain sharp, and the rest of the image below that area will appear blurred. If you choose Auto, then the camera will select the area to remain sharp, based on the area that was focused on by the autofocus system and by the camera's sensing how you are holding the camera. You will not see how the effect will alter your image while viewing the scene, although the camera will place gray areas on the parts of the image that will ultimately be blurred, to give you a general idea of how the final product will look. I used the RX100 for an image of this sort in Figure 4-80, with the Miniature effect set to its Vertical orientation, leaving the road running up and down the center of the image in focus.

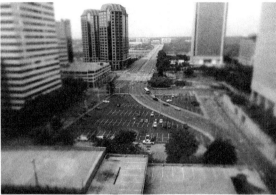

Figure 4-80: Miniature

This effect can provide a lot of fun if you are willing to experiment with it; it can take some work to find the right subject and the best arrangement of sharp and blurry areas to achieve a satisfying result.

One disappointing note is that this effect cannot be used for movies with the RX100. I was surprised to find this, because miniature effects are often used for making movies with subjects that look like speeded-up models of trains, cars, and the like. But not with the RX100, for some reason.

Watercolor

The Watercolor effect is designed to blur the colors of an image somewhat and make it look as if it were painted with watercolors that are bleeding together. You need to choose a subject that lends itself to this sort of distortion. For example, I have found that the faces of dolls and other figures can be pleasantly altered to have an impressionistic appearance; larger objects may not be affected significantly by this somewhat subtle effect. I have also had some pleasing results with plants, as shown in Figure 4-81.

185

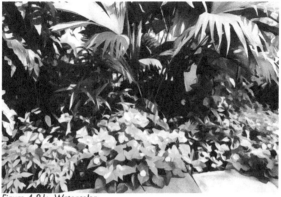

Figure 4-81: Watercolor

Illustration

The final option for the Picture Effect setting, Illustration, is one of my favorites. This effect finds edges of objects within the scene and adds contrast to them, making it appear as if they are outlined with dark ink as in a pen-and-ink illustration that has been colored in. You can set the intensity of the effect to Low, Mid, or High using the right and left direction buttons. If you choose a subject that has a fair number of edges that can be outlined and has a repeating pattern, you can achieve a very pleasing appearance. This is another one of the effects whose final result you cannot judge while viewing the live scene; you need to see the recorded image to know what the actual effect will look like.

As you can see in Figure 4-82, which was shot with Illustration set to the Mid level, this effect can transform an ordinary scene, here a yard with trees and grass, into an exotic picture. The images that are produced with this effect are more suited as decorative items than as depictions of actual objects or locations, but their appearance can be very striking and unusual.

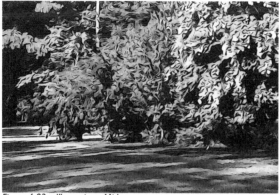

Figure 4-82: Illustration - Mid

Here are some more notes about the Picture Effect settings. First, as noted for the Miniature effect, several of the options are not available when you are shooting movies. Besides Miniature, these settings are Soft Focus, HDR Painting, Rich-tone Monochrome, Watercolor, and Illustration. If one of these effects is turned on when you press the red Movie button, the camera will turn off the effect while the movie is being recorded, and turn it back on after the recording has ended. You also cannot use Drive Mode with any of these effects. Also, even for the other effects, which can be used when shooting movies, you cannot take still images while shooting video. Finally, note that there are two other ways to create some of these effects: with the Photo Creativity feature in the Auto shooting modes, as discussed in Chapter 2, and with the Picture Effect setting in Playback mode, as discussed in Chapter 6.

Clear Image Zoom and Digital Zoom

This first option on the fourth screen of the Shooting menu, Clear Image Zoom, is a powerful feature that gives the RX100 extra zoom range without compromising the quality of your images very much. Digital Zoom, the next item on the menu, is a more conventional feature that magnifies the image but reduces the quality. In order to explain these features in context, I need to discuss all three zoom methods that the camera offers—optical zoom, Clear Image Zoom, and Digital Zoom.

Optical zoom is what could be called the camera's "natural" zoom capability—that is, moving the lens elements so they magnify the light that reaches the sensor, just as binoculars or a telescope do. You might call optical zoom a "pure" or "real" zoom, because it actually increases the amount of information that the lens gathers. The optical zoom of the RX100 operates within a range from 28mm at the wide-angle setting to the fully zoomed-in telephoto setting of about 100mm.

Just to complicate matters a bit, I should point out that the actual optical zoom range of the RX100's lens is 10.4mm to 37.1mm; you can see those numbers on the end of the lens. But the numbers that are almost always used to describe the zoom range of a compact camera's lens are the "35mm-equiv-alent" figures, which translate the actual zoom range into what the range would be if this were a lens on a camera that uses 35mm film. This translation is done because so many pho-tographers are more familiar with the zoom ranges and focal lengths of lenses for traditional 35mm cameras, on which a 50mm lens is considered "normal." I use the 35mm-equivalent figures throughout this book.

The Digital Zoom feature on the RX100 magnifies the image electronically without any special processing to improve the quality. This type of zoom does not really increase the infor-mation gathered by the lens; rather, it just increases the appar-ent size of the image by enlarging the pixels within the area captured by the lens. On some digital cameras, the amount of digital zoom can be very large, such as 50 times normal, but those large figures should be considered as marketing ploys to lure customers, rather than as a feature of real value to the photographer.

The third option on the RX100, Clear Image Zoom, is a special type of digital zoom developed by Sony. With this feature, the RX100 does not just magnify the area of the image; rather, the camera uses an algorithm based on analysis of the image to add pixels through interpolation, so that the pixels are not just multiplied. Instead, the enlargement is performed in a way that produces a smoother, more realistic enlargement than the standard Digital Zoom feature. Therefore, with Clear Image Zoom, the camera achieves greater quality than with Digital Zoom, though not as much as with the "pure" optical zoom.

Finally, there is one more way in which the RX100 can achieve a zoom range greater than the normal range of 28mm to 100mm, with no reduction in image quality. The standard zoom range of 28mm to 100mm is available when Image Size is set to Large. However, if Image Size is set to Medium or Small, then the camera needs only a portion of the pixels on the image sensor to create the image at the reduced size. It can use the "extra" pixels to enlarge the view of the scene. This process is similar to what you can do using editing software such as Photoshop. If the overall image size does not need to be of the Large size, you can crop out some pixels from the center (or other area) of the image and enlarge them, thereby retaining the same overall image size with a magnified view of the scene.

Therefore, if you set Image Size to M or S, the camera can zoom to a greater range than with Image Size set to L, and still retain the full quality of the optical zoom. You will, of course, end up with lower-resolution images, but that may not be a problem if you are going to post them on a web site or share them via e-mail.

In summary, optical zoom provides the best quality for magnifying the camera's view of a scene; Clear Image Zoom provides excellent quality, and Digital Zoom provides magnification that is accompanied by deterioration of the image.

With that introduction, here is how to use these settings. I will assume for this discussion that you are leaving Image Size set to L, because that is ordinarily the best setting to use to achieve excellent results in printing and otherwise distributing your images. Clear Image Zoom and Digital Zoom, the first two options at the top of the fourth screen of the Shooting menu, both have only two settings: Off and On. If you turn on Clear Image Zoom, you will achieve a greater zoom range than normal, as discussed above, and with minimal loss in quality. If you also turn on Digital Zoom, you will achieve an even greater zoom range, but the quality will deteriorate as the lens is zoomed past the range in which Clear Image Zoom operates. If you turn on Digital Zoom but leave Clear Image Zoom turned off, you will achieve a greater zoom range, but the image quality will deteriorate as soon as you pass the range for optical zoom.

When these various settings are in effect, you will see different indications in the viewfinder.

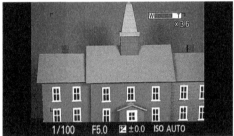

Figure 4-83: Image Size Large, Optical Zoom Only

In Figure 4-83, Image Size is set to L and both Clear Image Zoom and Digital Zoom are turned off. The zoom indicator at the top of the screen goes only as far as 3.6 times normal.

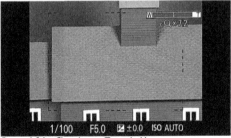

Figure 4-84: Clear Image Zoom In Use

In Figure 4-84, Clear Image Zoom is turned on. In this case, the zoom indicator goes up to 7.2 times normal. There is a small vertical line in the center of the zoom scale; that line indicates the point at which the zoom changes from optical-only to expanded (either Clear Image Zoom or Digital Zoom, depending on the settings). The icon of a magnifying glass with the letter C beneath the scale means that Clear Digital Zoom is turned on.

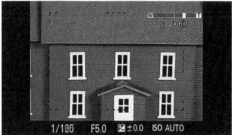

Figure 4-85: All Zoom Types Turned On, Zoom in C Range

In Figure 4-85, both Clear Image Zoom and Digital Zoom are turned on, and the zoom indicator goes up to 14 times normal. Up to a certain point in the zoom range, the magnifying glass icon will have a C next to it showing that Clear Image Zoom is in effect, as shown in Figure 4-85.

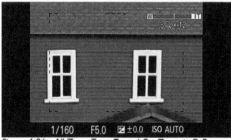

Figure 4-86: All Zoom Types Turned On, Zoom in D Range

When the zoom range extends beyond that point, the C will change to a D, showing that Digital Zoom is in effect, as shown in Figure 4-86.

191

The following table shows the zoom ranges that are available when Image Size is set to Large, Medium, and Small, with various settings of Clear Image Zoom and Digital Zoom. In all cases, Aspect Ratio is set to 3:2; with other settings, results would be different.

Available Zoom Range at Various Image Sizes			
	Large	Medium	Small
Optical Zoom	100mm	143mm	200mm
Clear Image Zoom	200mm	280mm	392mm
Digital Zoom	392mm	560mm	784mm

To summarize the situation with zoom, when Image Size is set to L, you can zoom up to 100mm with no deterioration, using optical zoom. You can zoom to about 200mm with minimal deterioration, using Clear Image Zoom. You can zoom to about 400mm using Digital Zoom, but with deterioration.

My personal preference, and that of quite a few photographers, is to limit the camera to optical zoom, and avoid any deterioration. However, many photographers have found that Clear Image Zoom yields surprisingly good results, and it is certainly worth trying when you cannot get close to your subject and you need to get a magnified view. I do not like to ever use Digital Zoom in order to take a picture. However, it can be useful to zoom in on a subject to meter a specific area of a distant subject, or to check the composition of your shot before zooming back out and taking the shot using Clear Image Zoom or optical zoom.

Note that Clear Image Zoom is not available in several situations, including when shooting RAW images, in Sweep Shooting mode, and with continuous shooting.

Also, note that Digital Zoom is always active when shooting movies, and cannot be turned off. If you don't want to use it, you need to be careful to avoid zooming beyond the optical range.

Long Exposure Noise Reduction

This next option, when activated, turns on special processing to reduce the visual "noise" or graininess that affects images during exposures longer than 1/3 second. This option is turned on by default so as to reduce these artifacts. However, in some cases this processing may remove details from your image. In addition, in certain situations you may prefer to leave the noise in the image for aesthetic reasons, because the graininess can be pleasing in some contexts. Or, you may prefer to remove the noise using post-processing software. If you want to turn off this option, use this menu item to do so.

High ISO Noise Reduction

High ISO Noise Reduction is available in three settings: Low, Normal, and High; it is set to Normal by default. This type of processing, like the previous menu option, removes visual noise that is caused when the camera is set to high ISO level. One negative aspect of this sort of noise reduction is that it takes time to process your images after they are captured. So, you may want to set this option to Low in order to minimize the delay before you can take another picture. If Quality is set to RAW, this option will be unavailable on the menu screen, because this type of noise reduction is not available for RAW images.

AF Illuminator

The AF Illuminator menu item gives you the option of disabling the use of the reddish lamp on the front of the camera for autofocusing. By default, this option is set to Auto, which means that, when you are shooting in a dim area, the camera will turn on this lamp briefly if needed, to light up the subject and assist the autofocus mechanism in gauging the distance to the subject. If you would rather make sure the light never comes on for that purpose, to avoid causing distractions in a museum or other sensitive area, or to avoid alerting a subject of candid photography, you can set this option to Off. In that case, the lamp will never light up for focusing assistance, though it will still illuminate if the self-timer, Smile Shutter, or another option that uses the lamp is activated.

SteadyShot

SteadyShot is Sony's optical image stabilization system, which compensates for small movements of the camera in order to avoid the blur that is caused by that motion, especially during exposures of longer than about 1/30 second. This setting is turned on by default, and I recommend leaving it on at all times, except when the camera is on a tripod. In that case, SteadyShot is not needed, and there is some chance it can "fool" the camera and result in an attempt to correct for motion that does not exist. Note that there is a different Steady-Shot setting for movies; I will discuss that Movie menu item in Chapter 8.

Color Space

With this option, you can choose whether to take your images using the "color space" known as sRGB, the more common choice and the default, or using the Adobe RGB color space. The sRGB color space includes fewer colors than Adobe RGB, and therefore is considered more suitable for producing images for the web and other forms of digital display than for printing. If your images are likely to be printed commercially in a book or magazine or it is critical that you be able to match a great many different color variations, you might want to consider using the Adobe RGB color space.

Shooting Tip List

This first menu item at the top of the fifth Shooting menu screen does not control any function. Instead, it is a collection of helpful tips about photography in general. To use it, press the center button when this option is highlighted, then scroll using the up and down direction buttons or the control wheel through the six main categories on the screen, including Basic techniques for shooting, Portraits and animals, and four others. Some of the tips are generic and would apply to any camera, and some discuss the use of a particular feature, such as the Smile Shutter. This little guide can be of some use if you are new to photography and need a few suggestions to get you started.

Write Date

This setting can be used to embed the current date in orange type in the lower right corner of your images, as shown in Figure 4-87.

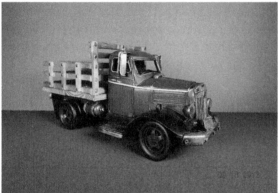

Figure 4-87: Write Date Option in Use

This embedding is permanent, which means that the information will appear as part of your image that cannot be deleted, other than through cropping or other editing procedures. You should not use this function unless you are certain that you want the date recorded on your images, perhaps for pictures that are part of a scientific research project. You can always add the date in other ways after the fact in editing software if you want to, because the camera always records the date and time internally with each image (if the date and time have been set accurately), so think twice before using this function. When you are shooting with this option activated, the word "DATE" appears in the upper right corner of the screen as you compose your shot, if you are using a shooting screen that displays detailed information.

Scene Selection

This next menu option is included here just because it comes next on the final screen of the Shooting menu. As discussed in Chapter 3, this option is used only when the camera is set to Scene mode; you use this menu item to select one of the various settings in that shooting mode, including Portrait, Anti Motion Blur, Sunset, Night Scene, and others. Note that you also can use the control ring to change Scene types, as long as the Control Ring option on the Custom menu is set to Standard and you are not using manual focus or DMF. In addition, the Scene Selection menu screen appears automatically whenever you turn the mode dial to the SCN position, if the Mode Dial Guide option on the Setup menu is turned on.

Memory Recall

The Memory Recall menu option is used only when the mode dial is set to MR, for Memory Recall mode. When the mode dial is turned to that setting, this menu item appears on the screen, with one of the three numbers at the upper right highlighted, as shown in Figure 4-88.

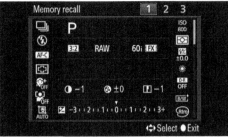

Figure 4-88: Memory Recall Screen

You can then turn the control wheel or use the right and left direction buttons to choose slot 1, 2, or 3 for the Memory Recall setting. Next, press the center button, and the camera will be set up with all of the shooting settings that were assigned to that numbered slot of the Memory Recall shooting mode. This procedure was discussed in Chapter 3.

Memory

The final option on the Shooting menu, Memory, also was discussed in Chapter 3 in connection with the Memory Recall shooting mode. Once you have set up the RX100 with all of the menu options and other settings that you want to store to a particular slot of the Memory Recall shooting mode, you select the Memory menu option, and choose one of those numbered slots, as shown in Figure 4-89.

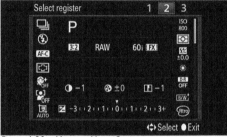

Figure 4-89: Memory Menu Option

Finally, press the center button, and all of the camera's current settings will be stored to that slot for the Memory Recall mode. You then recall those settings by turning the mode dial to the MR position and selecting slot number 1, 2, or 3.

Chapter 5: Other Controls

The Sony RX100, like many very compact cameras, does not have a great number of physical controls. It relies to a large extent on its system of menus to give you the ability to change settings. But the RX100 is at the upper end of the scale of high-quality compact cameras, and one aspect of its quality is that, although it does not have more actual controls than many cameras of this size, these controls can be configured to control a great many settings on the camera. Advanced photographers often prefer to be able to make settings with a knob or a dial whenever possible, for speed of access, and Sony has made it possible to set up the camera's controls in a way that suits your preferences. In this chapter, I'll discuss each of the camera's physical controls and how they can be used to best advantage, starting with the controls on top of the camera, shown in Figure 5-1.

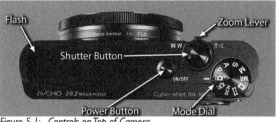

Figure 5-1: Controls on Top of Camera

Mode Dial

The mode dial, located at the right side of the camera's top, has just one function—to change the camera from one shooting mode to another. The shooting modes were discussed in Chapter 3. If you need to take a quick still picture, just turn this dial to the setting marked by the green camera icon and fire away. If you want to take a quick video sequence, turn the dial to that same position and then press the red Movie button, just below the mode dial at the top of the camera's back. It is important to remember that you can record a movie with the mode dial set to any position. There is a Movie mode on this dial, marked by a movie-film icon, but you do not have to select that icon in order to record movies.

Shutter Button

The shutter button is the single most important control on the camera. When you press it halfway down, the camera evaluates exposure and focus (unless you're using manual exposure or manual focus). Once you are satisfied with the settings, you press the button all the way down to take the picture. When the camera is set for continuous shooting, you hold this button down while the camera fires repeatedly. You also can press this button halfway to exit from playback mode and from menu and help screens, to get the camera set to take its next picture. Also, you can press this button to take a still picture while the camera is recording a movie.

Zoom Lever

The zoom lever is a small ring with a short handle, surrounding the shutter button. Its primary function is to change the focal length of the lens between its wide-angle setting of 28mm and its telephoto setting of 100mm. If you have the camera set for Clear Image Zoom or Digital Zoom, the lever will take the zoom to higher levels, as discussed in Chapter 4. Note that you can also use the control ring to zoom the lens, if you have the camera set up with that function using the Control Ring option on the Custom menu.

In playback mode, moving the zoom lever to the left produces index screens with increasing numbers of images, and moving the lever to the right enlarges your current image. These operations are discussed in Chapter 6.

Power Button

This button in the middle of the camera's top is used to turn the camera on and off. The orange light in the center of the button glows when the battery is being charged in the camera. You also can turn the camera's power on by pressing the Playback button, which places the camera into playback mode.

Built-in Flash

The camera's built-in flash unit is normally retracted and hidden in the left side of the camera's top. In order to set the flash so it will pop up, you have to use the Flash button, which is the right edge of the control wheel on the back of the camera. Even after you have selected a flash mode that will require the use of flash, such as the Fill-flash mode, the flash will not pop up into place until you press the shutter button halfway down to evaluate the exposure. (An exception is when you are using an automatic shutter release option, such as the Smile Shutter; the camera will pop up the flash if it needs to, even though you are not touching the shutter button.)

If you want the flash to be stowed away again, you need to press it gently back down into the camera until it clicks into place. If you want to use "bounce flash," which causes the flash to "bounce" off of the ceiling to reduce its intensity, you can pull the flash unit back carefully with a finger and hold the flash so that it is aiming upwards while it fires.

Next, I will discuss the two items on the front of the camera, as seen in Figure 5-2, before turning to the controls on the back.

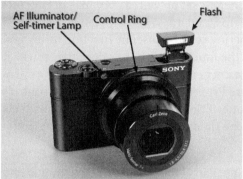

Figure 5-2: Items on Front of Camera

AF Illuminator/Self-timer Lamp

The small lamp on the front of the camera next to the control ring has multiple functions. Its reddish light blinks to signal the operation of the self-timer, the Self-portrait self-timer, and the Smile Shutter. It also turns on in dark environments to assist with autofocusing. You can control its function for helping with autofocus through the AF Illuminator item on the fourth screen of the Shooting menu, as discussed in Chapter 7.

Control Ring

The control ring is the very useful ridged circle that surrounds the lens, where the lens connects with the camera. As I noted earlier, it is a sign of a more advanced camera to have physical controls that let you make adjustments without navigating through menus. This particular control is of great use, first, because it is large, so it is easy to find and turn by feel, and, second, because you have the option of assigning various functions to it, so it can suit your particular needs as a photographer.

In order to assign functions to the control ring, you use the Control Ring menu option, which is the first item on the second screen of the Custom menu (the menu whose icon is a gear). When the camera is set up with its original, default settings, this item is set to Standard. When the Standard setting is in effect, the control ring controls just one function in any given shooting mode; the function it controls depends on which shooting mode the camera is set to. For example, if the camera is set to the Aperture Priority mode, the control ring controls the aperture; in Shutter Priority mode, the ring controls shutter speed. In the Scene shooting mode, the ring controls Scene setting selection.

Personally, I am quite happy to leave the Control Ring menu item set to Standard, because the functions the ring controls in the various shooting modes in that case are quite useful. However, if you want to use the ring for one, dedicated function no matter what shooting mode is in effect, you can use the Control Ring item on the Custom menu to choose one of the following items, which then will stay assigned to the ring until you make another change: exposure compensation, ISO, White Balance, Creative Style, Picture Effect, Zoom, Shutter Speed, or Aperture. You also can choose Not Set, in which case turning the ring will have no effect (unless you activate a function, such as manual focus, that requires use of the ring).

Of course, a function assigned to the ring will only work if the context permits it. For example, if you assign Aperture to the control ring, the ring will control aperture if the camera is set to Aperture Priority or Manual exposure mode. In any other shooting mode, turning the ring will have no effect, because aperture cannot be controlled manually in other modes.

On the next page I'm including a table with the functions that are assigned to the control ring with the Standard setting.

Control Ring Functions with Standard Setting	
Shooting Mode	Function
Intelligent Auto	Zoom
Superior Auto	Zoom
Program	Program Shift
Aperture Priority	Aperture
Shutter Priority	Shutter Speed
Manual Exposure	Aperture
Sweep Shooting	Direction
Scene	Scene Selection

The control ring also is used in two other situations, regardless of how you have set its assigned function. When you press the Function button (discussed later in this chapter), the camera activates a menu that shows several options, including items such as White Balance, ISO, exposure compensation, or others, depending on the settings you have chosen. Once you have pressed the Function button to pop up that menu, you can then turn the control ring (or the control wheel) to select the value for the setting that is active.

Finally, whenever the camera is set to manual focus or DMF (direct manual focus), you use the control ring to adjust the focus. In addition, if the MF Assist option is turned on through the third screen of the Custom menu, the display will be magnified to assist with focusing, as soon as you start turning the control ring. When the camera is set to either of those focus modes, you cannot use the control ring for any other function.

Now it is time to discuss the several important controls on the back of the RX100, as seen in Figure 5-3.

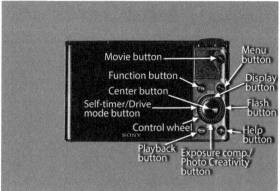

Figure 5-3: Controls on Back of Camera

Playback Button

This button to the lower left of the control wheel, marked with a small triangle, is used to put the camera into playback mode, which allows you to view your images on the LCD and lets you get access to the Playback menu. It also can be used instead of the power button to turn the camera on, placing the RX100 immediately into playback mode with the lens retracted. When the camera is in playback mode, you can then press the shutter button down halfway or press the Playback button again, to switch the camera into shooting mode.

Movie Button

The red button at the upper right of the camera's back has just one function—to start and stop the recording of movie sequences. You do not have to switch the camera into the Movie shooting mode; just press this red button at any time to start a video recording, and press it again to stop the recording.

The one problem I have had with this button is that I have found myself pressing it accidentally numerous times, resulting in many unwanted, short movies. To avoid doing this, I suggest resting your right thumb firmly on the rubbery pad to the left of the Movie button.

There are differences in how the camera operates for video recording in different shooting modes, though. I will discuss movie-making in detail in Chapter 8.

Menu Button

The Menu button, to the upper right of the control wheel, is quite straightforward in its basic function. Press it to enter the menu system, and press it once more to exit back to whatever mode the camera was in previously (shooting mode or play-back mode). The button also cancels out of sub-menus, taking you back to the main menu screen.

Function Button

The button marked Fn, for Function, is a control that gives you considerable flexibility for setting up the RX100 according to your own preferences. Using the Function Button menu option on the second screen of the Custom menu (discussed in Chapter 7), you can assign up to 7 functions to this button, from among 17 possibilities. The functions that can be assigned include important settings such as ISO, Drive Mode, White Balance, Metering Mode, and Picture Effect.

Once you have assigned your 7 (or fewer) chosen options to this button, it is ready for action. To use one of the options, just press the button when the camera is in shooting mode, and a menu of choices will appear along the bottom of the display, and in a circular menu at the top of the screen, as shown in Figure 5-4.

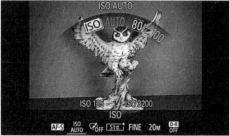

Figure 5-4: Function Button Menu

To scroll through these options, press the left and right direction buttons, moving the orange cursor underneath the one you want to select and moving through the matching choices at the top of the display. Do not press the center button to change the setting for the selected item; pressing that button will dismiss the menu without changing the setting. Instead, just turn either the control wheel or the control ring to change the value of the selected item.

For example, if you have moved the cursor under the ISO item, then, while the cursor and the ISO icon are on the screen, turn the wheel or the ring until the ISO setting you want to make appears. Then, press the center button to confirm the setting and exit from the Function button screen. Or, if you want to make multiple settings from the Function button options, you can scroll to another of the items in the horizontal menu at the bottom of the screen and change its value also, before exiting from the Function button screen.

Note that there may be some items at the bottom of the screen whose icons will be grayed out because the item is unavailable for selection in the current context. If you move the orange line under one of those items and then try to change the setting, the camera will display an error message.

The Function button system on the RX100 is very well thought out and convenient. I strongly recommend that you experiment and develop a list of seven items to assign to this button, and make use of this speedy way to change important settings.

Finally, when the camera is in playback mode, pressing the Function button brings up a screen allowing you to rotate the image that is currently displayed, as shown in Figure 5-5. If the currently displayed image is a movie, you will see an error message because the item cannot be rotated.

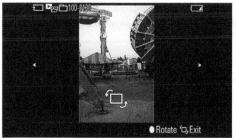

Figure 5-5: Function Button Rotate Screen

In-Camera Guide/Delete Button

The button marked with a question mark, to the right of the Playback button, is officially called the In-Camera Guide button or the Delete button. I prefer to call it the Help button or the Trash button. When the camera is in shooting mode, you can press this button to bring up a brief help screen with guidance or tips about the use of the camera. The help screen that is shown varies depending on the context. If the camera is ready to shoot, displaying the live view of the scene, pressing the Help button brings up the Shooting Tip List, the same option that is available from the fifth screen of the Shooting menu. Figure 5-6 is an example of the various types of photography tips that are available through this help system.

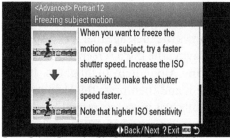

Figure 5-6: Example of In-Camera Guide Help Screen

When you are viewing these screens, you can scroll through the pages of tips using the control wheel or the up and down direction buttons. To dismiss the tip screen, press the Help button again. Press the Menu button to return to a previous screen. You also can press the shutter button down halfway to return to the shooting screen.

The Help button also has a special function when the camera is set to the Intelligent Auto or Superior Auto shooting mode. When you are using the Photo Creativity option in either of these modes and you have moved the indicator along the curved scale on the screen to change a setting (such as Brightness or Color), you can press the Help button to reset the option to its default value.

If the camera is displaying the main page of a menu screen with the highlight on a particular feature, then pressing the Help button will bring up a screen with a brief message explaining the use of that feature.

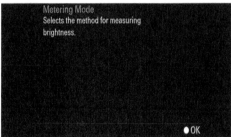

Figure 5-7: Help Screen for Metering Mode

For example, Figure 5-7 shows the message that was displayed when the camera was displaying the third screen of the Shooting menu, with the Metering Mode item highlighted. If you select an option for that item and then press the Help button, the camera will display a different message, providing details about that particular option. For example, Figure 5-8 shows the help screen that was displayed when I pressed the Help button after highlighting the Spot option for the Metering Mode item.

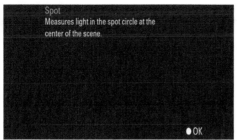

Figure 5-8: Help Screen for Spot Metering

This help system is quite detailed; for example, it provides varying guidance even for different ISO settings, such as ISO 80, 125, and 400, with tips about what shooting conditions might call for that setting. The shooting tips function operates with all of the RX100's menu systems, including Custom, Playback, Setup, and the others, not just the Shooting menu.

If the camera is set to playback mode and is displaying a recorded image or movie (and not a menu screen), then this button becomes the Delete button, or, as I prefer to call it, the Trash button, as indicated by the trashcan icon to the lower right of the button. If you press the button, the camera displays the message shown in Figure 5-9, prompting you to select Delete or Cancel.

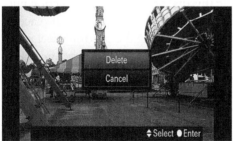

Figure 5-9: Trash Button Screen

If you highlight Delete and then press the center button, the camera will delete the image or video that was displayed on the screen. If you choose Cancel, the camera will return to the

209

playback mode screen.

Control Wheel and Its Buttons

The main controls on the back of the camera are within the perimeter of the control wheel, the ridged wheel with several icons around its outer edges. In the center of the wheel is the center button, a much-used control. At the four points of the wheel (up, down, left, and right), the edges of the wheel function as buttons. That is, if you press down on the wheel's rim at any of those four points, you are, in effect, pressing a button. These buttons all have at least two functions—as direction controls along with one or more other specific assignments. When they act as direction controls, the buttons are used to navigate through menu options and other choices for controlling the camera's settings. The other main functions of the buttons are indicated by one or more icons at each button's position on the control wheel. I will discuss all of these various controls in turn.

Control wheel

This wheel is one of the most versatile controls on the camera. In many cases, when you are able to choose a menu item or a setting, you can do so by turning this dial. In some cases, you have the choice of using this dial or pressing the direction buttons. One very helpful feature of the RX100 is that it places a round icon on the screen representing the control wheel when there is a value that can be adjusted at that point by the dial.

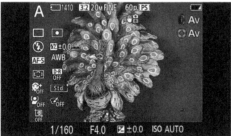

Figure 5-10: Icons Show Two Controls for Aperture

210

For example, in Figure 5-10, the icon, which looks like a gray ring facing directly out from the screen, is positioned next to the Av indicator, meaning that the control wheel can now control aperture. (The icon above that one shows that the control ring also can control aperture at this time.)

Figure 5-11 shows the camera in Manual exposure mode, in which case the icon for the control wheel is next to the Tv indicator, standing for Time value or shutter speed, indicating that you can adjust the shutter speed by turning the control wheel. (In this case, the icon above this one shows that the control ring can now adjust aperture.)

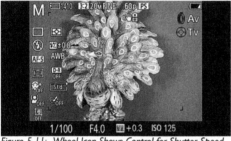

Figure 5-11: Wheel Icon Shows Control for Shutter Speed

The control wheel also has many other functions. When you are viewing a menu screen, you can navigate up and down through the lists of options by turning the wheel. When you are adjusting items using the Function button, you can change the value for the selected setting by turning the control wheel. When you are using manual focus and you have the Focus Magnifier option turned on, you can turn the control wheel to vary the portion of the scene that is being magnified.

In playback mode, the control wheel is used to navigate from one image to the next on the LCD. Also, when a video is being played on the screen and has been paused, you can turn the control wheel to play the video slowly, frame-by-frame, either forward or in reverse.

Center Button

This button in the center of the control wheel serves many purposes. On menu screens that have additional options, such as the Image Size screen, this button takes you to the next screen. It also acts as a selection button when you choose certain options. For example, after you select Focus Mode from the second screen of the Shooting menu and then navigate to your desired focus option, you can press the center button to confirm your selection and exit from the menu screen back to the shooting screen.

The center button also has several other possible uses, depending on how it is set up. The second screen of the Custom menu (discussed in Chapter 7) has an item called Function of Center Button. Using that option, you can set the center button to have its normal, default functions, by selecting the Standard option for Function of Center Button.

If you select the Standard option, then the center button is used to enable the Tracking Focus option when the camera is set to an autofocus mode (either Single-shot AF or Continuous AF), as long as the Autofocus Area is set to Multi or Center. If the Autofocus Area is set to Flexible Spot, then pressing the center button activates the screen for adjusting the location of the spot-focusing bracket. When the camera is set to manual focus and the MF Assist option is turned on, then pressing the center button roughly doubles the magnification of the Focus Magnifier display, from 8.6 times to 17.1 times. Pressing the button again toggles the display back to the 8.6 times magnification level.

If you would prefer not to use the Standard option, you can use the Function of Center Button option to set the center button to carry out any one of the following functions: AEL Toggle, AF/MF Control Toggle, or Focus Magnifier. I will discuss each of these options in turn.

AEL Toggle

If you set the center button to the AEL (Autoexposure Lock) Toggle option, then, when the camera is in shooting mode, pressing the center button will lock the exposure at the current setting as metered and set by the camera. If the camera is set to Manual exposure mode, pressing the center button as the AEL Toggle will lock the M.M. (Metered Manual) setting. The exposure will already be "locked," because you have set it manually, so using the AEL Toggle function will just keep the M.M. setting from changing further.

When the exposure is locked in this way, a large asterisk icon will appear in the lower right corner of the display and remain there until the lock is canceled. You will still be able to use the center button for changing the magnification on the MF Assist screen if necessary, without affecting the exposure lock. To cancel the exposure lock, press the center button again, when the shooting screen is in its normal mode (that is, when the MF Assist magnification screen is not displayed.)

Here is an example to illustrate the use of the AEL Toggle function. You might want to do this if you want to make sure your exposure will be calibrated for a particular object that is part of a larger scene, such as a dark painting on a light-colored wall. You could move close to the wall and lock the exposure while aiming the camera only at the painting, then move back to take the overall picture of the wall with that locked exposure, ensuring that the painting will be properly exposed.

To do this, assuming the camera is in Program mode, hold the camera close to the painting until the proper aperture and shutter speed appear on the screen. Then press and release the center button and an asterisk (*) will appear on the screen, as shown in Figure 5-12, indicating that exposure lock is in effect. Now you can move back (or anywhere else) and take your photograph using the exposure setting that you locked in. Once you have finished using the locked exposure setting, press the center button to make the asterisk disappear. The

213

camera is now ready to obtain a new exposure reading.

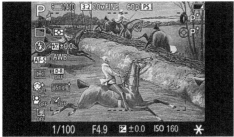

Figure 5-12: AEL in Use

AF/MF Control Toggle

If you select AF/MF Control Toggle for the setting of the center button's function, then pressing the button switches the camera back and forth between autofocus and manual focus. If the camera is set to any autofocus mode, then pressing the center button will switch the camera into manual focus mode. If the camera is set to manual focus mode, then pressing this button will switch the camera to Single-shot AF mode.

This function can be very convenient. First, it can be useful if you expect to encounter situations in which it may be difficult to use autofocus, such as dark areas or areas where you have to shoot through obstructions such as glass or wire cages. You can switch very quickly into manual focus mode and back again, as conditions warrant.

Second, having this capability can be useful if you want to set "zone" focusing so you can shoot quickly without having to wait for the autofocus mechanism to operate. For example, if you are doing street photography, you can set the camera to autofocus, and focus on a subject at about the distance you expect to be shooting from—say, 25 feet (7.6 m). Then, once focus is locked on that subject, press the center button to switch the camera to manual focus mode, and the focus will be locked at that distance in manual focus mode. You can then take shots of subjects at that distance without having to refocus. If you do need to set another focus distance, just press the center button to toggle back to autofocus mode and repeat the process.

Focus Magnifier

Finally, if you select the third option, Focus Magnifier, for the center button's function, then the button is used to magnify the focus area in manual focus mode. This option can be a bit confusing, because, as was discussed above, even when the center button is set to any of its other functions—Standard, AEL Toggle, or AF/MF Control Toggle, it always acts to magnify the focus area once you have started to focus using the control ring for the MF Assist function in manual focus mode. If you select the Focus Magnifier option, the difference is that pressing the center button will magnify the display before you start focusing with the control ring.

And there is another difference: With this option, pressing the center button once does not magnify the screen; rather, it changes the display to show that the magnification factor is 1.0 (no magnification), and places an orange frame in the middle of the screen. You can then move that frame around the screen using the control wheel (for vertical movement) or by pressing the direction buttons (for all directions). In this way, you can select exactly what part of the image you want to enlarge by moving the frame over that area. Then, when you press the center button again, that part of the image will be enlarged to 8.6 times normal. If you press the button again, that part of the display will be enlarged to 17.1 times normal. Throughout this process, you can still adjust the position of the orange frame, which will appear smaller as the display is enlarged. Another press of the center button returns the display to normal size, with the orange frame still displayed. To cancel out of the Focus Magnifier display, press the shutter button down halfway to return to the shooting screen.

In playback mode, you press the center button to start playing a video whose first frame is displayed on the camera's screen. Once the video is playing, you can press the center button to

215

pause the playback and then to toggle between play and pause. When a panoramic image is displayed, press the center button to make it scroll on the screen at a larger size, using the full expanse of the display screen. When you have enlarged an image using the zoom lever, you can return it immediately to its normal size by pressing the center button, and, when you are viewing a slide show, you can end it by pressing the center button. When you are selecting images for deletion or protection using the appropriate Playback menu options, you use the center button to mark or unmark an image for that purpose.

Direction Buttons

Each of the four edges of the control wheel—up, down, left, and right—is also a "button" that you can press to get access to a setting or operation. This is not immediately obvious, and sometimes it can be tricky to press in exactly the right spot, but these four direction buttons are very important to your control of the camera. You use them to navigate through menus and through screens for settings, whether moving left and right or up and down.

You also use them in playback mode to move through your images and, when you have enlarged an image using the zoom lever, to scroll around within the magnified image.

In addition to these navigational duties, the direction buttons are used for several miscellaneous functions in connection with various settings. For example, when the camera is set to Manual exposure mode, you can press the down button to toggle the action of the control wheel between setting aperture and setting shutter speed. And, as with the center button, the right and left buttons can be assigned to carry out other functions through the Custom menu, as discussed in Chapter 7.

Finally, each of the direction buttons has its own separate identity, as indicated by the one or two icons that appear on or near each of the buttons, as discussed below.

Up Button: Display

The up direction button, marked DISP, is used to switch among the various displays of information on the camera's LCD screen, in both shooting and playback modes. As is discussed in Chapter 7, you can change the contents of the shooting mode screens using the DISP Button (Monitor) setting on the first screen of the Custom menu. The various display screens that are available in playback mode are discussed in Chapter 6.

Right Button: Flash Mode

When the camera is in shooting mode, pressing the right button brings up a menu on the left of the display showing the options for setting the behavior of the flash unit. The options are Flash Off, Autoflash, Fill-flash, Slow Sync, and Rear Sync, although not all of them are available in any one shooting mode. This menu can also be summoned from the second screen of the Shooting menu. I discussed the use of these settings in Chapter 4.

One important point to note about the Flash button is that you have to use that button and its menu to bring the flash unit up into firing position. With some cameras, there is a physical button to pop up the flash, but that is not the case with the RX100—you have to use the settings on the little menu that comes up when you press this button. There is no way to pull the flash unit up by hand.

Down Button: Photo Creativity/Exposure Compensation

The down direction button has two icons directly below it, indicating that it has two different functions, depending on the shooting mode. In the Intelligent Auto and Superior Auto modes, pressing this button brings up the Photo Creativity options, which I discussed in Chapter 2. In the Program, Aperture Priority, Shutter Priority, Movie, and Sweep Shooting modes, this button controls exposure compensation, discussed below. In Manual exposure mode, in which exposure

217

compensation is not available, this button is used to toggle the control wheel's function between controlling aperture and controlling shutter speed.

Let's consider a specific situation in which you might use this exposure compensation control to adjust the camera's exposure to account for an unusual, or non-optimal, lighting situation. For example, consider Figure 5-13, in which I photographed an eagle figurine using the Program shooting mode.

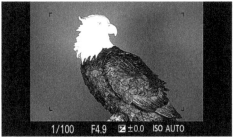

Figure 5-13: Before Using Exposure Compensation

The bird's head was a bright white, but the rest of the scene was quite dark. In this image, the camera's autoexposure system exposed properly for the larger, darker areas, but the head was overexposed and washed out.

One solution to this problem is to use exposure compensation to decrease the overall exposure of the image so that the head will not be overexposed. To accomplish this with the RX100, press the down button, which brings the exposure compensation scale up on the display, as shown in Figure 5-14.

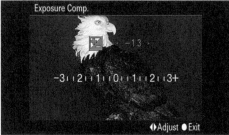

Figure 5-14: Setting Exposure Compensation

218

Adjust the amount of exposure compensation, positive or negative, by turning the control wheel or pressing the left and right direction buttons to move the orange triangle above the scale so that it points to a value to the left or right of the zero point.

As you do this, you will see the numbers change near the top of the display. With a negative value, the image will be darker than it otherwise would; with a positive value, it will be brighter. The LCD display will grow brighter or darker to indicate the effect of the adjustment.

In this case, with exposure compensation adjusted downward by 1.3 EV (exposure value), the eagle's head becomes darker and is no longer overexposed. This example demonstrates how the exposure compensation system works to adjust the brightness of your images.

Once you've taken the picture, you should return the exposure compensation setting back to the zero point, so you won't inadvertently change the exposure of later images that don't need the adjustment. (The exposure compensation setting will remain in place even after the camera has been turned off and back on again.)

There is one other duty performed by the down direction button: In playback mode, when a movie is being played the down button can be used to get access to a screen for adjusting the sound level of the movie.

Left Button: Self-timer/Drive Mode

The left direction button is labeled with the timer dial icon that indicates the self-timer, and the stack-of-frames icon that represents continuous shooting. When you press this button, the camera brings up the Drive Mode menu with its various options for self-timer, self-portrait shooting, continuous shooting, and bracketing. I discussed these options in Chapter 4, in connection with the Drive Mode option on the Shooting menu.

Chapter 6: Playback and Printing

If you're like me, you import the images you've shot into a computer, where you manipulate them with software, then post them on the web, print them out, e-mail them, or do whatever else the occasion calls for. In other words, I don't spend a lot of time viewing the pictures in the camera. But it's still useful to know how the various in-camera playback functions work. Depending on your needs, there may be plenty of times when you take a picture and then need to examine it closely in the camera. Also, the camera can serve as a viewing device like an iPod or other gadget that is designed, at least in part, for storing and viewing photos. So it's worth taking a good look at the various playback functions of the RX100. I'll also discuss options for printing images.

Normal Playback

Let's start with a brief rundown of basic playback techniques. First, you should be aware of your setting for the Auto Review function, which is found on the first screen of the Custom menu. This setting determines whether, and for how long, the image stays on the screen for review when you take a new picture. If your major concern with viewing images in the camera is to check them right after they are taken, this setting is all you need to be concerned with. As discussed in Chapter 7, you can leave Auto Review turned off, or set it to 2, 5, or 10 seconds.

If you want to control how your images are viewed later on, though, you need to work with the settings that are available in playback mode. For plain review of your images, the process is very simple. Just press the Playback button, marked by a small triangle, to the lower left of the control wheel on the back of the camera. Once you press that button, the camera is in playback mode, and you will see the most recent image saved to the memory card that is in the camera. To move back through older images, press the left direction button or turn the control wheel. To move back to the more recent images, use the right direction button or turn the control wheel to the right. To speed through the images, hold down the left or right direction button.

Index View and Enlarging Images

In normal playback mode, you can press the zoom lever on top of the camera to view an index screen of your images or to enlarge a single image. When you are viewing an individual image, press the zoom lever once to the left, and you will see a screen showing four images, one of which is outlined by an orange frame, as shown in Figure 6-1.

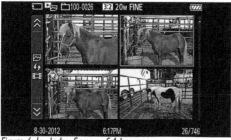

Figure 6-1: Index Screen of 4 Images

You can then press the center button to bring up the outlined image as the single image on the screen, or you can move through your images with the four-image index screen by pressing the left and right direction buttons or turning the control wheel (on the back of the camera).

If you press the zoom lever to the left once more, the camera will display an index screen of nine images. When either the four-image or the nine-image index screen is displayed, you

221

will see a thin vertical strip at the far left of the display. If you navigate to that strip by turning the control wheel or pressing the left direction button, that strip will become highlighted with an orange tint, as shown in Figure 6-2.

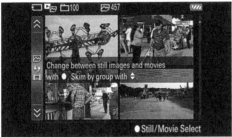

Figure 6-2: Image Selection Bar Highlighted in Orange

At that point, you can use the up and down direction buttons to choose a different folder of images, if there is one on your memory card. Also, you can press the center button while the strip is highlighted; that action will bring up the menu screen shown in Figure 6-3, which lets you choose to view still images, MP4 videos, or AVCHD videos. (Those video formats are discussed in Chapter 8.)

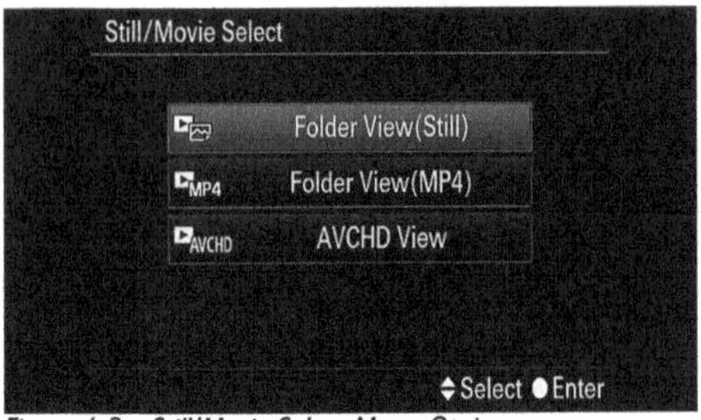

Figure 6-3: Still/Movie Select Menu Option

Highlight one of those options and press the center button to select it, in order to limit the camera's display to that one type of file.

When you are viewing a single image, one press of the zoom

lever to the right enlarges that image. You will then see a display in the lower left corner of the image showing a thumbnail of the image, with an inset orange frame that represents the portion of the image that is now filling the screen in enlarged view, as shown in Figure 6-4.

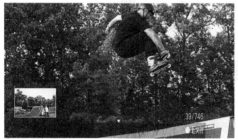

Figure 6-4: Enlarged Image with Inset Frame

If you press the zoom lever to the right repeatedly, the image will be enlarged to increasing levels. While it is magnified, you can scroll in it with the four direction buttons; you will see the orange frame move around within the thumbnail image. To reduce the image size again, just press the zoom lever to the left as many times as necessary or press the center button to revert immediately to normal size. To move to other images while the display is magnified, turn the control wheel.

Different Playback Screens

When you are viewing an image in single-image display mode, pressing the Display button (up direction button) repeatedly cycles through the three different screens that are available: just the full image with no added information; the full image with basic information, including date and time it was taken, image number, aspect ratio, aperture, shutter speed, ISO, and image size and quality, as shown in Figure 6-5; and a reduced-size image with detailed recording information, including aperture, shutter speed, ISO, shooting mode, white balance, and other data, plus a histogram, as shown in Figure 6-6.

223

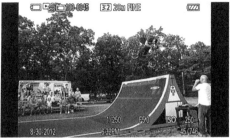

Figure 6-5: Playback Display with Basic Information

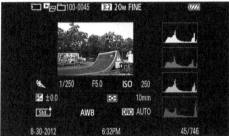

Figure 6-6: Playback Display with Detailed Information

A histogram is a graph showing the distribution of dark and bright areas in the image displayed on the screen. The darkest blacks are represented by vertical bars on the left, and the brightest whites by vertical bars on the right, with continuous gradations in between. With the RX100, the histogram displayed in playback mode includes four boxes with information. The top box provides information about the overall brightness of the image. The three lower boxes provide information about the brightness of the basic colors that make up the image: red, green, and blue.

If you have a histogram in which the brightness values are clearly bunched towards the left side of the scale, that means there is an excessive amount of black and dark areas (high points on the left side of the histogram), and very few bright and white areas (no high points on the right). The histogram in Figure 6-7 illustrates this degree of underexposure.

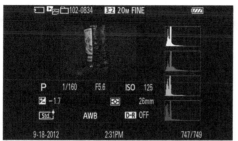

Figure 6-7: Histogram for Dark Image, with Peaks at Left

A histogram with its high points bunched on the right side of the screen means the opposite—too bright, as shown in Figure 6-8.

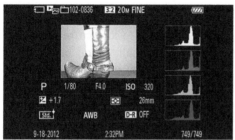

Figure 6-8: Histogram for Bright Image, with Peaks at Right

A histogram that is "just right" has its high points arranged evenly in the middle of the chart. That pattern, as illustrated by Figure 6-9, indicates a good balance of light, dark, and medium tones.

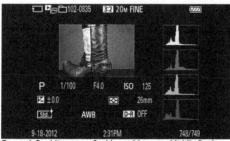

Figure 6-9: Histogram for Normal Image - Middle Peaks

When the histogram is on the screen, any areas containing highlights that are excessively bright will blink to indicate possible overexposure, thereby alerting you that you might need to take another shot with the exposure adjusted to avoid that situation.

The histogram is an approximation, and should not be relied on too heavily. It may be useful to give you some feedback as to how evenly exposed your image is likely to be. Also, there may be instances in which it is appropriate to have a histogram skewed to the left or right, for intentionally "low-key" (dark) or "high-key" (brightly lit) scenes.

Deleting Images with the Trash Button

As I mentioned in Chapter 5, you can delete individual images by pressing the Delete button, also known as the Trash button or Help button. This is the small, round button with a question mark on it at the far lower right of the camera's back. If you press this button when a still image or a video is displayed, whether individually or highlighted on an index screen, the camera will display the Delete/Cancel box shown in Figure 6-10.

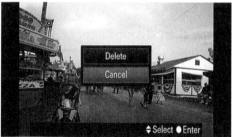

Figure 6-10: Trash Button Screen

Just highlight your choice and press the center button to confirm. You can delete only single images or videos in this way. If you want to delete multiple items, you need to use the Delete option on the Playback menu, discussed later in this chapter.

Rotating Images with the Function Button

As I also mentioned in Chapter 5, you can rotate a still image by pressing the Function button when the image is displayed on the camera's screen, either individually or on an index screen. When you press this button, you will see a screen like that shown in Figure 6-11, in which the camera prompts you to press the center button to rotate the image or to press the Function button again to cancel.

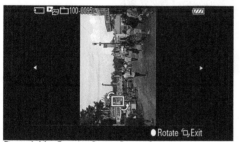

Figure 6-11: Function Button Rotate Screen

Each time you press the center button, the image will be rotated counter-clockwise by 90 degrees. After it has been rotated, it will be in the new position whenever it is displayed on the screen.

The Playback Menu

The other options that are available for controlling playback on the RX100 appear as items on the Playback menu, whose first screen is shown in Figure 6-12.

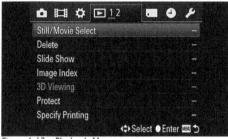

Figure 6-12: Playback Menu

You get access to this menu by pressing the Menu button when the camera is in playback mode. You enter playback mode by pressing the Playback button when the camera is turned on in shooting mode. Or, if the camera is turned off, you can turn it on in playback mode by pressing the Playback button instead of the power button.

Here is information about the items on the Playback menu:

Still/Movie Select

This first option on the Playback menu gives you a way to select whether to view just still images, MP4 movies, or AVCHD movies, as shown in Figure 6-13.

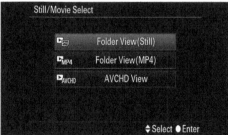

Figure 6-13: Still/Movie Select Menu Option

228

(MP4 and AVCHD are the two different movie formats available with the RX100; I will discuss those formats in Chapter 8.) The use of this menu option may not be immediately obvious, because it may seem to you that, whenever you take a still image you are immediately able to view it by pressing the Playback button, and, if you then take a video, you can immediately view the video by pressing the Playback button. In other words, it does not seem as if you have to switch the camera between viewing still images and viewing movies; it appears to do this switching automatically.

Actually, it is true that the camera switches automatically between these two viewing modes. However, that does not mean that this menu option is unnecessary. What happens is that, whenever you take a still picture or record a movie, the camera automatically switches into the proper mode for viewing that item. For example, suppose your memory card has an assortment of 50 videos and 50 still images stored on it. If you now take a still image, you can immediately press the Playback button and view that image. However, you will not be able to view any of the videos that are stored on the memory card. In order to view the videos, you would have to switch back to the mode for viewing those videos in one of two ways: either using the Still/Movie Select option, or by recording another video, which will automatically switch the camera back into the mode for viewing videos.

To put this another way, the camera has to be switched into either still-viewing mode or video-viewing mode for viewing either stills or videos. When you take a still or a video, that action automatically does this switching; otherwise, you have to use the Playback menu option to make the switch, or you have to go to the index screen, as discussed earlier in this chapter, and move to the far left of that screen, where you can press the center button to get access to the Still/Movie Select option.

Delete

The Delete command is available for you to use when you want to delete multiple images from your memory card in one operation. (If you just want to delete a few images, it's usually easier to display each image on the screen, then press the Trash button and confirm the erasure.) When you select the Delete command, the menu offers you various choices, as shown in Figure 6-14.

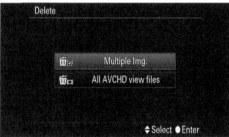

Figure 6-14: Delete Menu Option

These choices may include Multiple Images, All in Folder, or, if the current folder contains movies in the AVCHD format, All AVCHD View Files, depending on the current setting for the Still/Movie Select option, discussed above.

If you choose Multiple Images, the camera will then display an index screen showing the still images or videos, with a check box at the left side of each image, as shown in Figure 6-15.

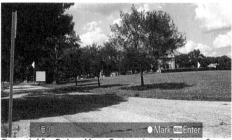

Figure 6-15: Delete Menu Option - Image Selection Screen

230

The images and videos may be shown individually or on an index screen, depending on current settings. You can change between full-screen and index views using the zoom lever.

Scroll through the images using the control wheel or the direction buttons. When you come to an image you want to mark for deletion, press the center button to mark it, which will place a check mark in the check box on that image. Continue with this process until you have marked for deletion all images you want to delete. Then, press the Menu button to move to the next screen, where the camera will prompt you to highlight OK or Cancel, and press the center button to confirm your choice. If you select OK, all of the marked images will be deleted.

If, instead of Multiple Images, you choose All in Folder, the camera will display a screen asking you to confirm deletion of all files in the current folder. Note that, because of the RX100's limitation of showing only still images or movies at any one time, this command will delete only stills or movies, not both. If you want to delete all files from a folder, you will have to carry out this process once for stills, once for MP4 videos, and once for AVCHD videos. Finally, if you select All AVCHD view files, you will have the opportunity to delete just the AVCHD-format video files.

Slide Show

This feature lets you play your still images in sequence, at an interval you specify and with transitions that you can choose. When you select this menu item, the next screen has three options that you can set: Repeat, Interval, and Image Type, as shown in Figure 6-16.

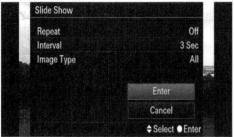

Figure 6-16: Slide Show Options

Repeat can be set either on or off. If it is turned on, the show will keep repeating; otherwise it will play only once. The camera will not power off automatically in this mode, so be sure to stop the show when you are done with it. Interval, which controls how long each image stays on the screen, can be set to 1, 3, 5, 10, or 30 seconds. The Image Type setting lets you choose whether to display all still images, or only 3D images. (This option seems somewhat odd, given that the RX100 has no built-in ability to shoot 3D images. However, the camera can display 3D images shot with other cameras.) You cannot include movies in the slide show.

Once the options are set, navigate to the Enter box at the bottom of the screen using the control wheel or the direction buttons, and then press the center button to start the show. You can move forward or back through the images with the left and right direction buttons. Hold those buttons down to fast-forward or fast-reverse through the images. You can stop the show by pressing the center button or the Playback button.

The Slide Show menu option does not provide any elaborate settings such as different transitions, effects, or music for the show. You cannot select which images to play; this option just lets you play all of your still images (or only 3D images, if you happen to have some from another camera).

Image Index

This menu option does not add anything new to what you can

232

already do in playback mode. It just lets you select and view either the 4-image or the 9-image index screen. This option does not change how the zoom lever calls up index screens; no matter how this menu option is set, pressing the zoom lever to the left in playback mode will call up the 4-image screen first, and then, with one more press of the lever, the 9-image screen. This menu option just gives you another way to get access to one or the other of those index screens, in case you prefer to use menu options rather than pressing the zoom lever. The index screen will display either still images or videos, depending on how the Still/Movie Select option is currently set.

3D Viewing

The 3D Viewing menu option is for use only when you have the RX100 connected to a 3D-capable TV using an HDMI cable. In order to use this function, once the camera is connected to the TV, select this menu option and then use the buttons on the control wheel to control the playback of the images.

Protect

With the Protect feature, you can "lock" selected images or videos so they cannot be erased with the normal erase functions, including using the Trash button and using the Delete option on the Playback menu, discussed above. However, if you format the memory card using the Format command, all data will be erased, including protected images.

To protect images using this menu option, the procedure is similar to the procedure for deleting images, discussed above, but the only available option is to mark images for protection individually; there is no option for selecting all images. Once you select this menu option, the camera will display an image, and you can mark its check box for protection by pressing the center button. Any image that is protected will have a key icon in the upper right corner, to the left of the battery icon, as shown in Figure 6-17.

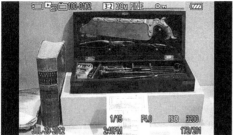

Figure 6-17: Protected Image with Key Icon

The key icon will be visible when the image is viewed with the detailed information screen or the basic information screen, but it will not appear in the image-only view.

If you want to unprotect all images or videos in one operation, you can select that option from the Protect item on the Playback menu. The option will prompt you to Cancel All Images, Cancel all Movies (MP4), or Cancel all AVCHD View Files, depending on which type of file is currently being displayed with the Still/Movie Select option.

Specify Printing

This menu option lets you use the DPOF (Digital Print Order Format) function, which is built into the camera. The DPOF system lets you mark various images on your memory card to be added to a print list, which can then be sent to your own printer. Or, you can take the memory card to a commercial printer to print out the selected images.

To add images to the DPOF print list, select the Specify Printing option from the Playback menu. Then, on the next screen, shown in Figure 6-18, set the DPOF Setup option to Multiple Images. You also can turn the Date Imprint option on or off to specify whether or not the pictures will be printed with the dates they were taken. Then highlight the Enter option at the bottom of this screen and press the center button to confirm.

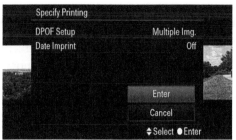

Figure 6-18: Specify Printing Menu Option

The camera will then display the first image or index screen of images, as shown in Figure 6-19, with an orange frame around the currently selected image and a check box in the lower left corner of each image thumbnail.

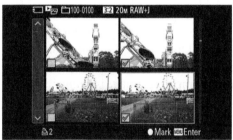

Figure 6-19: Selection Screen for Specify Printing Menu Option

(You can display individual images or index screens using the zoom lever.) There will be a small printer icon in the lower left with the number zero beside it, meaning no copies of any images have been set for printing yet. Use the control wheel or all four direction buttons to move through the images. When an image you want to have printed is displayed, press the center button to mark it for printing or to unmark it. You can then keep browsing through your images and adding (or subtracting) them from the print list. As you add various images to the print list, the DPOF counter in the lower left corner of the display will show the total number of images selected for printing.

When you have finished selecting images to be printed, press the Menu button to confirm your choices and exit from the selection screen. Then confirm the OK message on the screen by pressing the center button. You can then take the memory card to a service that prints photos using the DPOF system, or you can connect the camera to a PictBridge compatible printer to print the selected images.

If you want to cancel a DPOF order, you can do so quickly by going to the Specify Printing menu item and selecting the Cancel All option instead of Multiple Images on the initial screen.

Picture Effect

The Picture Effect option, the first selection on the second screen of the Playback menu, gives you a very limited selection of the options that are available through the Picture Effect item on the Shooting menu. Only two of the many effects from that menu are available: Watercolor and Illustration. When you select this option, if a compatible image is being displayed, the camera will display a screen giving you the option to apply one or the other of these effects. Highlight the one you want and press the center button to confirm. The camera will process the image for a while and then display the new version of the image.

At that point, press the Menu button, and the camera will ask whether you want to save a copy of the image with that effect. The result is similar to what you get with the Picture Effect option in shooting mode; an example of the Watercolor effect applied in Playback mode is shown in Figure 6-20. You can select OK or Cancel. If you go ahead, the camera will save a copy of the processed image and leave the original image intact, so there is no harm in going through with this procedure.

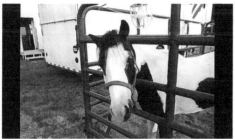

Figure 6-20: Watercolor Effect - Playback Menu

There are no adjustments available for intensity or other options. Also, these effects will not work with videos, panoramas, 3D images, or RAW images. However, these two effects can produce very pleasing results, so there may be situations in which it would be worthwhile to try them out.

Volume Settings

This menu option lets you set the volume for playback of movies in the camera, anywhere from 0 to 7. You can also set this level from the movie playback screen by pressing the down direction button to get access to the volume setting screen.

Playback Display

This final item on the Playback menu controls whether images shot with the camera held vertically appear in that orientation when you play them back on the camera's horizontal screen. By default, this option is set to Auto Rotate, meaning the images taken vertically are automatically rotated so that the vertical shot appears right-side-up on the horizontal display. If you change the setting to Manual Rotate, then the images will appear sideways on the screen. If you use the Auto Rotate option, vertical images will be displayed at a fairly small size, as shown in Figure 6-21. So, you might want to set the Playback Display option to Manual Rotate, and just rotate the camera itself, so you can see the image at a size that uses most or all of the display area on the screen. Also, if you use the Manual Rotate setting, you can always press the Function button to

237

rotate an image manually, as discussed earlier in this chapter.

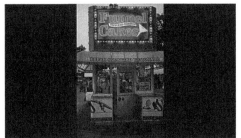

Figure 6-21: Image Taken with Camera Held Vertically

Chapter 7: Custom, Setup, and Other Menus

In previous chapters I discussed the options available to you in the Shooting and Playback menu systems. The Sony RX100 has several other menu systems that help you set up the camera and customize its operation. In this chapter, I will discuss all of the options on those menus: Custom, Memory Card Tool, Clock Setup, and Setup. (I'll discuss menu options for Movie mode in Chapter 8.)

Custom Menu

The Custom menu gives you control over numerous items that affect the ways in which you use the camera to take pictures and videos, but that do not change the photographic settings such as white balance, ISO, focus modes, and matters of that nature. With this menu, the items to be adjusted are more in the categories of control and display options. Following are details on each of the options on the three screens of this menu.

Red Eye Reduction

This first option on the Custom menu lets you set up the RX100's flash so as to combat "red-eye" in your images—the eerie red glow in human eyes that results when on-camera flash lights up the blood vessels on the retina. The way Sony has chosen to deal with this issue in the RX100 is through this menu item, which can be set either to On or Off. If it is turned on, then, whenever the flash is used, it fires a few pre-flashes before the actual flash that illuminates the image. The pre-flashes are intended to cause the subject's pupils to narrow, thereby reducing the ability of the later, full flash to enter the eyes, bounce off the retinas, and produce the unwanted red glow in the eyes.

My own preference is to leave this menu option turned off and to deal with red-eye effects by removing them with editing software, if necessary. However, if you will be taking flash photos at a party, you may want to use this menu option to minimize the occurrence of red-eye effects in the first place.

Grid Line

With this next option, you can select one of four possible settings for a grid of lines to be superimposed on the shooting screen. By default, there is no grid on the screen. If you choose one of the options to use a grid, the lines will appear, in your chosen configuration, whenever the camera is in shooting mode, regardless of whether the detailed display screen is selected or not. The four options are shown in Figure 7-1.

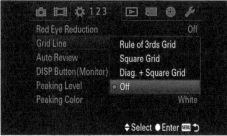

Figure 7-1: Grid Line Menu Option

Following are descriptions of these choices, other than Off, which leaves the screen with no grid.

Rule of Thirds Grid

This arrangement consists of two vertical lines and two horizontal ones, dividing the screen into nine blocks, as shown in

Figure 7-2.

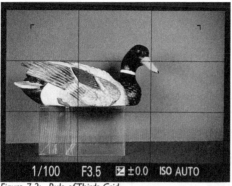

Figure 7-2: Rule of Thirds Grid

The concept behind this grid is the Rule of Thirds, a classical rule of composition that calls for placing the most important subject at the intersection of two of these lines, which will place the subject one-third of the way from the edge of the image. This arrangement seems to impart a pleasing amount of interest and asymmetry to an image.

Square Grid

With this setting, the camera sets up five vertical lines and three horizontal ones, dividing the display into 24 blocks, as seen in Figure 7-3.

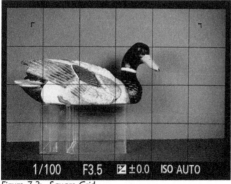

Figure 7-3: Square Grid

In this way, you can still use the Rule of Thirds, but you also have additional lines available for lining up items such as the horizon or the edge of a building or table that need to be straight in the image.

Diagonal + Square Grid

The last option gives you a square grid of four blocks in each direction, and adds two diagonal lines, as shown in Figure 7-4.

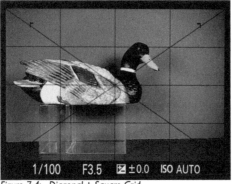

Figure 7-4: Diagonal + Square Grid

The idea with this option is that placing a subject, or, more likely, a string of subjects, along one of the diagonals can add interest to the image by drawing the viewer's eye into the image along the diagonal line.

Auto Review

The Auto Review option, shown in Figure 7-5, lets you set the length of time that an image appears on the LCD screen immediately after you take a picture. The default choice is 2 seconds, but you can set this time to 5 or 10 seconds, or you can turn the function off altogether. If you turn it off, the camera will return to shooting mode as soon as you have finished taking an image, once the camera has saved it to the memory card. When it is in use, you can always return to the live view by half-pressing the shutter button. The Auto Review option does not apply to movies; the camera does not display the beginning frame of a movie until you press the Playback button.

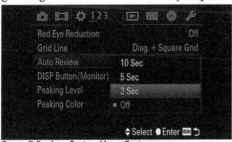

Figure 7-5: Auto Review Menu Option

Display Button (Monitor)

With this option, you are able to choose which of several available display screens appear when the camera is in shooting mode, as you press the Display button. There are five available display screens that you can select, shown below in Figures 7-6 through 7-9. (The screen displaying just the image, with no information, is not shown here.)

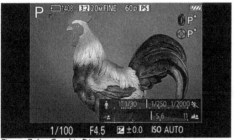

Figure 7-6: Graphic Display

Figure 7-6 shows the version of the screen with the graphic display in the lower right corner of the screen; that display is supposed to illustrate the use of faster shutter speeds to stop action and the use of wider apertures to blur backgrounds. I personally find it distracting and not especially helpful, but if it is useful to you, by all means select it.

I find the screen with full information, shown in Figure 7-7, to be rather cluttered and busy, but it does contain a lot of useful information about the camera's settings. You can always move away from this screen by pressing the Display button (if there is at least one other display screen available through this menu option), so I like to have it available for those times when I need to check to see what settings are in effect.

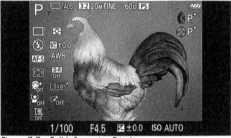

Figure 7-7: Full Information Display

The third screen, with no information other than the image, can be of great value in focusing and composing your image, so I definitely like to include it in the cycle of display screens.

The fourth screen, shown in Figure 7-8, displays the RX100's electronic level, which is a very useful tool for leveling the camera both side-to-side and front-to-back.

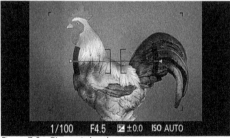

Figure 7-8: Electronic Level

You need to watch the small orange lines on the screen; when the two outer ones have turned green, the camera is level side-to-side; when the inner two lines have turned green, the camera is level front-to-back.

The final choice shown in Figure 7-9, is a screen with the histogram only.

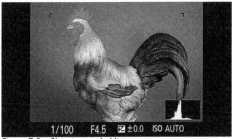

Figure 7-9: Shooting-mode Histogram

This shooting-mode histogram, unlike the one displayed in Playback mode, shows only basic exposure information, with no color data. However, it can give you an idea of whether your image will be well-exposed, letting you adjust exposure compensation and other settings as appropriate, while watching the live histogram on the screen. If you can make the histogram display look like a triangular mountain centered in the box, you are likely to have a good result.

Once you have selected the Display Button (Monitor) menu option and pressed the center button to get to the selection screen, you can scroll through the five choices using the control wheel or the up and down direction buttons. When a screen you want to have displayed is highlighted, press the center button to place an orange check mark in the small box to the left of the screen's label, as seen in Figure 7-10.

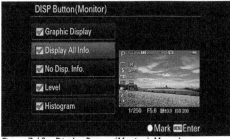

Figure 7-10: Display Button (Monitor) Menu Item

You can also press that button to un-mark a box. The camera will let you un-check all five of the items, but if you do that, the camera will display an error message as you try to exit the menu screen. You have to check at least one box so that some screen will display when the camera is in shooting mode.

After you have selected from one to five screens to be displayed, exit the menu by pressing the Menu button. Then, whenever the camera is in shooting mode, the selected screens will be displayed; you cycle through them by pressing the Display button (up direction button). If you have selected only one screen, then pressing the Display button will have no effect in shooting mode.

Note that, even if you select only the single screen that includes no information, the camera will still always display the shutter speed, aperture, exposure compensation, and ISO; all of those values are displayed in the black strip below the area where the image is displayed.

Peaking Level

Peaking Level, shown in Figure 7-11, controls whether the camera uses the Peaking display to assist with manual focus.

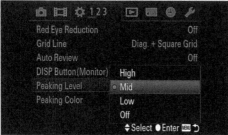

Figure 7-11: Peaking Level Menu Option

By default, this option is turned off. With this menu item, you can turn the feature on with a level of Low, Mid, or High. When it is turned on, whenever you are using manual focus, the camera places an outline with the selected intensity

246

around any area of the image that has edges that the camera can distinguish. The idea is that these lines provide a more definite indication that the focus is sharp than just relying on your judgment of sharpness. My own preference is to use the camera's very helpful MF Assist or Focus Magnifier function, either of which enlarges the view in manual focus mode. I find the Peaking display to be distracting and hard to make use of, but, as with many other options, this is a matter of taste, and you may find Peaking to be an excellent focusing aid. Note that it also works with DMF (Direct Manual Focus), even if you are using the autofocus function of that setting.

Peaking Color

This option lets you choose red, yellow, or white for the color of the lines that the Peaking feature places around the edges of in-focus items when you are using manual focus. It works along with the Peaking Level option, discussed above, which controls the intensity of the effect. The default color is white.

Control Ring

The Control Ring menu option, shown in Figure 7-12, is the first item on the second screen of the Custom menu.

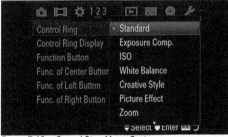

Figure 7-12: Control Ring Menu Option

This option lets you choose the function or functions of the control ring. As I discussed in Chapter 5 in connection with the control ring, by default this option is set to Standard. In that case, the control ring controls various functions in the

247

various shooting modes, as shown in the table in Chapter 5.

If you prefer to set the control ring to control a single function instead of the above group of functions, you can use this menu item to set the ring to control exposure compensation, ISO, white balance, Creative Style, Picture Effect, zoom, shutter speed, or aperture. Or you can leave the ring with no setting, in which case it will control only manual focus. In my opinion, the Standard option is the most useful, but you might prefer to use the control ring as an alternative zoom control for all shooting modes, or for one of the other available functions.

Control Ring Display

This option lets you choose whether or not a special circular display appears on the screen when you turn the control ring to control one of its assigned functions other than manual focus. For example, if the Control Ring menu option is set to Standard and you have the camera set to Program mode, turning the control ring will activate the Program Shift feature, moving through matched pairs of aperture and shutter speed settings that are equivalent to the original settings measured by the camera. As shown in Figure 7-13, as soon as you start turning the ring, the special display will appear on the screen.

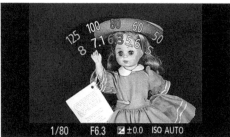

Figure 7-13: Control Ring Display - Program Shift

At the same time, the normal aperture and shutter speed figures in the lower left of the display will change, providing the same information.

To my mind, this feature is a distraction and I greatly prefer to turn it off. If you find that its additional display of information is helpful to you, by all means leave it turned on. (It is turned on by default.)

Function Button

The Function Button menu option is the means for selecting up to seven operations that can be controlled by pressing the Function button. As I explained in Chapter 5, pressing the button calls up a horizontal menu at the bottom of the display, with up to seven options to choose from. Using this menu item, you can select which options are included out of 17 possibilities. The choices are Exposure Compensation, Focus Mode, Autofocus Area, ISO, Drive Mode, Metering Mode, Flash Mode, Flash Compensation, White Balance, DRO/Auto HDR, Creative Style, Picture Effect, Soft Skin Effect, Quality, Image Size, Smile/Face Detection, and Aspect Ratio. You also can choose Not Set, leaving one or more of the seven slots unassigned to any function.

To use this menu item, scroll down through the entries for Function 1 through Function 7 by turning the control wheel or by pressing the up and down direction buttons. When a particular function number is highlighted, press the center button to select it and pop up a list of all 17 possible settings for that slot, as shown in Figure 7-14.

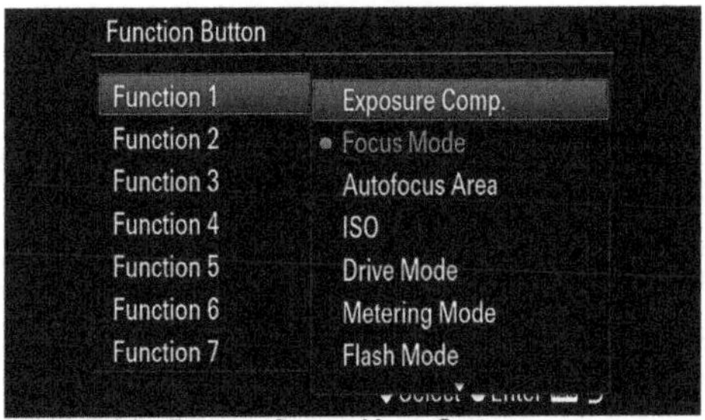

Figure 7-14: Function Button Menu Option

Highlight the setting you want to assign to that numbered slot

249

and press the center button to exit back to the main screen.

The default settings for the Function button are the following:

Default Settings for Function Button	
Function 1	Exposure Compensation
Function 2	ISO
Function 3	White Balance
Function 4	DRO/Auto HDR
Function 5	Picture Effect
Function 6	Not Set
Function 7	Not Set

I suggest you experiment with the settings for the Function button until you find those that are most useful to you. I certainly would not leave any slots with the "Not Set" choice. Personally, I would include Focus Mode, ISO, Picture Effect, Creative Style, Quality, Image Size, and DRO/Auto HDR as my choices, but that is just because those are settings I happen to use quite often. I would not include Exposure Compensation, because it is available with a press of the down direction button, and I find that Auto White Balance usually works quite well, so I don't change White Balance that often.

Function of Center Button

The next three options on the second screen of the Custom menu give you the ability to assign specific operations to the center, left, and right buttons on the control wheel. First is the center button. It can be assigned one of the following settings: Standard, AEL Toggle, AF/MF Control Toggle, or Focus Magnifier, as shown in Figure 7-15. I discussed these settings in Chapter 5, in connection with the discussion of the center button. If you plan to use the Tracking Focus option, you should leave this setting on Standard. If not, then you need to decide which function is more useful to you of those listed above. When I am doing photography through a telescope, as discussed in Chapter 9, I use the Focus Magnifier option. In other situations, I usually leave the center button set to its Standard option.

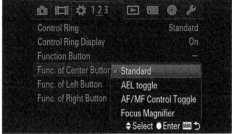

Figure 7-15: Function of Center Button Menu Option

Function of Left Button

The left direction button is, of course, ordinarily assigned to be the Drive Mode/Self-timer button, as indicated by the icons next to it on the camera's back. Using this menu option, as shown in Figure 7-16, you can assign any one of the following functions to it instead: Exposure Compensation, Flash Mode, Focus Mode, Autofocus Area, Smile/Face Detection, Auto Portrait Framing, Soft Skin Effect, ISO, Metering Mode, Flash Compensation, White Balance, DRO/Auto HDR, Creative Style, Picture Effect, Image Size, Aspect Ratio, Quality, Memory, AEL Toggle, AF/MF Control Toggle, or Focus Magnifier.

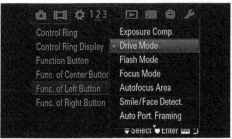

Figure 7-16: Function of Left Button Menu Option

My personal preference is to leave this button assigned to its standard function as the Drive Mode/Self-timer button, but it certainly gives you a lot of flexibility to have the other options available.

Function of Right Button

The right direction button, which normally is the Flash button, also can be reassigned to any of the options listed above for the left button. Again, my own preference is to leave this button set for Flash Mode, but it could be convenient to reset it to handle a setting such as DRO/Auto HDR, perhaps when you are on a photo shoot when you know you will not be using flash, but you will be encountering situations with wide variations in contrast, such as bright sunlight mixed with dark shadows, and you may need to quickly call up the dynamic range settings.

MF Assist

MF Assist is the first item at the top of the third and final screen of the Custom menu, as shown in Figure 7-17.

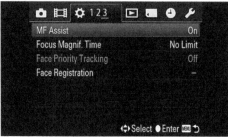

Figure 7-17: Final Screen of Custom Menu

I have discussed this option previously to some extent. When MF Assist is turned on, the camera enlarges the image on the display screen as soon as you start turning the control ring to focus manually. This enlargement can be of great assistance when you are trying to judge whether a particular part of the scene is in sharp focus. If you turn this option off, you can use another focusing aid, such as Peaking or Focus Magnifier, discussed earlier in this chapter. Personally, I find MF Assist to be extremely helpful, especially because you can set the camera to leave the enlarged screen in place indefinitely using the Focus Magnifier Time option, discussed immediately below. However, I find the Focus Magnifier option to be just as helpful, and preferable in a way because the screen does not become magnified until you press the center button, select the area to be magnified using the orange frame, and then magnify the screen.

Focus Magnifier Time

This option lets you select how long the display will stay magnified when you use either the MF Assist option, discussed directly above, or the Focus Magnifier option, which is available only if you have set the center, left, or right button to control that function. The choices are 2 or 5 seconds or No Limit, as shown in Figure 7-18.

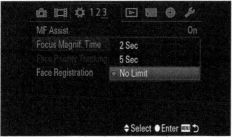

Figure 7-18: Focus Magnifier Time Menu Option

If you choose No Limit, then the image will stay magnified until you press the shutter button down to take the picture, or press it down halfway to dismiss the enlarged view.

My preference is to use the No Limit option, so I can take my time in adjusting manual focus precisely.

Face Priority Tracking

This menu option performs a very specific function, which is available for selection only if the camera is set for autofocus with the Smile/Face Detection option on the Shooting menu turned on. If you turn Face Priority Tracking on, then, when you use the Tracking Focus option (activated by pressing the center button), the focus-tracking feature will give priority to any human face it detects. If this option is turned off, then the focus-tracking function will give priority to the subject that is closest to the camera when you activate tracking.

Face Registration

This last option on the Custom menu lets you register human faces so the RX100 can give those faces priority when it uses face detection. You can register up to eight faces, and assign each one a priority from one to eight, with one being the highest priority. Then, when you set the option for Smile/Face Detection to On (Registered Faces), the camera will try to detect the registered faces first, in the order you have assigned them.

This feature is not one that I find any need for, but it could be useful if, for example, you take pictures at school functions and you want to make sure the camera focuses on your own children rather than on other kids.

To use this setting, select this menu option, and, on the next screen, select New Registration. Press the center button, and the camera will place a large square on the screen. Compose your shot with the face to be registered inside that frame, as shown in Figure 7-19, and then press the shutter button to take a picture of that face.

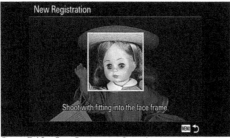

Figure 7-19: Face Registration Procedure

If that process is successful, the camera will display a screen with that face inside the frame, with the message, Register face? Highlight the Enter bar and press the Menu button to complete the registration process.

Later, you can use the Order Exchanging menu option to change the priorities of the faces that have been registered, and you can delete registered faces individually or all at once using other menu options.

Memory Card Tool Menu

The next menu to be discussed, whose tab is found to the right of the tab for the Playback menu, is the Memory Card Tool menu, shown in Figure 7-20.

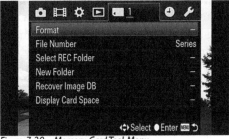

Figure 7-20: Memory Card Tool Menu

This single-screen menu contains several commands whose functions have to do with storing images and videos on your memory card. I will discuss them all below.

Format

The first option at the top of the screen—Format—is an extremely important command. This command is used to prepare a new memory card to store images and videos with the appropriate data format. The Format command also is useful when you want to wipe all the data off a card that has become full, or whose images you have copied to your computer or other storage device. Choose this process only when you want or need to completely wipe all of the data from a memory card. When you select the Format option, as shown in Figure 7-21, the camera will warn you that all data currently on the card will be deleted if you proceed.

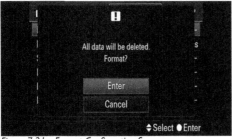

All data will be deleted.
Format?

Enter

Cancel

Select ● Enter

Figure 7-21: Format Confirmation Screen

If you reply by highlighting Enter and pressing the center button to confirm, the camera will proceed to format the card that is in the camera, and the result will be a card that is empty and properly formatted to store new images recorded by the camera.

With this procedure, the camera will erase all images, including those that have been protected from accidental erasure with the Protect function on the Playback menu. It's a good idea to periodically save your images and videos to your computer or other storage device and then re-format your memory card, to make sure it is properly set up to start recording new images and videos. It's also a good idea to use the Format command on any new memory card when you first insert it in the camera. Even though it likely will work without that procedure, it's best to make sure the card is set up with Sony's own particular method of formatting for the RX100.

File Number

This option gives you control over the way in which the camera assigns numbers to your images and videos. There are two choices: Series and Reset, as shown in Figure 7-22. If you choose Series, then the camera continues numbering where it left off, even if you put a new memory card in the camera. For example, if you have shot 112 images on your first memory card, the last image likely will be numbered 100-0112, for the folder number (100, the first folder number available), and 0112 for the image number. If you then switch to a new memory card with no images on it, the first image on that card will be numbered 100-0113, because the numbering scheme continues in the same sequence. If you choose Reset instead, the first image on the new card will be numbered 100-0001, because the camera resets the numbering to the first number.

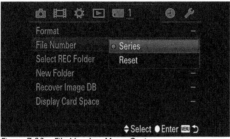

Figure 7-22: File Number Menu Option

Select REC Folder

When you select this menu item, the camera puts an orange bar on the screen with the name of the current folder, as shown in Figure 7-23.

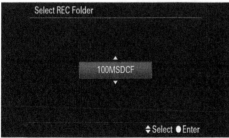

Figure 7-23: Select REC Folder Menu Option

You can then use the up and down direction buttons or turn

257

the control wheel to scroll to the name of another folder on the memory card, if one exists, so you can store future images and videos in that folder. It might be worthwhile to use this function if you are taking photos or movies for different purposes during the same photography outing. For example, if you are taking some photos for business and some for pleasure, you could create a new folder for the business-related shots (see the next menu item, below). The camera would then use that folder. Afterwards, you could use the Select REC Folder option to select the folder where your personal images are stored, and take more personal images that will be stored there.

New Folder

This menu item lets you create a new folder on your memory card for storing images and videos. Just highlight this item on the menu screen and press the center button; you will then see a message announcing that a new folder has been created, as shown in Figure 7-24.

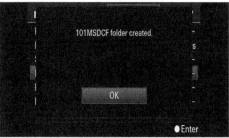

Figure 7-24: Create New Folder Menu Option

The camera will then begin storing new images and videos in that folder until you select another folder using the Select REC Folder option, discussed above. The camera also will create a new folder automatically once a folder contains 4,000 images.

Recover Image Database

This menu item activates the Recover Image Database function. If you select this option and then press the center button to confirm it on the next screen, as shown in Figure 7-25, the camera runs a check to test the integrity of the file system on the memory card.

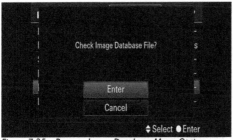

Figure 7-25: Recover Image Database Menu Option

This option pops up automatically when you place a brand new memory card in the camera, or a card that has previously been used in a different camera. I have never chosen this menu option myself, but if the camera is having difficulty reading the images on a card, using this option might recover the data.

Display Card Space

The final item on the Memory Card Tool menu screen gives you another way to see how much space is remaining on the memory card that is currently inserted in the camera.

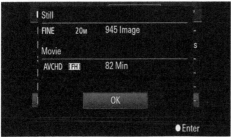

Figure 7-26: Display Card Space Menu Option

When you select this item and press the center button, the camera displays a screen like that in Figure 7-26, with information about the number of still images or the number of

259

minutes of video that can be recorded. It may be nice to have this option available, although the number of images that can be recorded is also displayed on the detailed shooting screen, and the number of minutes of video that can be recorded is displayed on the video recording screen once a recording has been started.

Clock Setup Menu

Sony has created a very short menu, with only two items, shown in Figure 7-27, for setting up the date and time.

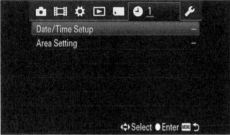

Figure 7-27:   Clock Setup Menu

I briefly discussed the first item, Date/Time Setup, in Chapter 1. When the camera is new or has not been used for a long time, it will prompt you to set the date and time and will display this menu option. If you want to call up these settings on your own, you can do so at any time.

Once you have chosen this item and pressed the center button, the camera will display a screen like that shown in Figure 7-28.

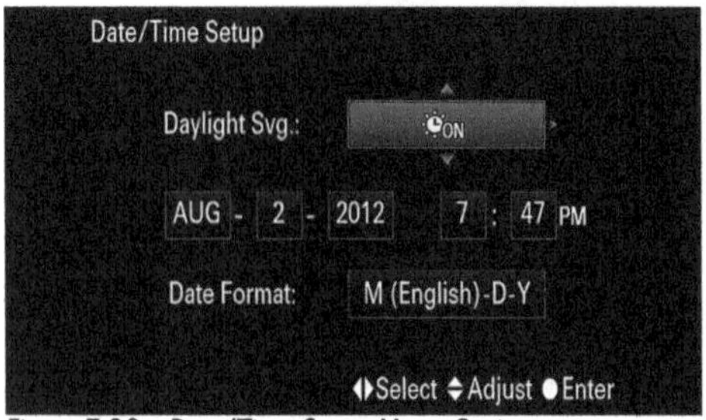

Figure 7-28:   Date/Time Setup Menu Option

You scroll through the various options for setting Daylight Savings Time, month, date, year, and other items by turning the control wheel or pressing the left and right direction buttons. As you reach each item, adjust its value using the up and down direction buttons. When all of the settings are correct, press the center button to confirm them and exit from this screen.

The other option on this menu, Area Setting, lets you select your current location, thereby adjusting the date and time for a different time zone when you are traveling. When you highlight this item and press the center button, the camera displays the map shown in Figure 7-29.

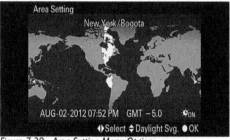

Figure 7-29: Area Setting Menu Option

Just turn the control wheel or press the left and right direction buttons to move the light-colored highlight over the map until it covers the area of your current location, then press the center button. The date and time will be adjusted for that location until you change the location again using this menu item.

Setup Menu

The Setup menu, reached through the last menu tab on the right of the menu screen, gives you various choices for housekeeping matters like screen brightness and operational sounds. This menu is designated by the wrench icon at the top of the screen, as shown in Figure 7-30.

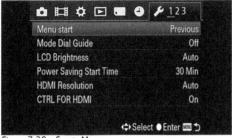
Figure 7-30: Setup Menu

Following are details about the items on the three screens of this menu.

Menu Start

This first menu option provides an important capability: It lets you choose what screen the RX100 displays when you press the Menu button to get access to the menu system. There are two choices, Top and Previous, as shown in Figure 7-31.

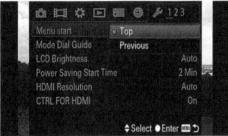
Figure 7-31: Menu Start Menu Option

If you choose Top, the camera always displays the first screen of the first menu for the camera's current mode (Shooting or Playback). So, for example, if the camera is in shooting mode and you press the Menu button, you will see the first screen of the Shooting menu. If the camera is in Playback mode, you will see the first screen of the Playback menu.

On the other hand, if you choose Previous, the behavior will be different. In that case, the camera will always display whatever menu screen it was last displaying, whenever you press the Menu button. I personally prefer the Previous setting, because it seems I generally am likely to work in the same area of the menus for a while, and there is a good chance it will be convenient to return to the most recent menu screen I was using. Of course, your habits may be different, and you may prefer the predictability of starting from a known location in the menu system whenever the Menu button is pressed.

Mode Dial Guide

This menu item gives you a way to turn on or off the Mode Dial Guide, a graphic display that appears on the camera's screen when you turn the mode dial to select a different shooting mode, as shown in Figure 7-32.

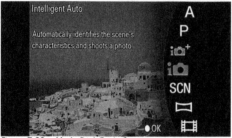

Figure 7-32: Mode Dial Guide Screen

This guide can be helpful if you need advice or reminders about each mode, but it can be annoying if you don't need the advice, and you have to press the center button or press the shutter button halfway down to dismiss the screen. I leave this option turned off to speed up my shooting.

LCD Brightness

This option lets you control the brightness of the LCD display using one of three available settings: Auto, Manual, or Sunny Weather, as seen in Figure 7-33. If you choose Auto, the camera adjusts the screen's brightness using a small light sensor at the upper left corner of the LCD to gauge the ambient light.

263

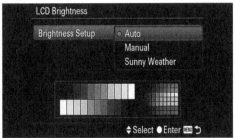

Figure 7-33: LCD Brightness Menu Option

If you choose Manual, the camera displays the screen shown in Figure 7-34.

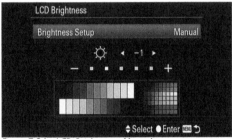

Figure 7-34: LCD Brightness - Manual

You can change the brightness to one or two units above or below normal. If you are shooting outdoors in bright conditions, you can choose the Sunny Weather setting, which sets the display to a very bright level so that you can see the screen despite the bright sunshine. I have found the Sunny Weather setting to be useful in that situation, because the screen can be very difficult to see when the sun is shining, and the RX100 does not have a built-in viewfinder for you to use, as some cameras do. (See Appendix A for a discussion of accessories that can help with composing your images in bright conditions.) The Sunny Weather setting drains the camera's battery fairly rapidly, so you should turn it off when it is no longer needed. For everyday shooting, I use the Auto setting, which is usually quite adequate.

Power Saving Start Time

This menu option lets you set the amount of time before the camera turns off automatically to save power, when no controls have been operated. The default setting is 2 minutes; with this option you can also choose 1, 5, or 30 minutes, as shown in Figure 7-35.

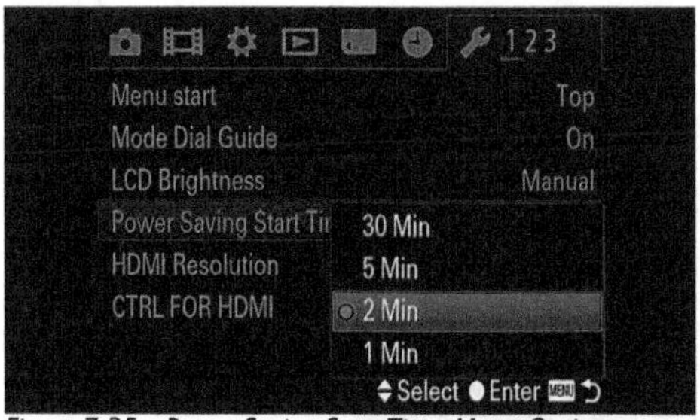

Figure 7-35: Power Saving Start Time Menu Option

You cannot turn the power-saving function off. However, the camera will not power off automatically when you are recording movies, when a slide show is playing, or when the camera is connected to a computer.

HDMI Resolution

The HDMI Resolution menu item can be set to Auto, 1080p, or 1080i. Ordinarily, the Auto setting will work best; the camera will set itself for the optimum display according to the resolution of the high-definition (HD) TV set it is connected to. If you experience difficulties with that connection, you may be able to improve the image on the HDTV's screen by trying one of the other settings.

CTRL for HDMI

This menu option is of use only when you have connected the camera to an HDTV set and you want to control the camera with the TV's remote control, which is possible in some situations. If you want to do that, set this option to On, and follow the instructions for the TV and its remote control.

Upload Settings

This option appears as the first item on the second screen of the Setup menu as shown in Figure 7-36, but only when an Eye-Fi card is inserted in the camera. If no Eye-Fi card is present, this menu option is not grayed out; it just does not appear at all.

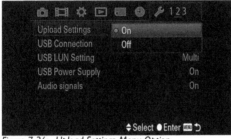

Figure 7-36: Upload Settings Menu Option

As discussed in Chapter 1, an Eye-Fi card is a special type of memory card that includes a transmitter to send your images to a computer over a wireless (WiFi) network, or directly to a wireless device if you use Direct Mode. This menu item has only two settings—On and Off. You might want to use the Off setting if you are on an airplane, where you may be required to turn off radio transmitters. Or, if you know you will not be using the Eye-Fi uploading capability for a while, you can turn this menu option off in order to save some battery power.

USB Connection

When no Eye-Fi card is present in the camera, this menu item is the first one on the second screen of the Setup menu. It sets the technical standard that the camera uses for transferring images and videos to your computer when the camera is connected to it by the USB cable. This option has three choices, as shown in Figure 7-37: Auto, Mass Storage, and MTP, which stands for Media Transfer Protocol, a standard developed by

Microsoft for transferring media files over a USB connection.

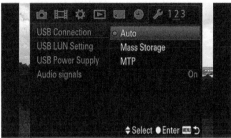

Figure 7-37: USB Connection Menu Option

You should ordinarily select Auto for this setting, and the RX100 should be able to detect which standard is used by the computer you are connecting the camera to. If the camera does not automatically select a standard and start transferring images, you can try one of the other settings to see if it works better than the Auto setting.

USB LUN Setting

This menu option is a rather technical one that will probably not often be used. LUN stands for Logical Unit Number. This option has two possible settings—Multi or Single. Ordinarily, it should be set to Multi, the default setting. In particular, it should be set to Multi when you have the RX100 connected to a computer and are using Sony's PlayMemories Home software to manage your images. If you ever encounter a problem with a USB connection to a computer, you can try the Single setting to see if it helps rectify the problem.

USB Power Supply

The USB Power Supply option, which can be turned either on or off, controls whether or not the camera's battery will be charged when the camera is connected to a computer or other USB device (such as an iPad, for example). This option also can be used if you have a portable USB charger available—a device that uses battery power to charge your cell phone and other portable gadgets.

Turning this option on gives you another avenue for keeping the RX100's battery charged. The only problem is that, if your computer is running on its battery, then that battery will be discharged more rapidly than usual. If you are plugging the camera in to a computer that is plugged into a wall power outlet, then there should be no problem in using this option.

Of course, as I will discuss in Appendix A, in my opinion you should get an external battery charger and at least one extra battery for the RX100, because, even if you can charge the battery in the camera using the USB cable, you don't have the ability to insert a fully charged battery into the camera when the first battery is exhausted.

Audio Signals

This option lets you choose whether or not to activate the various sounds the RX100 makes when an operation takes place, such as pressing the shutter button, confirming focus, or pressing a control button. By default, the sounds are turned on, but it can be helpful to turn them off when you are shooting in a quiet area or during a religious ceremony, or when you are doing street photography and want to avoid alerting your subjects that a camera is being used.

Version

This first entry on the third and final screen of the Setup menu gives you a way to find out the current version of the firmware that is installed in your camera. The Sony Cyber-shot DSC-RX100, like other digital cameras, is programmed at the factory with firmware, which is a semi-permanent set of computer instructions that are electronically implanted in the camera. These instructions control all aspects of the camera's operation, including the menu system, functioning of the controls, and in-camera processing of your images. The reason you might want to check to see what version is installed is that, in many cases, the manufacturer will release an updated version of the firmware that may fix problems or bugs in the system, provide minor enhancements, or, in some cases, even provide major improvements, such as including new shooting modes or menu options.

To determine what firmware version is currently installed in your camera, highlight this menu option, then press the OK button or the right direction button, and the camera will display the version number, as shown in Figure 7-38.

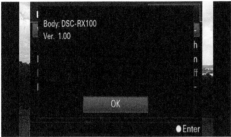

Figure 7-38: Version Menu Option

To determine whether any firmware upgrades have been released, I recommend that you visit Sony's support web site at http://esupport.sony.com. Find the link for Drivers and Software, and then the link within that category for Cyber-shot Cameras, and look for a link to any updated version. The site will provide detailed instructions for downloading and installing the new firmware.

Language

This option gives you the choice of language for the display of commands and information on the camera's LCD screen. Once you have selected this menu item, as shown in Figure 7-39, scroll through the language choices using the control wheel or the direction buttons and press the center button when your chosen language is highlighted.

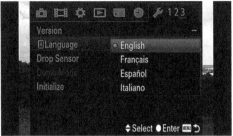

Figure 7-39: Language Selection Screen

Drop Sensor

The Drop Sensor option is turned on by default. This feature is an internal monitoring system that detects the motion of the camera if it is dropped, and quickly retracts the lens to avoid damage. Once this has happened, the camera displays the message shown in Figure 7-40.

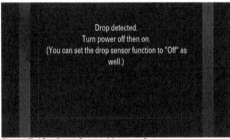

Figure 7-40: Drop Sensor Message Screen

This is an excellent safety measure, and I recommend leaving it on in all normal situations. The only time you might want to turn it off is if you are doing activities in which the camera will be subjected to strong forces, such as skydiving, bungee jumping, mountain climbing, and the like, and you want to avoid having the camera shut down in this way.

By the way, this item is not particularly concerned with the camera's image sensor; the word "sensor" in the title of this item is used generically to describe the system that senses the gravitational force the camera is being subjected to.

Demo Mode

The Demo Mode menu item is intended to provide an automated demonstration of movie playback, if the camera has not had any controls operated for about one minute. This feature is designed for use by retail stores so they can leave the camera turned on with a continuous demonstration on its screen. I certainly don't need this option, but I do like to know how each menu item works, and at first it was grayed out and could not be selected.

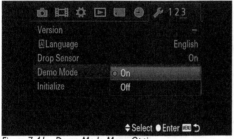

Figure 7-41: Demo Mode Menu Option

I eventually figured out that, for this feature to be available on the menu screen, as shown in Figure 7-41, the camera has to be plugged in to AC power using the included AC power adapter. Then, when the Demo Mode option is turned on and the camera is in shooting mode, after one minute of inactivity the camera enters the demo mode. At that point the camera is supposed to play a movie. You have to provide the movie. However, whenever I tried this, after the one minute passed, the camera's screen went black and displayed the message No Movies. This happened no matter how I tried to fix the situation. I placed both MP4 and AVCHD movies on the memory card, recorded new ones, and moved them to various locations on the card, all to no avail. I e-mailed Sony and then spoke to three different technical support people, none of whom could provide a solution. If anyone can explain how this works, please let me know.

Initialize

This final option on the Setup menu is useful when you want to reset some or all of the camera's settings back to their original (default) values. This action can be helpful if you have been playing around with different settings and you find that something is not working as expected.

When you select this item, the camera presents you with three choices: Reset Default, Record Mode Reset, and Custom Reset, as shown in Figure 7-42.

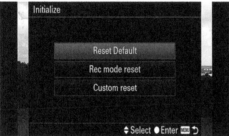

Figure 7-42: Initialize Menu Option

If you choose Reset Default, the camera resets all major settings to their original values. With Record Mode Reset, only the values from the Shooting menu are reset. If you select Custom Reset, only the values from the Custom menu are reset.

Chapter 8: Motion Pictures

Nowadays it seems that it's a necessity for any advanced compact digital or DSLR camera to include movie-making capabilities. Most recently, it's become standard practice for camera manufacturers to incorporate high-definition (HD) video recording into their premium cameras, and the Sony Cyber-shot DSC-RX100 is one example of that trend. The RX100's video abilities are very strong for a camera this small; they provide you with an excellent level of flexibility in capturing video. Before I get into the specific settings you can make for your movies, I'll begin with a brief overview of the process.

Movie-making Overview

In one sense, the fundamentals of making videos with the RX100 can be reduced to four words: "Push the red button." (That is, the red Movie button at the upper right corner of the camera's back.) Having a dedicated motion picture recording button makes things easy for users of this camera. Anytime you see a reason to take some video footage, you can just press and release that easily accessible red button while aiming at your subject, and you will get results that are likely to be quite usable. You do not need to worry about making any particular settings, particularly if you have set the camera to one of the Auto modes. To stop recording, press the red button again.

If you want to take a still photo while the movie is being recorded, go right ahead and press the shutter button and a still image will be recorded. (There are some limitations, which I will discuss later in this chapter.)

If you're mainly a still photographer and not that interested in movie-making, you don't need to read any further. Be aware that the red button exists, and if a newsworthy event starts to unfold before your eyes, you can get some excellent footage to post on YouTube or elsewhere with a minimum of effort.

But for those RX100 users who would like to delve further into their camera's excellent motion picture capabilities, there is considerably more information to discuss.

Before I get into details about how to record videos, I should note that the RX100, like most cameras in its class, has built-in limitations that prevent it from recording any sequence longer than 29 minutes. You can, of course, record multiple sequences adding up to any length, depending on the amount of storage space available on your memory cards. If you plan on recording a significant amount of high-definition (HD) video, you should get one of the highest-capacity and fastest memory cards you can find. For example, a 16 GB card can hold about 75 minutes of the highest quality of AVCHD video, about 2 hours of lower-quality AVCHD video, or about 2 hours 45 minutes of MP4 HD video. (I will discuss these video formats later in this chapter.)

If you want to fit both still images and HD video sequences on a card, you might be better off with a 32 GB card, or even with an SDXC card having a capacity of up to 128 GB. You should try to get a card rated in Class 6 or higher, so it will have the necessary speed for recording HD video.

Details of Settings for Shooting Movies

As I noted above, the one step that is a necessity for recording a movie with the RX100 is to press the red Movie button.

However, there are numerous settings that affect the way in which the camera records a movie when that button is pressed. I will discuss four categories of such settings: the selections you make on the Movie menu; the position of the mode dial on top of the camera; the selections you make on the Shooting menu; and selections you make with control buttons. I will discuss these four areas in turn, below.

The Movie Menu

First, I will discuss the Movie menu, which is of great importance because the items on this menu control the format and other options for all movies you record with the RX100. This is the one menu system I have not discussed previously. It is designated by the icon that looks like a single frame of movie film, just to the right of the Shooting menu in the line of menu icons, as shown in Figure 8-1.

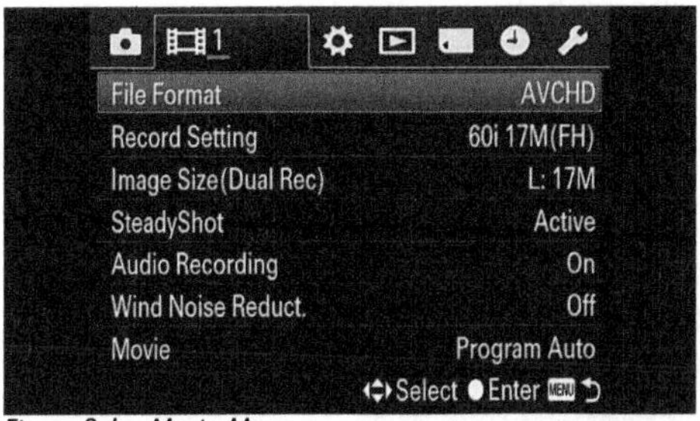

Figure 8-1: Movie Menu

The Movie menu is available in every shooting mode, including all of the modes for shooting still images and Movie mode itself. In other words, no matter what position the camera's mode dial is set to, you can get access to the Movie menu and make settings for video recordings. Those settings will affect only video recordings, not still images, with one exception. The exception is the Image Size (Dual Recording) item, which sets the size of still images captured during movie recording.

While I'm mentioning still images, I need to point out one limitation that might not be obvious, and could lead to problems: When the mode dial is set to Movie mode, you cannot shoot still images until you have started recording a movie. When the mode dial is set to any other position, you can pick up the RX100, turn it on, press the shutter button, and get some sort of still image. When the mode dial is turned to the Movie icon, though, pressing the shutter button will have no effect until a movie is being recorded. At that point, the camera will use the special setting for recording still images during video recording.

Because you can press the red Movie button to start a video recording at any time and in any shooting mode, you are always able to change the settings for movie recording using the Movie menu. I will discuss each item on the menu below.

File Format

The first item on the single screen of the Movie menu, File Format, gives you a choice between the two available movie recording formats on the RX100—AVCHD and MP4, as shown in Figure 8-2.

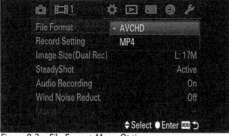

Figure 8-2: File Format Menu Option

If you want the highest-possible quality of video for viewing on an HDTV set, you should choose AVCHD, which stands for Advanced Video Coding High Definition. This format, developed jointly by Sony and Panasonic, has become increasingly common in advanced digital cameras in recent years. As noted, it provides excellent quality, and movies recorded in this format on the RX100 can be used to create Blu-Ray discs.

However, files recorded in the AVCHD format can be complicated to edit on a computer. In fact, just finding the AVCHD video files on a memory card can be a challenge. When you take a memory card from the RX100 camera and insert it into a memory card reader for viewing on your computer, you can find the still-image files within the folder labeled DCIM and then within sub-folders with names such as 100MSDCF. The AVCHD files, however, are not within that folder; they are within a different folder named PRIVATE. Inside that folder you will find another one called AVCHD, and within that one another one called BDMV. Open that folder and you will see more files or folders, including a folder called STREAM. With the card whose contents I am looking at now on my Macintosh, that folder contains numerous files with the extension .mts. Those .mts files are the actual AVCHD files that can be edited with compatible software packages, such as Adobe Premiere Pro. (You don't have to worry about finding the file names if you connect your camera to the computer using the USB cable, only if you use a card reader, as I do.)

If you want to record movies with excellent video quality but in a video format that is easier to edit with a computer, you can choose MP4. The MP4 format is compatible with Apple Computer's QuickTime software, and can be edited with various software programs, including QuickTime, iMovie, Windows Movie Maker, and many others.

Record Setting

The second item on the Movie menu lets you set another quality-related option for recording video. (The accent is on the second syllable of "Record.") The choices for this item are different, depending on whether you chose AVCHD or MP4 for File Format.

If you chose AVCHD, the three choices for Record Setting are 60i 24M(FX), 60i 17M(FH), and 60p 28M(PS), as shown in Figure 8-3. In each case, the number 60 stands for the number of video fields or frames recorded per second. (This number is 50 rather than 60 in countries that use the PAL video standard rather than the NTSC system used in the United States and some other locations.)

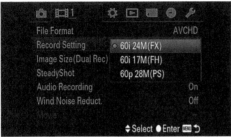

Figure 8-3: Record Settings Menu Option for AVCHD Format

The letter that comes next, either i or p, stands for interlaced or progressive. With interlaced video, the camera records 60 fields per second; a field is equal to one-half of a frame, and the two halves are interlaced together to form 30 full frames. The video frame rate of about 30 frames per second (fps) is the standard video playback rate in the United States.

If the letter is p, for progressive, that means that the camera records 60 full frames per second, which yields higher quality than interlaced video. The 60 frames are later translated into 30 frames for playback at the standard rate of 30 fps. However, if you want to, and your video editing software has this capability, you can play back your 60p footage in slow motion at one-half the normal speed and still maintain full HD quality. This possibility exists because, as noted above, the 60p footage is recorded with twice the number of full frames as 60i footage, so the quality of the video does not suffer if it is played back at one-half speed. (With other video formats, playback at half speed will appear choppy or jerky, because not enough frames were recorded to play back smoothly at that speed.) So, if you think you may want to slow down your footage significantly for playback, you should choose the 60p setting.

The next number-letter combination, either 28M, 24M, or 17M, provides the "bit rate," or volume of video information that is recorded—either 24 megabits per second or 17 megabits per second. Not surprisingly, the higher-numbered settings provide greater quality at the cost of using more storage capacity on the memory card and requiring greater computer resources to edit.

The final designations, FX, FH, and PS, are proprietary labels used by Sony for these various qualities of video. They have no particular meanings; they are just labels for various levels of video quality—PS is the highest, then FX, then FH.

Choose 60p 28M if you want the highest quality (including slow-motion capability), then 60i 24M for excellent quality, or 60i 17M for excellent quality that takes up fewer resources.

If, instead of AVCHD, you choose MP4 for File Format, then you are presented with just two choices for Record Setting: 1440 x 1080 12M and VGA 3M, as shown in Figure 8-4.

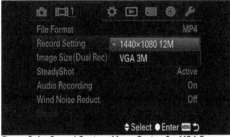

Figure 8-4: Record Settings Menu Option for MP4 Format

For the 1440 x 1080 setting, the numbers represent the numbers of horizontal and vertical pixels in the image. An image with 1440 pixels horizontally and 1080 vertically is considered to be widescreen. The other choice, listed on the menu as VGA, has only 640 x 480 pixels; this format produces images in the shape of traditional computer monitors, which were often designated as VGA, for Video Graphics Array. As you can see from the last numbers for these settings, 12M and 3M, they both have considerably lower data rates than any of the AVCHD settings. Therefore, the quality is not as great as for AVCHD, but the MP4 formats take up less space than AVCHD on a memory card, and, as noted above, are

279

easier to manipulate with a computer and to send by e-mail.

If you decide to choose the MP4 file format, I recommend you always select the 1440 x 1080 setting, because the quality of VGA video is very low. You should use that setting only if you have a drastic shortage of space on your memory card or you are recording the video for a purpose that may not require high quality, such as making a record of household possessions for an inventory.

Image Size (Dual Recording)

The next item on the Movie menu is different from the other settings on the menu, because it does not control the appearance or nature of your videos. Instead, this option sets the image size for still photographs that you capture while the camera is recording a video. The RX100 has an excellent capability in this regard. After you have pressed the red Movie button to start a video recording, you can, while the video is being recorded, press the camera's shutter button to take a still picture without interrupting the movie recording. This function works very well, though it is available only for the non-progressive standards. That is, you cannot use this feature when the Record Setting option is set to 60p 28M(PS). However, for every other video setting it works well.

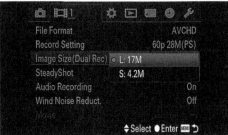

Figure 8-5: Image Size (Dual Rec) Menu Option

There are two choices for the Image Size (Dual Recording) option, which vary depending on what video setting you select. For all video settings other than the MP4-VGA setting, the choices are L:17M and S:4.2M, as shown in Figure 8-5. The Large size is suitable for printing at fairly large sizes, including A3 (297 by 420 mm) or 11 by 17 inches; the Small size is best only for smaller prints or for viewing on a TV screen.

If you have selected the MP4-VGA setting, the choices for Image Size for the still image change to L:13M and S:3.2M. The printing considerations for these image sizes are the same as for the larger sizes, except that the quality will be reduced somewhat.

My recommendation is to always choose the Large setting for this menu option unless you want the still image only for a technical record or some other non-critical purpose.

SteadyShot

The SteadyShot item on the Movie menu, shown in Figure 8-6, is somewhat different from the same-named option on the Shooting menu, which applies only for still photography.

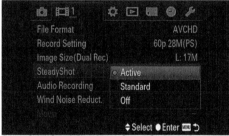

Figure 8-6: SteadyShot Menu Option for Movie Recording

The Movie menu version provides three options: Off, Standard, and Active, whereas the Shooting menu version of SteadyShot is limited to being turned on or off. With the Movie menu option, if you select Standard, the camera uses the same optical stabilization system used for shooting stills. If you select Active, the camera also uses an additional, electronic stabilizing system that can compensate for unwanted camera movement to some extent. With this feature, the camera will crop out

281

parts of the image at the edges to compensate for the required processing of the image.

If you are using a tripod, as I recommend for all movie shooting whenever possible, you probably should set the SteadyShot option to Off. If you are hand-holding the camera, I advise you to use the Active setting. I would use the Standard setting only if you find that the Active setting does not provide good results or if you object to the cropping that results from using this setting.

Audio Recording

The Audio Recording item on the Movie menu can be set either on or off. If you are certain you won't need the sound recorded by the camera, then you can turn this option off. Personally, I would never turn it off, because you can always turn down the volume of the recorded sound when playing the video, or, if you are editing the video on a computer, you can delete the sound and replace it as needed, but you can never recapture the original audio after the fact.

Wind Noise Reduction

This option activates an electronic filter designed to reduce the volume of sounds in the frequencies of wind noise. Here, again, as with the previous item, I recommend not using this feature unless you are certain it will help, because you are reducing the sounds that are recorded. With video (or audio) editing software, you can remove sounds in the frequencies that may cause problems for the sound track, but using the camera's built-in wind noise filter may permanently remove or alter some wanted sounds.

Movie (Exposure Mode)

The final item on the Movie menu, somewhat confusingly called simply Movie, is one of the most important options for advanced video shooting with the RX100, because it lets you choose an exposure mode, giving you control over aperture and shutter speed. This menu item is not available for selection except when the camera's mode dial is set to Movie mode, represented by the movie-film icon. In all other shooting modes, this choice is grayed out and cannot be selected.

When the camera is set to Movie mode, the Movie option on the Movie menu gives you the ability to select an exposure mode for shooting movies. If you have the Mode Dial Guide option turned on through the first screen of the Setup menu, the choices for the Movie menu item, as shown in Figure 8-7, will appear automatically when you select Movie mode with the mode dial and then press the center button after the initial Mode Dial Guide screen appears.

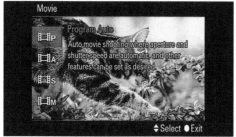

Figure 8-7: Movie Exposure Mode Choices on Movie Menu

If you do not have the Mode Dial Guide option turned on, then this menu screen will not appear unless you select it from the Movie menu. Navigate to the Movie menu and select the bottom item, Movie, and the same screen will appear, with its four options: Program Auto, Aperture Priority, Shutter Priority, and Manual Exposure. Move through these choices by turning the control wheel or pressing the up and down direction buttons. Following are details about the behavior of the RX100 when shooting movies with each of these settings.

Program Auto

With the Program Auto setting, the RX100 handles video recording the same way it does when it is set to any of the more advanced modes for still photography—Program, Aperture Priority, Shutter Priority, or Manual Exposure. In other words, the camera sets the aperture and shutter speed according to its metering system, and it uses the several settings from the

Shooting menu that carry over to video recording, including ISO, White Balance, Metering Mode, Face Detection, and DRO.

I personally do not find any advantage to using this setting. It does not provide any options beyond those that are available when the camera is set to a still-shooting mode, such as Intelligent Auto, Program, Aperture Priority, or Shutter Priority. And it has the disadvantage that the camera's mode dial must be set to the Movie mode. In that mode, you cannot shoot still images, unless you take one during the recording of a video. So, if you want to shoot movies with the camera making all of the exposure decisions for you, I recommend that you set the camera to the Intelligent Auto or P position on the mode dial. With that setup, you have the option of taking still images with the settings you want, and you still can press the red Movie button at any time to record a video.

Aperture Priority

With this setting, you are able to set the aperture, just as in the same-named mode for shooting still images, and the camera will set the shutter speed based on the exposure metering. There are some important differences to how the camera operates in this mode for recording videos, though. You still can set the aperture anywhere from the fully open f/1.8 to the most narrow f/11.0, depending on the zoom level. However, the camera will never set the shutter speed slower than 1/60 second in Aperture Priority mode, although it will do so in Shutter Priority and Manual Exposure modes. (The 1/60 second shutter speed corresponds to the standard video frame rate of 60 fields or frames per second in the United States; a shutter speed slower than 1/60 gives an unnatural, blurry appearance to the video.)

Also, it is important to note that the ISO setting when shooting movies cannot be higher than 3200. As a result, the low-light performance of the RX100 for video is somewhat limited. However, if you set the aperture at f/1.8 and ISO to Auto ISO with an upper limit of 3200, the camera will do very well in normal conditions.

Another feature of the RX100 that is very useful and somewhat unusual for cameras in this class is that you can adjust the aperture during the recording. This may not be something you need to do very often, but it can be useful in some situations. For example, you may be recording at a location with a variety of subjects, such as a garden show, and at some point you may want to open the aperture wide to achieve a blurred background as you focus on a small plant or other object. Afterwards, you may want to close the aperture down to a narrow value to achieve a broad depth of field to keep a large area in focus.

In general, as was discussed in Chapter 3, Aperture Priority can be an excellent mode to use when you need to have either a wide depth of field, as when shooting landscapes, or a shallow depth of field, when you want to blur the background.

Shutter Priority

The Shutter Priority exposure mode for movies lets you set the shutter speed, and the camera will set the aperture. Unlike the situation with Aperture Priority mode, in which the camera will not set the shutter speed slower than 1/60 second, you are able to set the shutter speed as slow as 1/4 second in this mode. You can select any shutter speed from that rate all the way to the maximum shutter speed of 1/2000 second. Of course, in order to expose your video normally at a shutter speed of 1/2000 second, you must have bright lighting or a high ISO setting, or both. Using a fast shutter speed for video can yield a crisper appearance to your shots, especially when there is considerable movement in them.

With the slower shutter speeds, particularly those below the normal video speed of 1/60 second (equivalent to 60 frames per second), the footage can become somewhat blurry with the appearance of smearing, particularly with panning motions. If you are shooting action scenes with strong lighting, this setting can be very useful. Or, if you are shooting a scene in which you want to have the drifting, dreamy appearance that a slow shutter speed brings, you can try that option.

Manual Exposure

The last setting for the Movie item on the Movie menu, Manual Exposure, is the setting to use for full control over the exposure of your videos. Just as with the Manual mode for shooting stills, you can adjust both the aperture and the shutter speed to achieve your desired effect. With video shooting, you can adjust the aperture from f/1.8 to f/11.0, and you can adjust shutter speed from 1/2000 second to 1/4 second. Using these settings, you have the ability to create effects such as fades to and from black as well as similar fades to and from white.

For example, if you begin a recording in normal indoor lighting using settings of 1/60 second at f/3.2 with ISO set to 800, you can record your scene, and then, whenever you want to fade out, start turning the control wheel slowly clockwise, increasing the shutter speed smoothly until it reaches 1/2000 second. Depending on how bright the lighting is, the result may be complete blackness. Of course, you can reverse this process to fade in from black.

If you want to fade to white, here is one possible scenario. Suppose you are recording video with shutter speed set to 1/400 second and aperture to f/1.8 at ISO 3200. When you want to start a fade to white, turn the control wheel smoothly to the left until the shutter speed decreases all the way to 1/4 second. In fairly normal lighting conditions, as in my office as I write this, the result will be a fade to a bright white screen.

There are, of course, many other uses for Manual Exposure mode when recording videos, such as shooting "day for night" footage, in which you underexpose the scene by using a fast shutter speed, narrow aperture, or both, in order to turn day into night for creative purposes. Also, you might want to use this mode when you are recording a continuous scene in which the lighting may change, but you do not want the exposure to change. In other words, for creative purposes, you may want some areas to remain in the dark and some to be unusually bright, rather than have the camera automatically adjust the exposure. In some cases, having a constant exposure setting can be preferable to seeing the scene's brightness change as the metering system adjusts the exposure.

In order to adjust the aperture and shutter speed when shooting videos, you use the same controls as when shooting still images. That is, you adjust both aperture and shutter speed using the control wheel on the back of the camera, and switch back and forth between those functions by pressing the down direction button. Also, if the Control Ring menu item (on the second screen of the Custom menu) is set to Standard, you can adjust the aperture by turning the control ring around the lens.

One important point to remember when shooting movies in Manual Exposure mode is that, just as with Manual mode for shooting still images, you cannot set ISO to Auto. You have to set it to a specific value. If it was set to Auto before you select this exposure mode, the camera will set it to the default of 125, which may be fine in bright conditions, but which will limit your options if the lighting is dim. I tend to use an ISO of 400 or 800 in most cases, so there is some leeway for adjusting exposure with both aperture and shutter speed.

Effect of Mode Dial Position on Recording Movies

The second category of settings that have an effect on the recording of movies with the RX100 is the position of the camera's mode dial. As I discussed above, you can shoot movies no matter what position this dial is set to, and you can get access to the Movie menu no matter what position the dial is in. However, as I also noted above, the shooting mode the camera is set to does make some difference for your movie options. I will provide more details here.

First, as noted earlier, you cannot get access to the Movie option—the final option on the Movie menu—unless the mode dial is set to Movie mode. The Movie option, which I would prefer to call Movie Exposure Mode, lets you select one of the advanced exposure modes for shooting movies: Program Auto, Aperture Priority, Shutter Priority, or Manual Exposure. In the last three of those modes, you have the ability to set the camera's aperture, shutter speed, or both for movie recording.

Second, the mode the camera is set to has an effect on what options are available on the Shooting menu and with the control buttons, as discussed in the next two sections. For example, if the shooting mode is set to Intelligent Auto, Superior Auto, or Scene, the Shooting menu options are limited. However, if the shooting mode is set to Program, Aperture Priority, Shutter Priority, or Manual, the options are greater. This point is important for video shooting because, as discussed below, several important Shooting menu options carry over to movie recording. In other words, if the camera is set to Program mode (P on the mode dial), you are able to make several settings that will control the recording of videos, if you press the red Movie button to start a recording while the mode dial remains in that position.

Next, I will discuss the details of which Shooting menu options have an effect on the recording of movies.

Effects of Shooting Menu Options on Recording Movies

As I discussed above, one of the factors that affect how the RX100 handles video recording is the shooting mode the camera is set to using the mode dial. One of the main reasons the shooting mode is important is that, just as with still photography, as discussed in Chapter 4, some Shooting menu options are not available in some shooting modes. For example, if you have the camera set to a mode such as Aperture Priority or Program, video recording will be affected by the current settings for White Balance, ISO Metering Mode, Face Detection, DRO, Focus Mode, and some others of less importance for movie shooting (such as Shooting Tip List).

Note that all of these settings have to be made before you press the red Movie button to start recording the movie, and once the recording is underway, you cannot get access to the menu system to change the settings unless you end the recording. In addition, there are some built-in limitations. For example, the ISO cannot be set any higher than 3200, and, not surprisingly, you cannot set ISO to Multi Frame Noise Reduction, which would cause the camera to take multiple shots.

There are some other settings on the Shooting menu that have no effect for recording movies. Some of these settings are clearly incompatible with shooting movies, such as Drive Mode, Flash Mode, and Auto Portrait Framing. Some are less obvious, including Autofocus Area, Soft Skin Effect, and Write Date. Also note that Clear Image Zoom and Digital Zoom options cannot be turned on for movie shooting, but there is a twist. Digital Zoom is always active when you are shooting movies; you cannot turn it on, but you also cannot turn it off. I recommend that you be careful to stop zooming before Digital Zoom takes effect, because of the image quality reduction.

There are two other settings that are worth some additional discussion. First, the Creative Style setting is available for shooting movies whenever the camera is set to a shooting mode that supports Creative Style (*i.e.*, all modes except the Scene and Auto modes). So, for example, if you have been shooting black-and-white still images using the Creative Style setting in Program mode or Sweep Shooting mode, and you then record a movie by pressing the red Movie button, your movie will be in black and white.

The situation is somewhat different with the Picture Effect menu option. Here, again, if a Picture Effect setting was selected while the camera was set to a shooting mode that supports this option (all modes other than the Scene, Auto, and Sweep Shooting modes), then, in some cases, that effect will still be active if you press the red button to record a movie.

Some of these settings do not work for recording movies. Specifically, only the following Picture Effect settings will carry over to your movies: Toy Camera, Pop Color, Posterization, Retro Photo, Soft High-key, Partial Color, and High Contrast Mono. None of the other effects will work for movies; if one of them was set before you press the red button, the camera will turn it off. The effects that do not work for movies are Soft Focus, HDR Painting, Rich-tone Monochrome, Miniature, Watercolor, and Illustration.

There are two other points that should be made about the ability of the RX100 to use Shooting menu settings for movies while the camera is set to a still-shooting mode. First, on the positive side, you have a great deal of flexibility in choosing settings for your movies, even when the camera is not set to the Movie position on the mode dial. You can set up the camera with the ISO, Metering Mode, White Balance, Creative Style, Picture Effect (to some extent) and other settings of your choice, and then just press the red Movie button to record using those same settings. In this way, you could, for example, record a black and white movie in a dark environment using a high ISO setting. Or, you could record a movie that is monochrome except for a broad selection of red objects, using the Partial Color-Red effect from the Picture Effect option, with the red color expanded using the color axis adjustments of the White Balance setting.

On the negative side, you have to be careful to check the settings that are in effect for still photos before you press the red Movie button to record a movie. For example, if you have been shooting stills using the Posterization setting from the Picture Effect menu option and then suddenly see an event that you want to record on video, if you just press the red Movie button the movie will be recorded using the Posterization effect, making the resulting footage hard to use as a clear record of the events. Of course, you may notice this problem as you record the video, but it takes time to stop the recording, change the menu setting to turn off the Picture Effect option, and then start recording again, and you may have missed a crucial part of the action you wanted to record by the time you have started recording again.

One way to lessen the risk of recording video with unwanted Shooting menu options is to switch the mode dial to the Intelligent Auto position (green camera icon) before pressing the red Movie button; that action will cause the camera to use more automatic settings, and will disable the Creative Style and Picture Effect options altogether.

In fact, shooting movies in the more automatic still-shooting modes, such as Intelligent Auto, Superior Auto, and the Scene mode types, works quite well. You can press the red Movie button and record your video in any of those modes. Note, though, that any special aspect of a Scene shooting mode will have no effect on your movies. For example, if you turn the mode dial to the Scene setting and then select Sunset as the Scene type on the Shooting menu, any movies you record with that setting will not have the emphasis on reddish hues that Sunset mode gives to still photographs.

Effects of Physical Controls When Recording Movies

The last group of settings that carry over to some extent from still-shooting modes to video recording is the category of functions controlled by physical buttons and switches. In this situation, as with Shooting menu items, there are differences depending on what shooting mode the camera is set to. Some of the behavior of the physical controls is quite variable, and I will not attempt to describe every possible combination of shooting mode and physical control. I will give some examples and discuss the most important settings to be aware of.

For example, consider the behavior of the direction buttons and the control wheel when the camera is set to the Intelligent Auto shooting mode. When the camera is set to this mode for shooting still images, as discussed in Chapter 2, the down button activates the Photo Creativity feature, and the left and right buttons scroll through the various options on the Photo Creativity menu at the bottom of the screen: Background Defocus, Brightness, Color, Vividness, and Picture Effect. Once one of these options is selected, turning the control wheel or pressing the up and down buttons adjusts the value of the setting for that option.

If you press the red Movie button to start recording a video in Intelligent Auto mode, and then press the down button, the camera displays an error message and the button has no effect. However, if you activate one of the Photo Creativity options using the down button *before* pressing the red Movie button, then that effect will carry over after you press the red button. For example, if you turn on one of the Picture Effect settings, such as Toy Camera or Posterization, that effect will be active when you press the Movie button, and will remain in effect while the movie is recorded. And, what is more, if you activated one of those settings (or just called up the Photo Creativity menu) before starting the video recording, then the control slider will appear at the right side of the screen, and it will control the Background Defocus option, even though you may have selected a different option. In that case, you could have both a Picture Effect and the Background Defocus features being used at the same time while recording your video. See Figure 8-8 for an example of this situation.

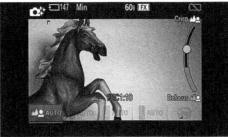

Figure 8-8: Photo Creativity Controls for Video Recording

I don't recommend that you try using any of the settings described above, because of the fairly complicated relationships among them. If you want to use a Picture Effect setting while shooting a movie, you should set the camera to Movie mode and select Picture Effect from the Shooting menu. However, it is useful to be aware that some of the settings made with the various physical controls will still operate when the camera is shooting movies, even in the most automatic shooting modes.

Without attempting to catalog the behavior of every physical control in every possible combination of shooting mode with menu options, here are what I consider to be the major points about these controls.

First, you can use exposure compensation when shooting movies by pressing the down direction button when the mode dial is set to the P, A, S, M, Movie, or Sweep Shooting setting. (Note that you can use exposure compensation even with the mode dial set to M when recording movies, even though you cannot do so for still images.) However, the range of adjustments available is only plus or minus 2.0 EV, rather than the plus or minus 3.0 EV that is available when shooting still images. If you set exposure compensation to a value greater than 2.0 (plus or minus), the camera will set it back to 2.0 after you press the red Movie button to start shooting a movie.

Second, you can press the center button to activate Tracking Focus for shooting movies when the mode dial is set to any position other than Sweep Shooting. As a matter of fact, you can even use this option in certain varieties of Scene mode in which you cannot use Tracking Focus for shooting stills: Anti Motion Blur, Hand-held Twilight, and Fireworks. This is because, when you are shooting movies, the special features of Scene settings are disabled, so the multi-shot or long shutter speed characteristics of these settings do not interfere with the Tracking Focus feature, as they do for still shooting. Of course, to use Tracking Focus you have to have an autofocus mode selected using the Focus Mode option on the Shooting menu.

Third, the Function button operates normally, depending on the shooting mode that is currently set. So, for example, if the camera's mode dial is set to the P position for Program mode, then, after you have pressed the red Movie button to start re-

293

cording a movie, you can press the Function button, and it will bring up the Function button menu on the screen. This menu will let you control only those items that can be controlled under current conditions, including the various settings that are in effect, as seen in Figure 8-9.

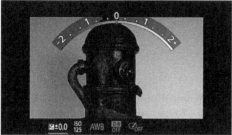

Figure 8-9: Function Menu for Video Recording - Program Mode

If you start recording a movie while the mode dial is set to a mode such as Superior Auto, in which the various functions on the Function button menu are not available, the RX100 will display the menu, but none of the items can be selected, as shown in Figure 8-10.

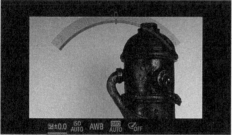

Figure 8-10: Function Menu for Movie Recording - Super Auto Mode

Summary of Options for Recording Movies

As I have discussed, there is a considerable degree of complication in trying to explain all of the relationships among the controls and settings of the RX100 for recording movies. In order to cut through that complication, here is a summary of your options for recording movies with the RX100.

If you just want to record a quick video clip with standard settings, you can leave the mode dial set to either of the Auto modes or the Scene position and fire away with the red button. The camera will adjust the exposure automatically and you can set Focus Mode to Autofocus or Manual Focus. (If you select Single-shot Autofocus, the camera will use Continuous Autofocus for video recording). Other menu options cannot be adjusted.

If you want a bit more control over your video shooting, you can set the mode dial to the P, A, S, or M position. In those cases, you can control several additional Shooting menu options, including ISO, White Balance, Metering Mode, Creative Style, and Picture Effect, among others. You can also choose either Autofocus or Manual Focus, in the same way as for the Auto modes. However, the camera will still adjust the exposure automatically.

If you want the maximum control for movie recording, set the mode dial to the icon that looks like a frame of film, representing Movie mode. Then select an option from the Movie item, which is the last item on the Movie menu. If you want to control the aperture, choose Aperture Priority; to control shutter speed, choose Shutter Priority; to control both aperture and shutter speed, choose Manual Exposure. Other options can be selected from the Shooting menu.

Control buttons operate during movie recording if the context permits. The main buttons that will be of use during movie recording are the down button (exposure compensation), center button (Tracking Focus), and Function button (various options, as set by the user).

If you want to have the RX100 ready to record good, standard video footage at a moment's notice without having to remember a lot of settings, I recommend that you set up one of the three slots (I use slot 3) of the Memory Recall shooting mode with a solid set of movie-recording settings. Here are the settings I recommend: (Settings not listed here can be set however you like.)

Suggested Settings for Recording Movies	
Mode Dial	Program Mode (P)
Shooting Menu	
Image Size	L:20M
Aspect Ratio	3:2
Quality	Fine
Focus Mode	Continuous AF
Smile/Face Detection	Off
ISO	ISO Auto
Metering Mode	Multi
White Balance	Auto White Balance
DRO/AUTO HDR	DR Off
Creative Style	Standard
Picture Effect	Off
Movie Menu	
File Format	AVCHD
Record Setting	60p 28M(PS)
Image Size (Dual Rec)	L:17M
SteadyShot	Active
Audio Recording	On
Wind Noise Reduction	Off

Movie Playback

As with still images, you have the option of transferring your movies to your computer for editing and playback, or playing them back right in the camera, for displaying either on the camera's LCD or on a TV, when the camera is connected via an optional HDMI cable.

If you want to play your movies in the camera, there is one basic aspect of this camera you need to be mindful of. As I discussed in Chapter 6, the RX100 cannot play both movies and still images in a single sequence; you have to set the camera to play one or the other type of file. In other words, if you scroll through the saved items on your memory card by pressing the left and right direction buttons or by turning the control wheel, you will see either all still images or all videos, never a mixture. In order to switch from stills to videos or vice-versa you need to switch the camera into the proper mode for displaying the selected type of file.

There are three ways to switch the camera between viewing still images and viewing movies. First, you can use the Still/ Movie Select option, which is the first item on the first screen of the Playback menu. This option lets you choose to view either still images, MP4 videos, or AVCHD videos.

Second, you can make the switch between stills and movies from a playback index screen. To do this, press the Playback button to enter playback mode. Then press the zoom lever once to the left, to bring up an index screen showing four images (if that many exist). Press the left direction button to move the highlight into the narrow strip at the far left of the screen. At that point, the camera will display a message at the lower right of the display telling you to press the center button for the Still/Movie Select option. If you press the center button, you will get access to that menu option, and you can choose which kind of file to view.

The third, and sometimes the quickest, way to switch playback modes is just to take a still photo by pressing the shutter button or record a very short video by pressing the red Movie button twice in fairly rapid succession. Either of these actions will automatically switch the camera into the respective viewing mode, for stills or movies. Of course, this method has the disadvantage of cluttering your memory card with unnecessary files, though you can delete them later if you want to.

Once you have selected the proper mode to view your videos, the only files you will see in playback mode will be files of that type. Once the first frame of a video is displayed on the screen, you will see the word Play next to an icon representing the center button, as shown in Figure 8-11. (If you don't see the Play message, press the Display button to switch to the more detailed information screen.)

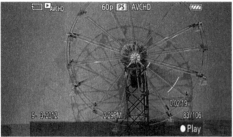

Figure 8-11: Movie Ready to Play by Pressing Center Button

Once you press the center button to start the movie playing, you will see additional icons at the bottom of the screen, as shown in Figure 8-12.

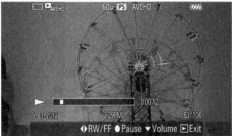

Figure 8-12: Movie Playback Controls While Playing

These icons indicate, from left to right, that you can press the left/right direction buttons for Rewind/Fast Forward; center button for Pause; down button for Volume; Playback button to Exit from the playback. If you press the down button for the volume control, you can then turn the control wheel or press the up and down direction buttons to set the volume level. If you press the center button to pause the playback, you will see a slightly different screen, as shown in Figure 8-13.

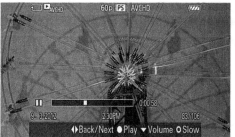

Figure 8-13: Playback Controls While Movie Paused

In this case, the icons are the same, except that the last icon on the right indicates that you can turn the control wheel in either direction to play the movie back slowly, one frame at a time. When you are finished with frame-by-frame playback, press the center button to pause, and then press the center button again to resume normal playback.

Editing Movies

The RX100 does not have any capability for editing your movies in the camera. If you want to do any editing, you will have to do it with a computer. For Windows, you can use software such as Windows Movie Maker or the PlayMemories Home software that comes with the RX100. To install PlayMemories Home on your computer, you need to connect the camera to the computer using the USB cable that comes with the camera, and follow the prompts that appear on your computer. (If you do not see the prompts, consult the online Sony Cyber-Shot User Guide.) This software does not work with Macintosh computers. If you are using a Mac, you will have to use iMovie or any other movie editing software that can deal with .mp4 and AVCHD files. I use Adobe Premiere Pro on my Mac, and it handles these files very well.

One issue you may encounter when first starting to edit movie files from the RX100 is finding the files. When you insert a memory card into a card reader, the still images are easy to find; on my computer, the SD card shows up as No Name

299

or Untitled; then, beneath that level, there is a folder called DCIM; inside it are folders with names such as 100MSDCF, which contain the still images.

The movie files are a bit trickier to find. As I mentioned earlier in this chapter, the AVCHD files that you need to find and import into your software are the files with the .mts extension. Here is the pathway to a sample file, assuming the file name at the level of the SD card is Untitled: Untitled\Private\ AVCHD\BDMV\Stream\0006.MTS. The file called 0006.MTS is an AVCHD file that can be imported directly into compatible software for editing.

To find your MP4 files, locate files using a pathway such as the following: Untitled\MP_ROOT\100ANV01\MAH1430. MP4. The file named MAH1430.MP4 is an MP4 file that can be played by Apple's QuickTime software or imported into iMovie for editing.

You can avoid the complications of finding the movie files on a memory card by connecting the camera to your computer using the USB cable. With most video-editing software, the camera should be detected and the software should import the movie files automatically, ready for you to edit them.

Chapter 9: Other Topics

Macro (Closeup) Shooting

Macro photography is the art or science of taking photographs when the subject is shown at actual size (1:1 ratio between size of subject and size of unenlarged image) or slightly magnified (greater than 1:1 ratio). So if you photograph a flower using macro techniques, the image on the camera's sensor will be about the same size as the actual flower. You can get wonderful detail in your images using macro photography, and you may discover things about the subject that you had not noticed before taking the photograph.

The RX100 is quite capable of shooting macro photographs in various shooting modes. For example, I took the shot of the butterfly in Figure 9-1 with the lens at its full wide-angle setting using the Portrait setting in Scene mode. The camera exposed the image for 1/160 second at f/4.0 using ISO 125.

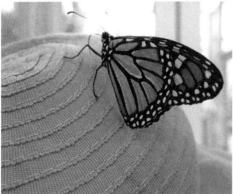

Figure 9-1: Portrait, f/4.0, 1/160 Second, ISO 125

301

There are several ways to take macro photographs with the RX100. First, you can set the mode dial to the Scene setting and select the Macro option, as shown in Figure 9-2.

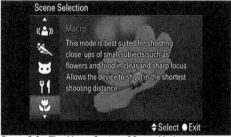

Figure 9-2: The Macro Setting of Scene Mode

With this setting, as discussed in Chapter 3, the camera will be set up for good close-up shots, and you can still make a number of advanced settings, including choosing RAW or RAW & JPEG for the Quality setting. However, you will not be able to select several other important Shooting menu items, including continuous shooting, Autofocus Area, ISO, White Balance, Metering Mode, Creative Style, and others.

Another way to take close-ups is to set the camera to the Intelligent Auto or Superior Auto mode, in which case, when you get close to subject, the camera is likely to select the Macro mode using its Scene Selection technology. Here, again, you will likely get good results, but you will not be able to make advanced settings.

The best way to take macro shots with the RX100, in my opinion, is to use one of the advanced shooting modes—Program, Aperture Priority, Shutter Priority, or Manual exposure. In that way, you will have the full range of Shooting menu options available. Also, depending on the subject, you can choose a shooting mode that makes the most sense. For example, if you are photographing flowers or other items that are not moving significantly, you may want to use Aperture Priority for one of two reasons: so you can use a wide aperture to focus sharply on the subject while blurring the background, or so you can use a more narrow aperture so you can get the whole subject in focus, with expanded depth of field. The shot shown in Figure 9-3 was taken in Program mode at f/2.8 with an exposure of 1/100 second at ISO 125.

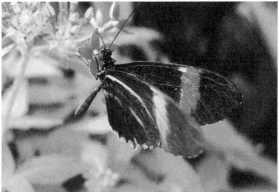

Figure 9-3: Program, f/2.8, 1/100 Second, ISO 125

There is one aspect of the RX100's focusing system that makes macro photography particularly easy: There is no special "macro" focusing mode, as there is on many other cameras. If you just set the camera to one of its autofocus modes—either Single-shot or Continuous—it will focus on objects as close as 2 inches (5 cm) when the lens is zoomed out, and as close as 22 inches (55 cm) when the lens is zoomed in to its maximum telephoto range.

You don't have to use any autofocus setting at all to take macro shots if you don't want to; if you set the camera to manual focus, you can also focus on objects very close to the lens. You do, however, lose the benefit of automatic focus, and it can be tricky finding the correct focus manually. If you use the DMF (Direct Manual Focus) setting, though, you have the ability to check your manual focusing by pressing the shutter button halfway and having the camera use its autofocus system.

When shooting extreme close-ups, you should use a tripod

303

if possible, because the depth of field is very shallow and you need to keep the camera steady to take a usable photograph. It's also a good idea to take advantage of the two-second self-timer setting. If you take the picture using the self-timer, you will not be touching the camera when the shutter is activated, so the chance of camera shake is minimized. You should also leave the built-in flash retracted (or set to Forced Off) so it can't fire. Flash from the built-in unit at such a close range would likely be of no use. If you need extra lighting, you might want to consider using a small lamp that can illuminate the subject without overwhelming it.

Using RAW Quality

I've discussed RAW a couple of times. RAW is an available setting for Quality on the Shooting menu. It applies only to still images, not to movies. When you set the image type to RAW, as opposed to JPEG, the camera records the image without any in-camera processing; essentially, it just takes in the "raw" data and records it.

There are both advantages and drawbacks to using RAW in this camera. First, the drawbacks. A RAW file takes up a lot of space on your memory card, and, if you copy it to your computer, a lot of space on your hard drive. Second, there are various functions of the RX100 that won't work when you're using RAW. The menu options that don't work with RAW mode include Image Size, Soft Skin Effect, Auto HDR, Picture Effect, Clear Image Zoom, Digital Zoom, High ISO NR, and Write Date. In addition, you cannot use RAW quality with the Sweep Shooting mode, and you cannot use the DPOF feature to mark RAW images for printing directly from a memory card.

Let's talk about the advantages, and how much (or little) to worry about the drawbacks. The main advantage is that RAW files give you an amazing amount of control and flexibility with your images. When you open up a RAW file (those from this camera have an .arw extension) in a compatible software program, the software gives you the opportunity to correct problems with exposure, white balance, contrast, color tints, and other settings.

For example, the image in Figure 9-4 is shown as it is being opened in Adobe Camera Raw, before being opened in Photoshop.

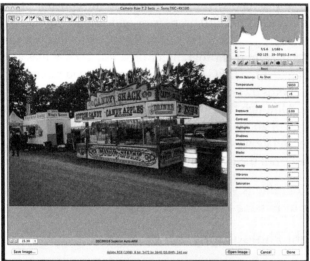

Figure 9-4: *RAW Image from RX100 Opened in Adobe Camera Raw*

If you had the aperture of the camera too narrow when you took the picture, and it looks underexposed, you can manipulate the Exposure slider in the software and recover the image to a proper exposure level. Similarly, you can adjust the white balance after the fact, and correct color tints. You can even change the amount of fill lighting. In effect, you get a second chance at making the correct settings, rather than being stuck with an unusable image because of unfortunate settings when you pushed the shutter button.

Therefore, the drawbacks are either not too severe, or they are counter-balanced by the great flexibility RAW gives you. The large size of the files may be an inconvenience, but the increasing size of hard drives and SD cards, with steadily dropping prices, makes file size much less of a concern than previously. I have heard some photographers grumble about the difficulties of having to process RAW files on the computer. That could be an issue if you don't regularly use a computer. I use my computer every day, so I don't notice. I have had problems with RAW files not loading when I didn't have the latest Camera RAW plug-in for Adobe Photoshop or Photoshop Elements, but with a little effort, you can download an updated plug-in and the software will then process and display your RAW images. Sony provides users of the RX100 with Image Data Converter, a computer program for processing RAW files and converting them to JPEG or other formats that you can use for sending photos by e-mail and manipulating them with editing software. Although the Adobe Camera RAW software was not updated until about six weeks after the camera was released, once the update was released, I had no problems processing RAW files from the RX100 for use in Adobe Photoshop.

The bottom line is you certainly don't have to use RAW, but you may be missing some opportunities if you avoid it.

Low-light Photography

The RX100 is equipped with a generous assortment of features for taking still images and movies in dimly lighted environments. With this many options, it sometimes can be confusing to decide which ones may work best in a particular situation. I am going to provide some guidelines here that may help you in making such decisions.

First, it's worth noting some aspects of the RX100 that make it so well-suited for this sort of photography. The camera's lens has a maximum aperture of f/1.8, which is very "fast" for a camera in this class. In other words, this aperture is a relatively wide one that lets in a lot of light. Because the aperture lets in a good deal of light, the camera is able to use relatively fast shutter speeds. The result is that the RX100 can stop action in fairly dim light by using shutter speeds of 1/30 second or faster, thereby avoiding the blurry images that come from using slow shutter speeds.

In addition, the RX100 has a broad range of high ISO values available, up to ISO 3200 in all situations, and well above that level, all the way up to a stratospheric 25600, in limited cases. The image quality at ISO 3200 and above may suffer because of the noise that results from such high ISO settings, but the images can be quite usable, as seen in Figure 9-5. This shot was taken at ISO 3200 in order to enable the use of a fast shutter speed of 1/800 second to freeze the action.

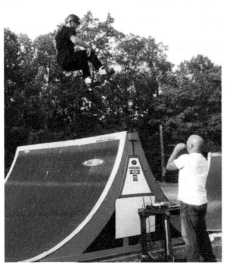

Figure 9-5: ISO 3200 Used to Stop Action

When you can set the ISO this high, you can use fast shutter speeds and avoid the use of flash or other artificial lighting in many cases. If you are shooting in dim light, there may be more noticeable noise than in a brightly lit shot like this one.

Finally, the RX100 has several special settings for use in dim light. When the mode dial is turned to the Scene position, you will find several Scene mode options for low-light photography: Anti Motion Blur, Night Scene, Hand-held Twilight, and Night Portrait. (The Night Portrait setting involves the use of flash, but it is included here because it involves low-light con-

307

ditions.) You also can set the mode dial to the Superior Auto position, in which the camera may automatically use one of the above settings as conditions may dictate.

Apart from the special shooting modes designed for dim light, the RX100, as noted, has a special ISO setting, Multi Frame Noise Reduction, that is actually more like a shooting mode than just an ISO setting. With this feature, the camera makes a rapid burst of exposures at ISO settings up to 25600 and then combines those exposures internally to create a single composite image that has reduced noise. Using this special setting is the only way to set ISO above 6400 with the RX100.

Now that I have mentioned the special features of the RX100 that make it an excellent camera for low-light photography, I will provide some guidelines for using these features. For this discussion, I will assume that you are not going to use flash or other artificial lighting (except when the camera needs flash for a special night setting, as discussed below).

I also will assume that you are not going to use one of the more advanced shooting modes, such as Program or Shutter Priority. (If you do use one of those modes, you can make several settings that will affect your low-light images, including shutter speed, ISO, and Long Exposure Noise Reduction.) Instead, I will assume that you are going to choose one of the shooting modes designed specifically for low-light shooting.

First, if you can use a tripod for a particular shot, you should consider using the Night Scene setting of Scene mode. With this option, the camera will use a low ISO value to maximize image quality and reduce noise, and will take a long exposure if necessary. For example, in Figure 9-6, using this setting, the RX100 exposed the image for 1/6 second at f/2.8 with an ISO setting of 125. The picture was taken well after dark, with the only lighting coming from within the store. I did not use a tripod for this particular shot, and I was just able to hold the camera steady enough to avoid noticeable blur from camera movement. If I try this shot again, I will use a tripod.

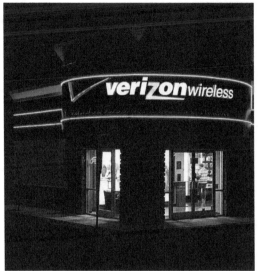

Figure 9-6: Scene Mode - Night Scene Setting, 1/6 Sec.

Second, you may have a situation in which you are taking a portrait at night. With the Night Portrait setting of Scene mode, the camera will use the flash for the portrait, but it will set the flash mode to Slow Sync so that the ambient lighting will have a chance to light up the background, as in Figure 9-7.

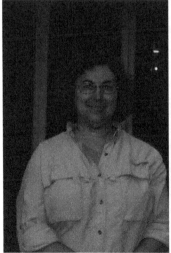

Figure 9-7: Scene Mode - Night Portrait

In this case, the RX100 shot the picture with a shutter speed of 2 seconds to allow the background to be visible, with an aperture of f/4.9 and an ISO of 250.

Third, you may have a situation in which the lighting is dim, but you cannot use a tripod or flash, and you want to record the scene as clearly as possible. For this sort of shot, you have several options with the RX100. Of course, these have all been covered in Chapters 3 and 4, but now I will mention them again to provide a brief comparison.

If you turn the mode dial to the SCN position, you have three options among the 13 available settings: Anti Motion Blur, Hand-held Twilight, and High Sensitivity. If you choose Anti Motion Blur, as in Figure 9-8, the RX100 will set its ISO as high as necessary to allow the use of a relatively fast shutter speed, so it can avoid motion blur.

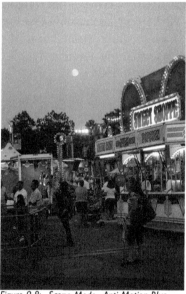

Figure 9-8: Scene Mode - Anti Motion Blur

The camera takes 6 shots that it combines into a single image to reduce noise; therefore, this setting does not work well with subjects in rapid motion, which could change positions while the 6 shots are being taken. For scenes with moderate motion, however, the camera is able to reject the images with the most motion blur, thereby optimizing the final composite image.

With the Hand-held Twilight setting, as seen in Figure 9-9, the camera places more emphasis on image quality, and therefore will use a slower shutter speed so it can use a lower ISO and avoid image noise.

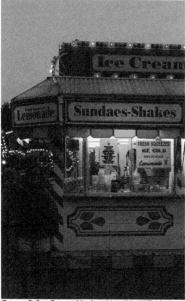

Figure 9-9: Scene Mode - Hand-held Twilight

Again, the camera combines 6 shots into one, so this setting works best for still or slow-moving subjects. In my experience, this setting works well when there is a fair amount of ambient lighting. For example, in the image shown here, the ice cream stand, which is lighted up, shows up quite well, but the woman to the left, in the shadowed area, is not seen clearly. (The settings for this shot were f/3.5, 1/100 second at ISO 125.)

The third Scene mode setting for this situation is High Sensitivity. With that option, the camera is likely to set the ISO level

311

quite high. In Figure 9-10, shot in a dimly lighted museum, the camera set itself to f/4.0 for 1/15 second at ISO 3200 in order to expose the subject adequately.

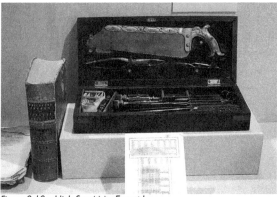

Figure 9-10: High Sensitivity Example

With this setting, the camera does not try to avoid using a slow shutter speed if needed in order to expose the image well. In this case, the camera takes only a single shot, rather than combining multiple images as it does with Anti Motion Blur and Hand-held Twilight. Therefore, this setting can work for moving subjects, as long as there is sufficient light for the camera to use a relatively fast shutter speed.

Finally, there is one more special setting to consider for use in dimly lit environments—the Auto ISO Multi Frame Noise Reduction setting. This option, which was discussed in Chapter 4 in connection with the ISO menu item, is not a shooting mode, though it acts like one to some extent. When you make this choice on the ISO menu, the camera will let you set the ISO anywhere from 200 all the way up to the expanded setting of ISO 25600. And, as the setting's name implies, the camera takes 6 shots and combines them together in order to reduce the noise that results from high ISO settings. In Figure 9-11, I used this setting with the ISO set to 6400; the shot was taken at f/5.6 with a shutter speed of 1/125 second.

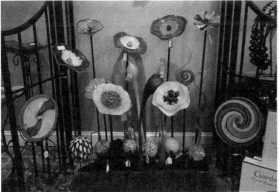

Figure 9-11: Auto ISO Multi Frame Noise Reduction Shot

The potential advantage from using this option is that it is selected from the Shooting menu when the camera is set to one of the more advanced shooting modes such as Program or Shutter Priority. Therefore, many of the other choices on the Shooting menu are available for selection, including White Balance, Metering Mode, and Creative Style. So, you might want to use this setting when the lighting is so low that you need the highest possible ISO settings, or when you need to make other settings, such as Creative Style and the others available on the Shooting menu. (You cannot use the RAW quality or Picture Effect options with this setting, however.)

To summarize, the following table has suggested guidelines for using the various special settings for low-light shooting.

Guidelines for Low-light Shooting Modes	
Night Scene	High image quality with use of a tripod.
Night Portrait	Portrait using flash, with background illuminated through use of slow shutter speed.

313

Guidelines for Low-light Shooting Modes	
Anti Motion Blur	Uses higher ISO; results in good, clear exposure for non-moving objects; also reduces motion blur for subjects in moderate motion.
Hand-held Twilight	Uses lower ISO; more emphasis on image quality for non-moving objects.
High Sensitivity	Can use high ISO and slow shutter speed; takes only a single shot, so can be used with moving objects in brighter light.
High ISO Multi Frame NR	Can use ISO as high as 25600; takes multiple shots; allows use of advanced settings from Shooting menu.

Street Photography

One of the reasons many users prize the RX100 is because it is very well suited for street photography—that is, for shooting candid pictures in public settings, often without the subject being aware of your activity. The camera has several features that make it well-suited for this type of work. It is small, lightweight, and unobtrusive in appearance, so it can easily be held casually or hidden in the photographer's hand. Its 28mm equivalent wide-angle lens is excellent for taking in a broad field of view, so can shoot from the hip without framing the image carefully on the screen. Its f/1.8 lens lets in plenty of light, and it performs well at high ISO settings, so you can use a relatively fast shutter speed to avoid motion blur. You can make the camera almost completely silent by turning off the beeps and shutter sounds.

What are the best settings for street shooting with the RX100? If you ask that question of many photographers, you are likely to get many different responses. I'm going to give you some fairly broad guidelines as a starting point. The answer depends in part on your own personal style of shooting, such as whether you will talk to your subjects and get their agreement to be photographed before you start shooting, or whether you will fire away from some distance with the camera at your waist and hope you are getting a usable image.

Here are a couple of approaches you can start with and modify as you see fit. One technique that some photographers use is to shoot in RAW, and then use post-processing software such as Photoshop or Lightroom to convert their images to black and white, along with any other effects they are looking for, such as extra grain to achieve a gritty look. (Of course, you don't have to produce your street photography in black and white, but that is a common practice.) If you decide to shoot using RAW quality, you can't take advantage of the various image-altering settings of the Picture Effect menu option. You can, however, use the Creative Style option on the Shooting menu. You might want to try using the Black and White setting; you can tweak it further by increasing contrast and sharpening if you want. (Of course, you may prefer a different look, so try reducing contrast and sharpening if that effect appeals to you.)

You also can experiment with your basic exposure settings. I recommend you shoot in Shutter Priority mode at a fairly fast shutter speed, say, 1/100 second or faster, to stop action on the street and to avoid blur from camera movement. You can set ISO to Auto, or possibly use a high ISO setting, in the range of 800 or so, if you don't mind some visual noise. Or, you can rely on the more automatic settings. For Figure 9-12, I used the Sports Action option of Scene mode in order to grab a candid shot of people at a local county fair.

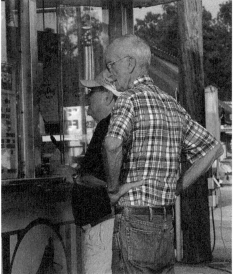

Figure 9-12: Candid Shot Taken with Sports Action Setting

In the alternative, you can set the image type to JPEG, at Large size and Fine quality, to take advantage of the camera's image-processing capabilities. To get the gritty "street" look, try using the High Contrast Monochrome setting of the Picture Effect item on the Shooting menu, with ISO set somewhat high, in the range of 800 or above, to include some visual grain in the image while boosting sensitivity enough to stop action with a fast shutter speed. I used that setting for the image in Figure 9-13.

Also, consider turning on continuous shooting, so you'll get several images to choose from for each shutter press.

One thing to try if the light is dim is to use the High Sensitivity setting of Scene mode, which I discussed earlier in this chapter in connection with low-light photography. You might want to try this option to see if the extra graininess that results from a high ISO level has a pleasing appearance in the context of your shooting.

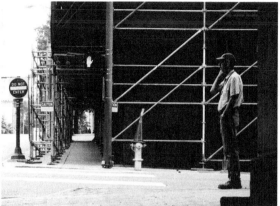

Figure 9-13: Street Photograph - High Contrast Monochrome

Finally, although you are likely to get fine results using the RX100's autofocus system, you may want to try focusing manually. Here is one approach to try. In preparation for shooting, use autofocus and focus on a practice subject at about the distance at which you expect your actual subjects to be. Then switch the camera to manual focus; the focus distance will remain at this distance for all future shots, so you will not have to re-focus, as long as you keep shooting subjects at the same distance. You should try to use a somewhat narrow aperture (f/4.0 or higher) to keep the depth of field broad. Also, for any of this sort of shooting, I suggest that you leave the lens zoomed back to its full wide-angle position, unless a specific situation comes up when you can hold the camera very steady and zoom in on a specific subject.

Making 3D Images

There's been a lot of attention paid to three-dimensional (3D) movies and images lately, with the advent of 3D televisions and the renaissance in 3D movies. Some digital cameras have appeared recently that have special features for creating 3D panoramas and other stereoscopic images, including the Sony NEX models, the Fujifilm FinePix Real 3D W3, the Panasonic Lumix LX7, and others. The RX100 has no such built-in capability. But why should its users feel left out of the 3D wave? It's

317

not that hard to create 3D images using just the RX100 (well, okay, or any other camera, for that matter). Anyway, for you experimental types, here is one way to get into 3D with the RX100.

First, you need to take two pictures of the same scene from two different positions, separated by a short distance.

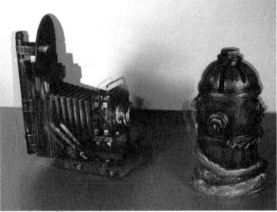

Figure 9-14: 3D Example Image

For Figure 9-14, I set up two tripods at the same height, about 4 inches (10 cm) apart, with the subject about 53 inches (1.3 m) distant. Then I took two pictures of the tabletop scene, first one from the left tripod, then one from the right. The camera needs to be facing straight ahead each time, not angled in toward the subject. I used manual exposure at f/4.0 with a shutter speed of 1/50 second and set the ISO to 500, to get good quality with no variation between the two exposures. I took the images in RAW format, but then converted them to JPEG in Photoshop without doing any manipulation of the exposure or white balance, and saved the images as JPEG files.

Next, I used a Windows program called Stereo Photo Maker, which can be downloaded free at http://stereo.jpn.org/eng/ stphmkr. From the program's File menu I selected Open Left/

Right images. I opened my two JPEG images with this command, which lets you load multiple images at once. Then, I went to the Stereo menu and, with both images appearing on the screen, I selected Color Anaglyph, and, on the sub-menu that appeared, Dubois (red/cyan). The program produced the single image shown in Figure 9-14, which looks blurry to the naked eye, with red and blue lines characteristic of 3D images you may have seen in comic books or other printed materials. (If you're using a Mac, there are other programs available, though I haven't used them. One possibility is Anabuilder, at http://anabuilder.free.fr. You also can use Photoshop, but you'll need to experiment a bit, or find instructions on the web.)

That's all there is to it! If you follow these steps with images that are properly aligned and taken from a good distance apart, the resulting image should be ready for viewing, either on screen or on paper, using old-fashioned red/blue 3D glasses. (The red side goes over the left eye.) If it doesn't pop out as a 3D image when viewed through the glasses, go to the Adjustment menu and try various commands, including Auto Alignment, Easy Adjustment, and others, until the image looks good. (I had to use those options to adjust the images that I worked with.)

Astrophotography and Digiscoping

Astrophotography involves photographing the stars, planets, and other celestial objects using a camera connected to (or aiming through) a telescope. Digiscoping is the practice of attaching a digital camera to a spotting scope in order to get clear shots of remote objects, generally birds and other wildlife. I can't say that using the Sony RX100 is the best possible way to engage in either of these activities; if you want to take close-ups of wild animals and birds, you might do better with a DSLR using a long telephoto lens, and for astrophotography you undoubtedly could do better with a special camera or imaging device that is designed for long exposures through a telescope. However, this book is about the RX100, and my goal here is to give you some suggestions about useful and enjoyable ways to use this camera, not to find the best possible methods for long-distance photography. That's not to say that the RX100 is a bad camera for these types of photography; it does have some features that equip it nicely for taking pictures through a scope, including light weight, a large sensor for a camera of its size, a high-quality f/1.8 lens, manual exposure, manual focus, RAW quality, and a self-timer.

One of the less-helpful features of the RX100 when it comes to astrophotography, however, is that it has a permanently attached lens. You cannot remove the lens and attach the camera's body directly to a telescope or spotting scope as you can with a DSLR. So, you have to use the lens of the RX100 in conjunction with the eyepiece and main lens or mirror of the scope. There are many different types of scope and several different ways to align the scope with the RX100's lens. I will not discuss all of the various methods; I will talk mainly about the one combination I have experience with, and hope that it gives you enough general guidance to explore the area further if you want to pursue it.

I used a Meade ETX-90/AT telescope, shown in Figure 9-15 with the RX100 connected to its eyepiece.

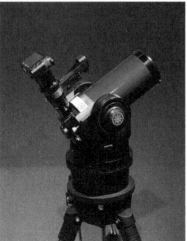

Figure 9-15: RX100 on Meade Telescope

This telescope has a diameter of 90mm (3.5 inches), an effective focal length of 1250mm, and a focal ratio of f/13.8. It is of the Maksutov-Cassegrain design, which uses both mirror and lens to focus light into a relatively small tube (compared to the tube of a comparable reflector or refractor).

One challenge in using a camera like the RX100 to take photos through this telescope is to find a way to get the image that the eye can see through the scope's 1.25-inch (32mm) diameter eyepiece into the camera's lens. There are various types of adapter available to accomplish this. The simplest way is to handhold the camera with its lens as close as possible to the scope's eyepiece and snap pictures until you get a usable image. Of course, this technique will not work with an exposure of any length, because you cannot get a sharp image when you handhold the camera for longer than about 1/30 second. Another way is to use a "universal adapter," which is a kind of clamp that attaches the camera to the eyepiece. I have found that sort of adapter to be bulky, and had problems aligning the camera's lens with the telescope's eyepiece, because that sort of adapter does not create a direct connection between the two.

A much better approach, and the one I used, is to obtain adapter rings that let you connect the camera directly to the telescope's eyepiece, providing a firm and continuous connection. For this system, you need a filter adapter, such as the 52mm version from Lensmate, discussed in Appendix A, as well as adapter rings that let you connect the filter adapter to the telescope's eyepiece. You can get the proper adapter rings by purchasing the 52mm Digi-Kit, part number DKSR52T, from the online site telescopeadapters.com. That is the setup that is shown in Figures 9-16 and 9-17. I took the image shown in Figure 9-18 with the RX100 connected to a 40mm eyepiece on the telescope using the adapter rings.

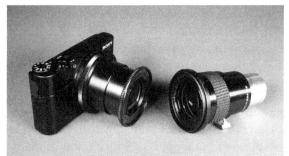

Figure 9-16: Telescope Eyepiece Beside RX100

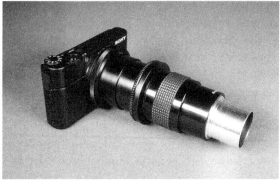

Figure 9-17: Telescope Eyepiece Attached to RX100

The camera was set to Manual exposure mode; through experimentation I arrived at an exposure of 1/400 second at f/9.0, with the ISO set to 1600. I used manual focus mode on the camera, setting the focus approximately at first, and then adjusting the telescope's focusing control until the image appeared sharp on the camera's LCD display. I used the Focus Magnifier option so I could fine-tune the focus with an enlarged view of the moon's craters. I used the self-timer, set to 2 seconds, to minimize camera shake as the exposure was taken, and had SteadyShot turned on. I set the image quality to RAW+JPEG so I would have a RAW image to give some extra latitude in case the exposure seemed incorrect. As you can see in Figure 9-18, the RX100 did a pretty good job of capturing the half moon. Because of the large sensor and relatively high resolution of the RX100, this image can be enlarged to a fair degree without deteriorating.

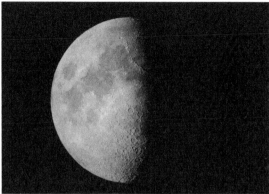

Figure 9-18:   Moon, f/9.0, 1/400 Sec., ISO 1600

You can also use this setup for digiscoping. I don't currently have a spotting scope, but I did try out the RX100 for terrestrial photography through the Meade telescope. I couldn't locate any birds or other animals, so I took a photograph of the stop sign shown in Figure 9-19, which was quite far from the camera.

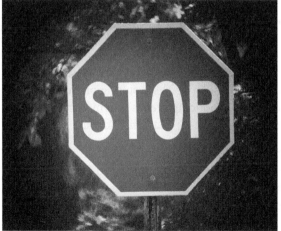

Figure 9-19:   View of Stop Sign Through Telescope

You can judge the distance in Figure 9-20, which was taken from the same place as the previous shot, using the camera's maximum optimal zoom setting of 100mm.

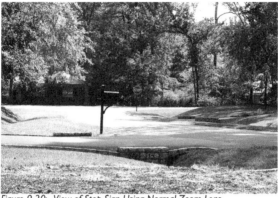

Figure 9-20: View of Stop Sign Using Normal Zoom Lens

Based on my experience in taking this photo, it appears that the RX100 would perform nicely if connected to a traditional spotting scope.

Infrared Photography

Infrared photography involves finding a way for the camera to record images that are illuminated by infrared light, which is invisible to the human eye because it occupies a place on the spectrum of light waves that is beyond our ability to see. In some circumstances, cameras, unlike our eyes, can record images using this type of light. The resulting photographs can be quite spectacular, producing scenes in which green foliage appears white and blue skies appear eerily dark.

Shooting infrared pictures in the times before digital photography involved selecting a particular infrared film and the appropriate filter to place on the lens. With the rise of digital imaging, you need to use a camera that is capable of "seeing" infrared light. Many modern cameras include internal filters that block infrared light. However, some cameras do not, or block it only partially. (You can do a quick test of any digital camera by aiming it at the light-emitting end of an infrared remote control and taking a photograph while pressing a button on the remote; if the remote's light shows up as bright white, the camera can "see" infrared light at least to some extent.)

The Sony RX100 is quite capable of taking infrared photographs. In order to unleash this capability, you need to get a filter that blocks most visible light, but lets infrared light reach the camera's light sensor. (If you don't, the infrared light will be overwhelmed by the visible light, and you'll get an ordinary picture based on visible light.)

As with most experimental endeavors, there are multiple ways to accomplish this. For example, on the internet you will find discussions of how to improvise an infrared filter out of unexposed but developed (*i.e.*, black) photographic film.

A more certain, if more expensive way to make infrared photographs with the RX100 is to purchase an infrared filter and use an adapter that lets you attach the filter securely to the camera, as shown in Figure 9-21.

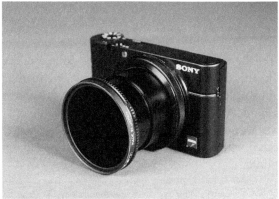

Figure 9-21: R72 Infrared Filter with Lensmate Adapter

As discussed above in connection with astrophotography and in Appendix A, you can obtain an adapter from Lensmate that lets you attach any filters with a 52mm thread. There also is a model available for use with 49mm filters.

The infrared filter I have seen most often recommended is the Hoya R72, which is what I use. It is a very dark red, and blocks most visible light, letting in mainly infrared rays in the part of the spectrum that tends to yield interesting photographs. For the image shown in Figure 9-22, I used the Black & White Creative Style setting. I set the camera to Manual exposure mode and exposed for 0.4 second at f/1.8, with ISO set to 200 on a bright, sunny day.

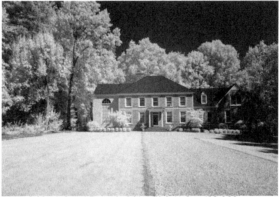

Figure 9-22: Infrared Example, B&W, f/1.8, ¼ Sec., ISO 200

Even though I really enjoy the other-worldly appearance of infrared shots like this, I could not resist tweaking it a bit further by using the Illustration setting of the Picture Effect menu option, set to its High level, as shown in Figure 9-23. The Illustration effect gives wonderful results with many types of image, and I was pleased with the added interest that it provided for the infrared photo.

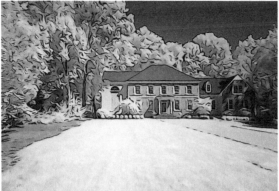

Figure 9-23: Infrared Shot With Illustration Effect - High

You can also shoot infrared images in color. When doing that, I set a custom white balance, using brightly sunlit green foliage as the base. That is, I call up the camera's white balance setting screen by pressing the WB button, and select the option for setting a custom white balance. To set the custom white balance, I fill the large white rectangle on the camera's screen with the green foliage and press the shutter release button to record the new white balance setting.

Infrared photography often yields images with leaves and grass that look unnaturally light, and other strange but pleasing effects. This sort of infrared photography often is most successful in the spring or summer, when there is a rich variety of green subjects available outdoors.

Connecting to a Television Set

The RX100 can readily play back its still images and videos on an external television set—either a standard-definition set or an HDTV. The camera does not come with any audio-video cable as standard equipment, so you have to purchase your own cable to connect to either type of set.

To connect to a standard TV, you need a cable with a micro-HDMI connector at the camera end and a standard HDMI connector at the TV end. These cables are widely available through retailers such as Amazon.com.

To connect the cable to the camera, you need to open the little flap on the bottom of the camera next to the tripod socket and plug the micro-HDMI connector into the port that is underneath that flap, as shown in Figure 9-24.

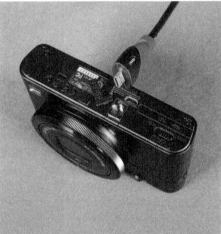

Figure 9-24: HDMI Cable Next to HDMI Port

Then connect the large connector at the other end of the cable to an HDMI input port on an HDTV set.

Once you have connected the camera to a TV set, the RX100 operates very much the same way it does on its own. Of course, depending on the size and quality of the TV set, you will likely get a much larger image, possibly better quality (on an HD set), and certainly better sound. When the camera is connected to a TV with an HDMI cable, it not only can play back recorded images; it also can record. When the RX100 is hooked up to a TV while in recording mode, you can see on the TV screen the live image being seen by the camera. In that way, you can use the TV screen as a large monitor to help you compose your photographs and videos.

APPENDIX A: Accessories

When people buy a new camera, especially a fairly expensive model like the RX100, they often ask what accessories they should buy to go with it. I will hit the highlights, sticking mostly with discussing items I have used personally.

Cases

I almost did not include a section on cases in this book, because the RX100 is such a compact camera that you don't really need a case. There is no separate lens cap to deal with as there is with some other models in this class, and, when the camera turns off and its lens retracts, the RX100 is ready to stow easily in your pocket, purse, briefcase, or other handy location.

But I do use a case with my RX100 and I know that other users do also, so I will provide some suggestions. One problem in doing so is that it would be hard to find a case that will not work for the RX100, because the camera is so compact.

First, I will mention the official Sony case, model LCJ-RXA, shown in Figure A-1. Before I bought the case I did not expect to like it, because the camera is so small and does not seem to need a fancy case.

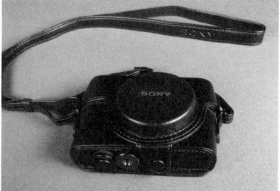

Figure A-1: Sony Leather-like Case LCJ-RXA

But I appreciated this case once I had it, and I have used it steadily. It is made of polyurethane but looks like leather, and it fits the camera neatly, with a tripod screw that secures the camera to the rear half of the case. Sony includes a matching shoulder strap with the case. If you don't care about having the genuine Sony case and the Sony logo, you can get a much cheaper version of the case on eBay.

The problem with a case of this sort is that you cannot store anything but the camera itself in the case. There is no room for an extra battery, memory card, filters, or anything else. But, if you want a very attractive case that does a fine job of protecting the camera, this one is an excellent choice.

Another case I have used a great deal for my RX100 is the Lowepro Tahoe 30, shown in Figure A-2. There is nothing fancy about this case; it is soft with a cushioned interior and it zips closed. It has a large belt loop and a small exterior pocket that also closes with a zipper. I carry my extra battery in that pocket. If I need to carry a tripod and other large items, I still keep the RX100 in this case and place the case and camera inside a larger bag or case along with the other items. I have heard good things about the LowePro Apex 30 case, also, but have not tried it myself.

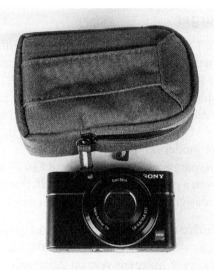

Figure A-2: Lowepro Tahoe 30 Case

If you want an even smaller case that still provides a good fit, try the Lowepro Tahoe 10 or the Case Logic TBC-302.

I occasionally go on a day trip using a waist pack made by Kata, model number DW-491, shown in Figure A-3, which has room for the camera, some accessories, and a couple of small water bottles in the two side pouches.

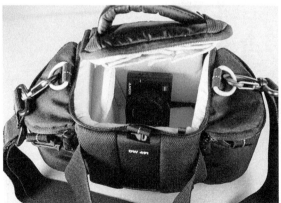

Figure A-3: Kata DW 491 Case with RX100 Inside

Batteries and Charger

Here's one area where I recommend you go shopping either when you get the camera or right afterwards. I use the camera heavily, and I find it runs through batteries fairly quickly. You can't use disposable batteries, so if you're out taking pictures and the battery dies, you're out of luck unless you have a spare battery (or the AC adapter and a place to plug it in, as discussed below). The model number of the Sony battery is NP-BX1. You can get a spare Sony battery for about $40.00 as I write this. It won't do you a great deal of good by itself, though, because the battery is designed to be charged in the camera.

There is an easy solution to this problem. You can find generic replacement batteries, as well as chargers to charge the batteries outside the camera, very inexpensively on Amazon.com, eBay, and elsewhere. I purchased a package including a generic replacement battery and a charger, shown in Figure A-4, for about $20.00 on eBay.

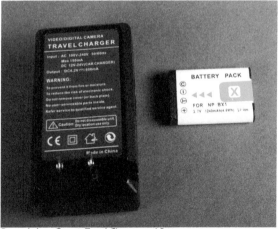

Figure A-4: Generic Travel Charger and Battery

The charger worked well, both for that battery and for the original Sony battery. The battery itself seemed fine, but I eventually concluded that it was giving me a somewhat shorter time between recharges than the genuine Sony battery, so I purchased another Sony one for daily use.

There is another type of third-party charger that some users have tried—a wall charger with a micro-USB plug. You may have a charger of this type that came with another electronic device, such as a tablet PC or a cell phone. I have not tried using that sort of charger myself, and I have read that users have had mixed results with using other chargers. Personally, I have found no reason to use any in-camera charger other than the one that came with the camera. However, if you are confident that the voltage and amperage of your charger match the requirements of the camera (5V and 1500 mA), then that may be a good way to obtain an extra charger for the RX100.

While I am on the subject of batteries and power, I should mention one positive aspect of the RX100 that is unusual, at least in my experience. The AC adapter that comes with the camera can be used to power the camera, as well as to charge the battery in the camera. With some other cameras, you can purchase an optional AC adapter, or one may come with the camera, but it cannot be used to power the camera; you need to purchase an additional, different adapter to power the camera. With the RX100, at least in the United States, you can connect the AC adapter, model number AC-UD11, to the camera and use it to power the camera indefinitely. This can be convenient if you are working with the camera indoors, or even outdoors if you have a power supply that it can be plugged into.

Add-on Filters and Lenses

There is no way to attach a filter or other add-on item, such as a close-up lens, directly to the lens of the RX100, as you can with DSLRs and other cameras whose lenses are threaded to accept filters and auxiliary lenses. With the RX100, in order to add such accessory items, you need to get an adapter. There is no such adapter made by Sony, but enterprising inventors have stepped into the breach. You can obtain a very workable adapter from Lensmate, at lensmateonline.com.

The adapter consists of two parts. The first part, shown in Figure A-5, is a plastic ring called the "receiver" that you glue onto the front of the lens barrel. This piece stays in place and does not interfere with the lens or the automatic lens cover.

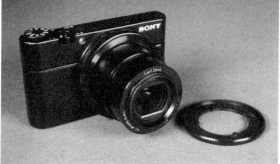

Figure A-5: Lensmate Filter Adapter, Receiver is on Lens

To use a filter, you attach a larger piece, the "filter holder," lying next to the camera in this image, which bayonets onto the receiver. Then you can screw any 52mm diameter filter or other auxiliary lens into the holder. (You also can purchase a model that accepts 49mm filters; I chose the 52mm version because I have filters of that size.) Figure A-6 shows a circular polarizing filter attached to the RX100 with this adapter.

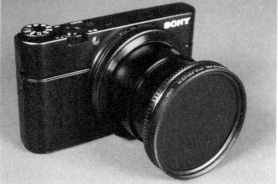

Figure A-6: Circular Polarizer Attached with Lensmate Adapter

The receiver is removable if you later want to take it off the lens; I removed a similar adapter from my Canon PowerShot S95 and installed it readily on my PowerShot S100, after obtaining a new installation adhesive patch from Lensmate.

As you might expect, this system is not as sturdy as the natural screw-on capability of other cameras, because everything depends on a plastic ring that is glued in place. So, don't expect to attach large items like teleconverters or anything heavier than a standard 52mm filter. Having the ability to attach filters, however, enhances the usefulness of the camera greatly. You can use infrared filters, ultraviolet filters, polarizers, or any of a wide assortment of close-up lenses, among others. Also, as discussed in Chapter 9, I used this system to attach the RX100 to the eyepiece of a telescope to take pictures through the telescope. The Lensmate adapter worked well for that purpose.

There is at least one other option available for attaching filters to the RX100—the "Magfilter" system, which involves gluing a very thin metallic ring to the front of the lens and then attaching a magnetic filter holder to that ring. I have not tried this system myself, but I have heard good things about it. You can get more details at www.carryspeed.com.

Grip

One of the points that some users make about the RX100 is that it can be difficult to get a firm grasp of the camera because it is small and has a smooth front surface with no place to take hold of it. The people at Lensmate, who provide the filter adapter discussed above, also offer a solution to this issue—the custom-made grip designed by Richard Franiec.

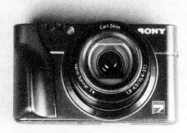

Figure A-7: Custom-made Grip on Front of RX100

This item, shown in Figure A-7, is well crafted from aluminum and contoured to fit on the camera's body with a low profile. It is attached with a strong adhesive supplied by Lensmate. This grip does offer you a solid ridge for keeping a tight hold on the camera. I do not find it necessary, but this is a matter of personal taste.

Cable Release

Another option you may want to consider for your RX100 is a cable release, which can trigger the camera's shutter without your having to press the shutter button with your finger. Using the cable can reduce the pressure that is placed on the camera, and thereby reduce the risk that the camera will move, causing blur in the image. This possibility is of particular importance when you are making time exposures of multiple seconds, and exposures using the BULB setting, which holds the shutter open until you close it.

Of course, you may well ask, where can you attach a cable release? With traditional film cameras, it often is possible to screw a release into the shutter button. This is the case even with some modern digital cameras such as the Fujifilm FinePix X100. It is not the case with the Sony RX100, though; there is no place to screw in a cable release and no place even to attach an adapter that will fit over the shutter button, such as the adapter sold for some Panasonic and Leica digital cameras, which fits into the flash shoe.

I have tested one product that offers a possible solution to this problem—the Hama Cable Release for Digital Cameras. This item consists of a standard cable release that is attached to a round plastic plunger and a Velcro strap, shown in Figure A-8. You wrap the strap tightly around the camera so that the round plunger is directly over the camera's shutter button, as shown in Figure A-9. Then, when you activate the cable release, the round plunger presses the camera's shutter button.

This device is designed to work with a variety of small cameras that do not have a way to screw in the standard connecting threads from a cable release. It takes some fiddling to get it properly situated so that it will activate the shutter button on the RX100. I had to shorten one side of the Velcro strap about one-half inch (1.2 cm) to get the strap to fit around the camera tightly. After a few attempts, though, I was able to get it to work. It does a good job, especially when I need to press the shutter button and keep it depressed during a fairly lengthy exposure using the BULB setting in Manual Exposure mode.

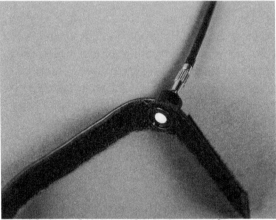

Figure A-8: Hama Cable Release, Showing Plunger and Strap

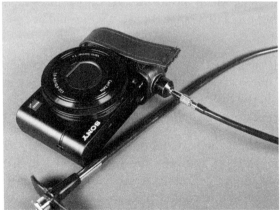

Figure A-9:   Hama Cable Release Attached to RX100

External Flash

Clearly, Sony did not consider the use of external flash units to be a high priority for users of the RX100, because the camera does not have an accessory flash shoe on top, as many other advanced compact cameras do. This decision by Sony makes perfect sense for this camera, because one of the virtues of the RX100 is its very small size. It would defeat the purpose of designing such a compact camera to load it up with a bulky flash unit that would make the camera top-heavy.

Also, you might decide that your RX100 does not need a very powerful flash, for a couple of reasons. First, the camera has a sensor that is very capable of taking excellent pictures in low light, with ISO settings reaching up to 6400 in most cases and as high as 25600 if you use the special Multi Frame Noise Reduction setting on the ISO menu. Second, even apart from the RX100's dim-light shooting prowess, for everyday snapshots that are not taken at long distances, the built-in flash should suffice. It works automatically with the camera's light-metering controls to expose the images well. It is limited by its power, though. According to Sony, at the wide-angle focal length, the range of the built-in flash is up to about 56 feet (17 m), which is a good range, but those figures are listed for a setting of Auto ISO, which means the ISO can range as high as 3200. The built-in flash's range at lower ISOs would be considerably shorter.

So, if you will often use the camera to take photos of groups of people in large spaces, or otherwise need additional power from your flash, you may need to supplement the built-in unit. Fortunately there are some options.

As far as I am aware, the best and probably the only way to synchronize an external flash with the Sony RX100 is to use an optical slave unit. An optical slave is a device that can either be built into a flash unit or come as a separate component that connects to a flash unit. The optical slave has a sensor that detects when the built-in flash of the RX100 fires, and immediately fires the external flash, thereby adding to the light for the image being taken by the camera.

There are many optical slave units available, and most of them work quite well with many compact cameras. However, there is a problem that has to be overcome with the RX100. That is, the camera's built-in flash always fires a pre-flash before it fires the flash that is synchronized with the exposure of the image. The pre-flash is fired in order to let the camera measure the light that will be available for the actual exposure. There is no way to turn the pre-flash off. Therefore, if you are using an ordinary optical slave unit, the optical slave's sensor will "see" the pre-flash and will trigger its flash at that instant, before the "real" flash is fired on the RX100. The result will be an image that does not get the benefit of the external flash.

There is a solution to this problem, which is to use an optical slave unit that can be set to ignore the pre-flash. I have heard about several units that may be able to do this, and I have test-ed a few. One unit that I have had success with is the Yongnuo Speedlite YN560.

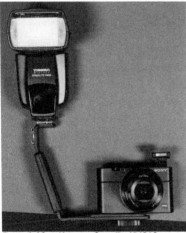

Figure A-10:   Yongnuo Speedlite YN560

As you can see in Figure A-10, this flash is quite large com-

339

pared to the RX100, but it is relatively powerful and can open up new possibilities for your flash photography. It has a rotating head that can bounce the flash off of walls and ceilings, and it has a built-in diffuser that slides down over the flash head. You can attach this unit and the RX100 to a flash bracket, as shown here, or you can put the Yongnuo flash on a separate tripod or light stand.

The feature that makes the Yongnuo unit so useful for this purpose is that it has three modes—Manual, S1, and S2, selected by the Mode button, seen in Figure A-11.

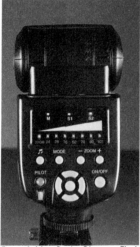

Figure A-11: Back of Yongnuo Flash

With the mode set to S2, the unit ignores the pre-flash from the RX100, and does not fire its flash until the RX100 takes the picture with the actual flash exposure. I set the RX100's flash to Fill-flash and the exposure mode to Manual. I experimented with the settings until I found the best exposure for a particular shot. This setup worked very well.

There also are two units made by Canon that work with the RX100. These are the HF-DC1 and HF-DC2 High-Power Flash, similar small units that fit well with the Sony RX100 in terms of looks and function and add a more powerful flash than the one that is built into the camera.

These flash units each come with a bracket that attaches to the underside of the camera, using the tripod socket. The flash is then screwed into the bracket, right up against the camera, as shown in Figure A-12.

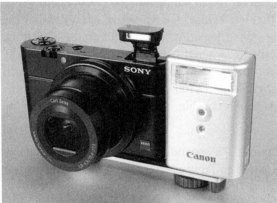

Figure A-12:   Canon HF-DC1 Flash with RX100

Each of these units has a built-in optical slave.

One limitation of the HF-DC1 is that it is a single unit with no rotating flash head, so that, if you mount it right next to the camera on its bracket, there is no possibility of bouncing the flash off of the ceiling or pointing it anywhere other than where the camera is pointing. However, because there is no direct connection between this flash unit and the camera, the flash can be mounted away from the camera, at any location within about 20 feet (6 meters). So, you can place the flash, with its bracket, on a separate tripod, or even hold it in your hand and aim it at the ceiling for a bounce effect.

In my experience, I have had the best results with the HF-DC1 unit by setting the external flash to its Auto mode, setting the camera to Manual exposure mode, and taking several test shots until I found the correct exposure.

There is a newer model of this unit, the HF-DC2, but I have

not tested it. There also are similar flash attachments available from other companies: the Sunpak PF20XD and the Metz 28 CS-2. I have not tested those, either.

There is one other flash unit I have tried that is specifically designed as a digital slave—the Zeikos Digital Slave Flash, which comes with a bracket for attaching it to the camera, and which has a switch that lets you set the way in which it handles the pre-flash issue. When I set the flash's switch to the S2 setting, meaning it would fire when it senses the second flash from the camera's built-in unit, it worked perfectly, and fired its flash in sync with that of the RX100. The Zeikos flash is very inexpensive, and is worth considering as an external unit for the RX100.

Finally, you could try a separate optical slave device such as the SYK-5, pictured in Figure A-13, which comes with a hot shoe for attaching any compatible external flash unit.

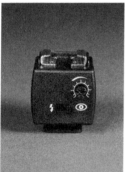

Figure A-13: SYK-5 Optical Slave

The SYK-5 has a knob that can be used to adjust the delay of its signal to trigger the flash, from 70 milliseconds to 1.5 seconds. I tried the unit with several flash units, but I could not get it to synchronize with the flash of the RX100 in most cases. I did get it to fire at the proper time with the Canon Speedlite 430EX II, with the flash set to manual mode and the SYK-5 set with its switch at the "red-eye" position and its delay knob turned all the way to the right. Other users have reported greater success with the SYK-5, so it is probably worth a try; it is quite inexpensive and is available from Amazon.com and other sellers.

Viewfinders

One other item that some users like to add to their RX100 is an optical viewfinder. It can be convenient to be able to view the scene through the bright window of one of these devices, rather than trying to make out an image on the LCD display that is washed out by bright sunlight. Personally, I have managed all right using the Sunny Weather setting of the LCD Brightness option on the Setup menu. But, if you prefer the classic looks and operation of a good optical viewfinder, it is not that difficult to attach one.

In my case, I used a Voigtlander 28mm viewfinder and attached it to the camera using double-sided tape, as shown in Figure A-14, because I was just experimenting with this setup.

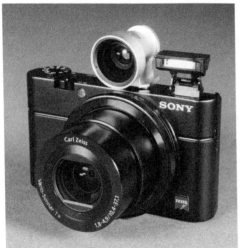

Figure A-14:   Voigtlander 28mm Viewfinder on RX100

If you want to be able to attach and remove the viewfinder repeatedly, you can attach an accessory shoe to the camera with strong tape or adhesive and then just slide the viewfinder in and out of the shoe.

Of course, there are many other optical viewfinders available. You just need to find one that fits well with the RX100 in size and appearance.

Another option that is more expensive and bulky but works well for some photographers is the Hoodman Hoodloupe 3.0. This is a viewing device that you hold up against the LCD screen, shading the display and letting you view the screen through an eyepiece, as shown in Figures A-15 and A-16.

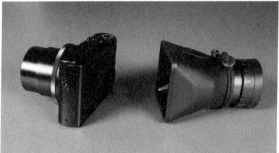

Figure A-15:   Hoodman Hoodloupe 3.0 Next to RX100

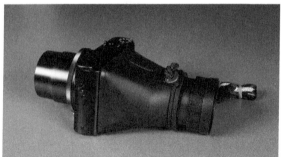

Figure A-16:   Hoodloupe in Viewing Position with RX100

With this setup, you can put the loupe's eyepiece up to your eye and see the screen without having it washed out by sunlight. Details are available at Amazon.com or at hoodmanusa.com.

Tripod Usage

Finally, I am going to discuss one last topic that is not really an accessory but a problem that can be solved with different accessories. Of course, it often is advisable to use a tripod with the RX100, as with any camera, especially for macro shots, low-light shots, and others where focus is critical, shutter speeds are longer than usual, and the like. When the camera is attached directly to a tripod with a standard release plate, as in Figure A-17, the control ring fits very snugly against the tripod's plate and is difficult to turn.

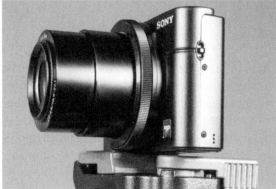

Figure A-17: RX100 Attached to Release plate on Manfrotto Tripod

There are several ways to deal with this problem. One way is to use a tripod whose plate is flat and hard, and therefore does not screw up tightly against the control ring. Figure A-18 shows the RX100 screwed onto the flat plate of a ZipShot tripod. Although it may be hard to see in this image, there is enough of a gap between the control ring and the tripod that the control ring can be turned easily. The problem with this solution is that the ZipShot, although it is a highly portable and convenient tripod that folds into a very small size, is not very sturdy and is not suitable for heavy uses.

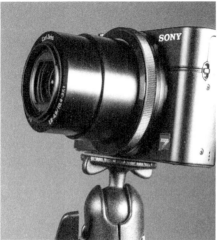

Figure A-18: RX100 Attached to ZipShot Tripod

A better solution is to use the Sony case, discussed earlier in this Appendix, which includes a tripod screw at the bottom that screws into the camera and secures it in the case. Then, when the case is screwed onto a tripod, the extra thickness of the case and its screw elevate the RX100 above the tripod's release plate and the control ring can turn freely, as shown in Figure A-19.

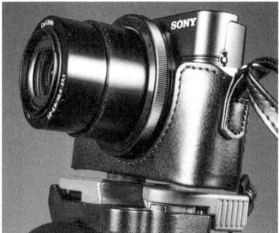

Figure A-19: RX100 in Sony Case on Tripod

There is one other way to deal with the problem of the control ring and tripods that I will mention here—using a small accessory like that shown in Figure A-20.

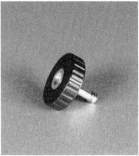

Figure A-20: Tripod Screw

This item, sold in a set of 5, is called a "tripod screw," sold by Hama; I purchased a set from B&H Photo Video online. When you attach this screw to the camera's tripod socket and to the tripod's release plate, there is plenty of clearance between the control ring and the tripod's plate, as shown in Figure A-21, using the same tripod and plate as in Figure A-17.

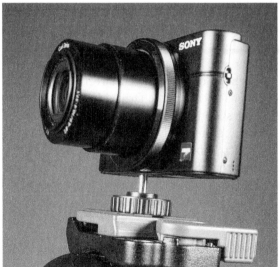

Figure A-21: RX100 with Tripod Screw Attached to Tripod

347

APPENDIX B: Quick Tips

In this section, I'm going to list some tips and facts that might be useful as reminders, especially if you are new to digital cameras like the RX100. My goal is to give you small chunks of information that might help you in certain situations, or that might not be obvious to everyone. I have tried to include points that you might not remember from day to day, especially if you don't use the RX100 constantly.

Use continuous shooting. I recommend that you consider turning continuous shooting on as a matter of routine, unless you are running out of storage space or battery power, or have a particular reason not to use it. In the days of film, burst shooting was expensive and inconvenient, because you had to keep changing film, and you had to pay for film and processing. With digital cameras like the RX100, it just gives you more options. Even with stationary portraits, you may get the perfect fleeting expression on your subject's face with the fourth or fifth shot. So, press the left direction button (or use the menu system) to call up the Drive Mode menu, scroll down to continuous shooting, and turn it on. Remember that continuous shooting is not available when the camera is set to the Movie or Sweep Shooting mode or to any of the Scene mode settings other than Sports Action. Also recall that you can shoot more rapidly if you set the camera to the Speed Priority setting, but the camera will not adjust its focus or exposure after the first shot.

Avoid the Shooting menu. You can't completely avoid using this menu, which includes many important settings, but you can speed up your access to your most often-needed settings by placing them on your Function button menu, for instant recall with a press of that button. In some cases, as with flash settings and Drive Mode, you can press a button (the right and left direction buttons, respectively) to get access to the features you need. When you do use the Shooting menu, speed through it by using the control wheel to move rapidly through the items on each screen, and use the right and left direction buttons to move through the menu system a full screen at a time.

Use the Memory Recall shooting mode. The MR position on the mode dial gives you a powerful way to customize the RX100. Most obvious, it lets you set up your three most important groups of settings. For example, right now I have slot 1 of the MR shooting mode set up for my latest settings for street photography: Aspect Ratio = 3:2; Quality = RAW; Drive Mode = Continuous Shooting; Focus Mode = Continuous AF; Autofocus Area = Multi; Smile/Face Detection = Off; ISO = 800; Metering Mode = Multi; White Balance = Daylight; DRO/Auto HDR = Off; Creative Style = Black & White with Contrast and Sharpness both at -1; SteadyShot = On. However, you can also use it for more specific purposes. One thing I like to do is have one slot set up to remove all "special" settings, such as Creative Style, Picture Effect, and self-timer, so I can quickly set up the camera to take a shot with no surprises. Another thing you can do is use one slot to set the camera at a particular zoom range, such as, say, 50mm. To do this, press the zoom lever to move the lens so you see the desired range below the zoom scale in the upper right corner of the display. The camera does not display the range in millimeters; only in multiples of the wide-angle 28mm range. So, 50mm is about 1.8X and 75mm is about 2.7X. When the range is set as you want it, save the settings to one of the MR slots. If you have more than three sets of favorite settings, consider jotting them down (or printing them with a computer printer) on small note cards so you can easily enter them into the camera as needed.

Remember the Extra Settings for White Balance and Creative Style. Don't forget the ability the RX100 gives you to tweak some settings. When you set White Balance, even to the Auto White Balance setting, you can press the right direction button and then use the amber-blue and green-magenta axes to achieve substantial variations in the color of your shots. This extra setting is not immediately obvious on the menu screen, but it gives you a great way to alter the appearance of images. Just remember to undo any color shift when you no longer need it. Also, you can press the right direction button after selecting a Creative Style option and then adjust the contrast, saturation, and sharpness settings. (Saturation is not adjustable for the Black and White setting.)

Consider using DMF as your standard focusing option. I originally did not consider DMF (Direct Manual Focus) to be a very important setting; I viewed it as a somewhat exotic option to be used in difficult focusing situations when I needed to move back and forth between manual focus and autofocus. I eventually realized that DMF works just the way standard single-autofocus works on many other cameras: the camera does not start focusing until you press the shutter button down halfway. When you do, the camera uses its autofocus quickly; after that you can still use manual focus to adjust further. For me, this is an excellent option because I do not want the camera to use autofocus constantly before I press the shutter button. Using DMF saves battery power and gets the job done efficiently.

Use macro shooting for subjects other than nature. Many photographers create beautiful images using the macro ability of the RX100, shooting insects, flowers, and other natural items. But, with its focusing down to 2 inches (5 cm), its wide-angle lens, and its great low-light performance, the RX100 can serve you in many other ways with its macro shooting. If you need a quick copy of a shopping list, memo, driving directions, sales receipt, or cancelled check, it might make sense to boost the ISO to 800 or so if the lighting is dim, and snap a quick image of it. When you get to your destination, you can display the image on the camera's LCD and enlarge it using the zoom lever, then scroll around in the document with the direction buttons. The RX100 can become a pocketable copy machine.

Don't forget the camera's audio capability. While we're on the subject of possible business-related and other non-photographic uses of the camera, here is one to consider: Although the camera's audio features are not that strong, it does have a built-in stereo microphone that is quite capable of recording voices clearly. If you need an audio recorder to record a spoken memo or to keep a record of a meeting, go to the Movie menu and set File Format to MP4 and Record Setting to VGA (to give more recording time and use less space on the memory card). Try to aim the voices at the two small holes for the stereo microphone, on the top of the camera just behind the lens.

Play your movies in iTunes, and on iPods, iPhones, and iPads. If you set the RX100 to record movies using the MP4 format (as opposed to AVCHD), the movie files are compatible with Apple Computer's QuickTime and iTunes software. You can use iTunes to copy your MP4 files to an iTunes-compatible device, such as an iPad. Just open a window on your computer to display the icon for a movie file (using Windows Explorer or Macintosh Finder), then open iTunes on the same computer, and drag the .mp4 file from the Explorer or Finder window to the panel for the Library in iTunes. You can then play the movie from iTunes. If you want to play it on an iPod, iPhone, or iPad, you will need to take a few more steps: Select the video in iTunes, then select Advanced from the iTunes menu, and, from that menu item, choose Create iPod or iPhone version, or iPad or AppleTV version, as appropriate. Then you can sync iTunes with your device, and the movie will play very nicely on that device. (If you have trouble locating the .mp4 files on your computer, see the last part of Chapter 8.)

Explore the RX100's creative potential. The RX100 is a very sophisticated camera, with several advanced features that give you the ability to explore experimental photographic techniques. Here are a few suggestions: Use Manual exposure mode with its shutter speeds as long as 30 seconds or the BULB setting to take night-time shots with trails or other patterns of lights from automobiles, storefronts, and other sources. Use shutter speeds as fast as 1/2000 second to freeze moving motorcycles, track runners, and other speedy subjects in mid-motion. Try "camera tossing," in which you toss the camera in the air, set to a multi-second shutter speed, to capture trails of light and color as the camera spins around. (But be sure to catch it on the way down!) Try panning or otherwise steadily moving the camera during a multi-second exposure. Use long exposures (on a tripod) to turn night into day. Take HDR images with partly blurred subjects, such as blowing flags.)

Take advantage of the RAW format. If you haven't previously used a camera that shoots RAW files, get to know the benefits of this capability and use them to improve your images. Install and use the Image Data Converter software that Sony provides for the RX100, or use other software, such as Adobe Photoshop or Photoshop Elements, to "develop" the RAW images. Learn how to adjust white balance, exposure, and other settings after the fact, using the flexibility of RAW shooting.

Diffuse your flash. If you find the built-in flash produces light that's too harsh for macro or other shots, some users have reported success with using translucent plastic pieces from milk jugs, other food containers, or broken ping-pong balls as homemade flash diffusers. Just hold the plastic up between the flash and the subject. Another approach you can try when using fill-flash outdoors is to use the Flash Compensation setting on the Shooting menu to reduce the intensity of the flash by -2/3 EV. Also, you can bounce the built-in flash by holding it back with a finger.

Use the self-timer to avoid camera shake. The RX100 has a self-timer capability that is very easy to use; just select it from the Drive Mode menu and choose your setting. This feature is not just for group portraits; you can use the 2-second self-timer whenever you'll be using a slow shutter speed and you need to avoid camera shake. It also can be useful when you're doing macro photography. And don't forget that you can set the self-timer to take multiple shots, which can increase your chances of getting more great images.

Set zone focusing. If you're doing street photography or are in any other situation in which you want to set the camera on manual focus for a specific zone or general distance, here is a quick way to do so. Set the focus mode to Single-shot autofocus, then aim the camera at a subject that is approximately the distance you want to be able to focus on quickly. Once focus has been confirmed, reset the camera to manual focus. Now you will have locked in the manual focus at your chosen distance, and you're ready to shoot any subject at that distance without the need to re-focus.

Understand the Differences Between Similar Settings. There are several ways to achieve some effects, but they have different characteristics. For example, you can take black-and-white photos with various settings: the B/W setting of the Creative Style option on the Shooting menu, or any of the following settings of the Picture Effect setting on that menu: Posterization B/W, High Contrast Monochrome, Partial Color, or Rich-tone Monochrome. Of course, the Picture Effect settings do more than just make the image monochrome, but there also are other important differences. If you use the Creative Style option, you can use the Sweep Shooting mode as well as the P, A, S, M, or Movie mode, and you also can use RAW quality if you're not shooting a panorama. If you use the Picture Effect settings, you cannot shoot an in-camera panorama and you cannot use RAW quality.

APPENDIX C: Resources for Further Information

Books

A visit to a good bookstore or a search on Amazon.com will reveal the vast assortment of books about digital photography that is currently available. Rather than trying to compile a long bibliography, I will list a few especially useful books that I consulted while writing this guide.

C. George, *Mastering Digital Flash Photography* (Lark Books, 2008)

C. Harnischmacher, *Closeup Shooting* (Rocky Nook, 2007)

J. Paduano, *The Art of Infrared Photography* (4th ed., Amherst Media, 1998)

D. Pogue, *Digital Photography: The Missing Manual* (O'Reilly Media, Inc., 2009)

S. Seip, *Digital Astrophotography* (Rocky Nook, 2008)

Web Sites

Since web sites come and go and change their addresses, it's impossible to compile a list of sites that discuss the RX100 that will be accurate far into the future. One way to find the latest sites is to use a good search engine such as Google or Bing and type in "Sony DSC-RX100." I just did so in Google and got more than 5 million results.

Another approach can be to go to Amazon.com, search for the camera, and read the users' reviews, though you have to be careful to weed out reviews by people who are disgruntled for reasons that don't have anything to do with the product itself. You can also visit a reputable dealer's site, such as that of B&H Photo Video, and read the users' reviews of the camera there. I will include below a list of some of the sites or links I have found useful, with the caveat that some of them may not be accessible by the time you read this.

Digital Photography Review

http://forums.dpreview.com/forums/forum.asp?forum=1009

This is the current web address for the "Sony Cyber-shot Talk" forum within the dpreview.com site. Dpreview.com is one of the most established and authoritative sites for reviews, discussion forums, technical information, and other resources concerning digital cameras.

Reviews of the RX100

The links below lead to reviews or previews of the RX100 by dpreview.com, photographyblog.com, and others.

http://www.dpreview.com/reviews/sony-cybershot-dsc-rx100/

http://www.photographyblog.com/reviews/sony_cybershot_dsc_rx100_review/

http://www.cameralabs.com/reviews/Sony_Cyber-shot_DSC_RX100/

http://reviews.cnet.com/digital-cameras/sony-cyber-shot-dsc/4505-6501_7-35326410.html

http://www.dcresource.com/reviews/cameraDetail.php?cam=1882

http://www.stevehuffphoto.com/2012/07/26/the-sony-rx100-digital-camera-review/

http://www.popphoto.com/gear/2012/08/tested-sony-cyber-shot-dsc-rx100-compact-camera

http://www.pcmag.com/article2/0,2817,2407795,00.asp

http://www.t3.com/reviews/sony-rx100-review

http://www.luminous-landscape.com/reviews/cameras/sony_rx100.shtml

http://www.imaging-resource.com/PRODS/sony-rx100/sony-rx100A6.HTM

http://www.theverge.com/2012/7/27/3187725/sony-rx100-review

http://www.eoshd.com/content/8499/sony-rx100-review

http://blog.mingthein.com/2012/08/06/the-sony-rx100-a-somewhat-comparative-review/

The Official Sony Site

The United States arm of the Sony company provides resources on its web site, including the downloadable version of the user's manual for the RX100 and other technical information.

http://esupport.sony.com/US/p/model-home.pl?mdl=DSCRX100&LOC=3#/howtoTab

Equipment Suppliers

Lensmate is a company that sells accessories for the RX100 and other cameras, including an adapter for attaching filters and a grip that lets you take firm hold of the camera.

http://www.lensmateonline.com/

Telescopeadapters.com is a site that sells adapters that let you connect the RX100 (as well as other cameras) to the eyepiece of a telescope, provided that you have a filter adapter.

http://www.telescopeadapters.com/

Carry Speed is a seller of many types of photographic accessories, including the Magfilter, a system for attaching filters to the RX100 and other cameras using a magnetic filter holder.

http://www.carryspeed.com/

Eye-Fi is a company that makes the series of Eye-Fi cards, which are SD memory cards containing tiny transmitters. With these cards, your images are uploaded wirelessly to your computer or other device over a WiFi (wireless) network.

http://www.eyefi.com/

Finally, I should note that my own site, White Knight Press, provides updates about this book and other books, offers support for download of PDFs, and provides a way for readers or potential readers to contact me with questions. I always look forward to hearing from readers.

http://www.whiteknightpress.com.

Index

G

H

J

K

L

Q

R

W